Southern Biography Series
William J. Cooper, Jr., Editor

CARTER G. WOODSON

CARTER G. WOODSON

A LIFE IN BLACK HISTORY

JACQUELINE GOGGIN

LOUISIANA STATE UNIVERSITY PRESS
BATON ROUGE AND LONDON

Louisiana Paperback Edition, 1997
06 05 04 03 02 01 00 99 98 97   5 4 3 2 1
DESIGNER: AMANDA McDONALD KEY
TYPEFACE: JANSON TEXT
TYPESETTER: G & S TYPESETTERS, INC.
PRINTER AND BINDER: THOMSON–SHORE, INC.

Library of Congress Cataloging-in-Publication Data

Goggin, Jacqueline Anne, 1953–
    Carter G. Woodson : a life in Black history / Jacqueline
Goggin.
      p.   cm. — (Southern biography series)
    Includes index.
    ISBN 0-8071-1793-5 (cloth) ISBN 0-8071-2184-3 (pbk.)
      1. Woodson, Carter Godwin, 1875—1950. 2. Historians—United
States—Biography. 3. Afro-American historians—Biography.
4. Association for the Study of Negro Life and History, inc.
5. Afro-Americans—Historiography. I. Title II. Series.
E175.5.W65G64   1993
973'.0496073'07202—dc20
    [B]   92-35980
                                                                  CIP

    The author gratefully acknowledges Moorland-Spingarn Research
Center for permission to quote from its collections, and Michael R. Winston, Literary Executor of the Estate of Rayford W. Logan, for permission to quote from the Logan Papers, housed in the Manuscript Division
of the Library of Congress.

    Frontispiece photograph courtesy of Morgan Sparks Smith, New
York City, copy held by Moorland-Spingarn Research Center, Howard
University.

*To my parents and teachers
with appreciation*

Contents

ILLUSTRATIONS

Preface

For African-American historian Carter G. Woodson, the collection, dissemination, and publication of materials about the black past were highly political acts. Woodson's impressions of the black past were anchored in the cultural and political history of post-Reconstruction Virginia; both his own and his family's experiences provided him with a framework for examining the larger black experience. Born in 1875, in the dark days of Reconstruction—the period that his colleague historian Rayford Logan termed the "Nadir"—Woodson grew to adulthood conscious of the importance of the black past. Appropriately, Woodson has been given the appellation "the father of Negro history" by those who recognize his achievements in founding and organizing the Association for the Study of Negro Life and History in 1915 and in editing the *Journal of Negro History* from 1916 to 1950. Yet no full-length biography of Woodson has ever been published.

Few biographies of black intellectuals have been written, partly because of the lack of primary source materials. Much of the difficulty I encountered in assessing Woodson's life and work stemmed from just such a paucity, preventing me from probing as deeply into Woodson's life and career as I would have liked. I found no Woodson family papers and no records of the association or the *Journal of Negro History*. Only two small collections of Woodson's papers exist. Therefore I expanded my search for information to libraries and archives across the country—public records, university archives, collections of organizational records, and personal papers. What I have assembled is an intellectual biography of Woodson that focuses on his scholarly career.

As with any research attempting to reconstruct the lives of slave families, many of my assertions regarding Woodson's parents and grandparents are tentative. Yet examination of Woodson's social origins explains, in part, his devotion to the cause of promoting black history. He obtained two bachelor's degrees, a master's degree, and a doctorate, taught school in West Virginia, the Philippines, and Washington, D.C., and formulated his ideas about the transformative influence of education. Woodson prepared himself for his life's work by reflecting on the various types of educational programs that would meet the needs of both the urban and rural black working classes and the black bourgeoisie.

In the ten years that Woodson spent in the Washington public schools, he deepened his belief in the uplifting power of education for blacks, and particularly in the need for accurate education about the black past. Acting on this belief, he founded the Association for the Study of Negro Life and History in September, 1915, and began the work that would engage him for the rest of his life. Woodson also began a career as a college professor and encountered the patronizing racism of white administrators and trustees. His experiences in black institutions of higher education further strengthened his resolve to devote all of his time to promoting black history through the association and the *Journal of Negro History*.

After securing a regular income and a firm financial base for his organization, Woodson began to write articles, book reviews, and monographs. And although he continued to struggle to raise additional funds, he pursued over a dozen research projects, trained a coterie of younger black scholars, and worked at a breakneck pace building his black history movement. When financial support from white foundations was no longer forthcoming in 1933, Woodson reached out to the black community for funds to continue his work. Thus he broadened the base of his movement to include the masses of black Americans and heightened the black community's racial pride and cultural consciousness.

From the early 1930s until his death in 1950, Woodson managed to keep the *Journal* and the association afloat and even began several new research projects and publishing ventures. He continued to put in long hours, undertaking scholarly tasks along with menial chores. These arduous struggles adversely affected Woodson's personality and temperament, and he became increasingly distant and possessive of the association. Yet Woodson's stubbornness and single-mindedness were his greatest strengths in keeping the association a viable institution, for he did not become drawn into black political power struggles and organizational disputes or allow his freedom of action to be undermined.

While he was most concerned with the promotion of black history, Woodson also used his scholarship to influence social and cultural change. He viewed his research and writing as a mechanism not only to inform but also to influence the solutions proposed by black protest organizations for black social and economic advancement in American society. Active in such black social welfare and protest organizations as the National Urban League and the National Association for the Advancement of Colored People (NAACP), Woodson later joined more radical groups, such as the Friends of Negro Freedom. He supported Marcus Garvey's Universal Negro Improvement Association, the New Negro Alliance and its "Don't Buy Where You Can't Work" campaign, and the leftist coalition that founded the National Negro Congress in 1935. He argued that blacks should organize along racial rather than class lines and lashed out against the class bias of the black bourgeoisie. As racism and the crisis in black education remain with us in the 1990s, many of Woodson's ideas about the relevance of black history continue to be important.

Woodson, to a greater degree than were other contemporary scholars, was influenced by his early formative experiences and by the racism and segregation he experienced. The wide range of his life experiences affected not only the subjects he chose for scholarly examination, such as slavery, black labor, the frontier, migration, and religion, but also the themes and tone of his work. To appeal to as broad an audience as possible, however, he felt compelled to be dispassionate in his scholarship. While his view of the black past was not shared by his white contemporaries, the historical framework he constructed was used by historians of African Americans from the 1960s through the 1980s. Indeed, present-day social historians have had to rediscover many of the methods, sources, and interpretations that were first proposed by Woodson more than half a century ago.

Acknowledgments

I have accumulated many debts of gratitude in the past fifteen years of work on this project. My greatest thanks goes to the fine staff of the Library of Congress, with whom I had the pleasure of working for eight years. Manuscript Reading Room colleagues Fred Bauman, Paul Chestnut, Chuck Kelly, Janice Ruth, and Mary Wolfskill witnessed the transformation of my manuscript into a book, and provided me not only with assistance for my research but also with friendship and good cheer. Many other staff members at the library offered moral and research support over the years, especially Diane and David Kresh.

Special acknowledgment is due several individuals at Howard University. Thomas C. Battle, Esme Bhan, Paul Coates, Karen Jefferson, and Wilda Logan Willis (now at the National Archives) guided me through the use of numerous manuscript collections, while Janet Sims-Wood and Betty Culpepper facilitated my research in the book collection at the Moorland-Spingarn Research Center. Others also have provided invaluable research assistance: Minnie Clayton, of Atlanta University; Susan Davis and Diana Lachatanere, of the New York Public Library's Schomburg Collection for Research in Black Culture; Larry Dowler, now my colleague at Harvard but formerly at Beinecke Library, Yale University; Lucious Edwards, at Virginia State University in Petersburg; Lyndon Hart, at the Virginia State Library; the late Sara Dunlap Jackson, at the National Archives; and Alan Gallay, formerly at the National Archives; Clifton Johnson, of the Amistad Research Center; Archie Motley, of the Chicago Historical Society; Mike Plunkett, at Alderman Library, University of Virginia; Pat Quinn, at Northwestern University; Judith Schiff, of Sterling Memorial Library, Yale University; Ann Allen Shockley, of Fisk University; Richard Shrader, at the Southern Historical Collection, University of North Carolina; James

Walker, of the Sumner School Archives, Washington, D.C.; and Danny Williams, at Tuskegee University.

Archivists and librarians from the following institutions assisted me in my search for materials on Woodson: Bowie State University, the University of Chicago, Columbia University, Harvard University Libraries, the Huntington Library, Illinois State Archives, the Social Science Research Council, Soper Library at Morgan State University, the State Historical Society of Wisconsin, West Virginia State University, and the Rockefeller Archive Center, which provided me with a travel grant to use its collections. In funding my next project, the American Council of Learned Societies also enabled me to finish this one. Randall K. Burkett, Associate Director of the W. E. B. Du Bois Institute for Afro-American Research, and other colleagues at Harvard, provided me with quiet space, where I put the finishing touches on the manuscript. Thanks are also due to Margaret Dalrymple, Catherine Landry, and Margaret Hart of Louisiana State University Press for getting the manuscript into print.

Many individuals read one or several versions of all or part of this manuscript, or offered advice and information. Thanks are due Herbert Aptheker, Richard Blackett, John Blassingame, John Bracey, Melinda Chateauvert, Bill Cooper, Merle Curti, Maceo C. Dailey, Jr., Dennis Dickerson, Howard Dodson, Walter Fisher, Philip Foner, Lorenzo Johnston Greene, Debra Newman Ham, Louis Harlan, Linda Henry, Evelyn Brooks Higginbotham, Darlene Clark Hine, Alton Hornsby, Nathan Huggins, Lawrence Levine, Arnett Lindsay, Fabian Linden, Rayford W. Logan, W. Augustus Low, August Meier, Louise Merriam, Fred Miller, Lynda Morgan, James Oberly, Michele Pacifico, Harold T. Pinkett, Marion Jackson Pryde, Armstead Robinson, Morey D. Rothberg, Elliott Rudwick, Sister Mary Anthony Scally, John David Smith, Kenneth Stampp, Jeffrey Stewart, Arvarh Strickland, Earl Thorpe, Joe Trotter, Clarence Walker, Charles H. Wesley, Minnie Shulmate Woodson, and Bob Zangrando. Incisive comments and very valuable advice on the manuscript were provided by John Hope Franklin, Robert L. Harris, Jr., Nell Irvin Painter, and Patricia Romero.

Two very close friends also need to be thanked: Robert L. Hall and Grace Palladino each read all or most of the manuscript more than once and offered helpful criticism and suggestions for revisions. Hall, my husband, will be relieved that finally he now is the only black historian to command the lion's share of my attention and affection.

My study of Carter Woodson began longer ago than I care to admit, in a course on comparative race relations taught by Donald Ramos at Cleveland State University. Ramos and my other professors at Cleveland State University, especially Melvin Drimmer, Timothy Runyan, and Curtis Wilson, provided me with regular encouragement, inspired me with their scholarship and teaching abilities, and urged me to seek advanced training in history. At the University of Rochester, Stanley L. Engerman, Elizabeth Fox-Genovese, Eugene D. Genovese, and Mary Young turned me into a historian. I owe an immeasurable debt to Engerman, Fox-Genovese, and Genovese for their unfailing support and sound advice as they read many versions of this work in its various stages.

Finally, I thank my mother, Carla Elizabeth Goggin, and my late father, James Martin Goggin, for insisting that I get more education than they did and for their curiosity about my interest in the past.

CARTER G. WOODSON

ONE

PREPARING FOR LIFE'S WORK, 1875–1915

Born in New Canton, in Buckingham County, Virginia, just ten years after the end of the Civil War, Carter Godwin Woodson was the first and only black American of slave parentage to earn a Ph.D. in history.[1] It is likely that he descended from slaves held by Dr. John Woodson, who migrated from Devonshire, England, to Jamestown, Virginia, in 1619. Woodson's paternal grandfather and father, however, were owned by John W. Toney, a small planter in Fluvanna County. By 1840, Toney held nine slaves, four females and five males. The ages of four of the male slaves corresponded roughly to those of Woodson's grandfather, Carter, born about 1810, his uncles, George and Carter, born in the mid-1830s, and his father, James Henry, born about 1837. Woodson never mentioned his paternal grandmother in any of his writings, but in 1830 one of Toney's female slaves was between twenty-four and thirty-six, the age span to which his grandmother would have belonged in order to bear three sons during the 1830s. Woodson's grandmother bore at least two more children, Bettie, born about 1845, and Schuyler, born about 1850.[2]

1. W. E. B. Du Bois, in 1895 the first black to earn a Ph.D. in history, came from a free northern background. Charles H. Wesley, in 1926 the third black to earn a Ph.D. in history, also came from a free background; his parents had been born free in Kentucky.
2. Henry Morton Woodson, *Historical Genealogy of the Woodsons and Their Connections* (Memphis, 1915), 10–11, 52, 91–92, 194–95, 302–303; Will of Joseph Woodson, October 2, 1783, in *The Edward Pleasants Valentine Papers: Abstracts of Records in the Local and General Archives of Virginia*, ed. Valentine Museum (3 vols.; Richmond, 1979), III, 1858–59; Census of 1830, Buckingham County, Va., in Record Group 29, Records of the Bureau of the Census, National Archives and Records Administration; Census of 1840, Buckingham and Fluvanna cties., Va., in RG 29; Slave Schedules, Census of 1850, Fluvanna Cty., Va., in RG 29; Slave Schedules, Census of 1860, Buckingham and Flu-

In 1850, Toney held fifteen other slaves in addition to the Woodson family. He grew wheat, corn, and oats, as well as tobacco, and Woodson's family probably worked as field hands. Woodson's grandfather and namesake also was trained as a skilled carpenter. When he was not needed to perform agricultural tasks, the elder Carter Woodson may have made most of the wooden articles used on Toney's farm. If the tasks performed by slave carpenters nearby on John Cocke's Fluvanna County plantation were typical, he would have made plows, oxcarts, wagons, tobacco hogsheads, churns, shingles, panels, flooring, and furniture. His greatest value to Toney, however, lay in the wages he commanded when he was hired out.[3]

Woodson remembered his grandfather as being an excellent carpenter and cabinetmaker and a skillful negotiator. Toney apparently allowed the elder Woodson to make his own contracts but required him to report in regularly and turn in his wages. There were both advantages and disadvantages for the hired slave. Uncertainty about working conditions was greater when serving temporarily under a new master, even if the slave could choose whom he would work for. Undoubtedly because of what his grandfather and father told him, Woodson believed that material and living conditions for hired slaves were worse and that they suffered abuse from skilled white craftsmen. Yet there also was greater freedom. Woodson recalled that his grandfather perceived himself to be more like a free man than a slave, and that his sense of independence and rebelliousness caused problems in relations with his master. On at least one occasion his grandfather got into a scrape with an overseer who tried to whip him but who was whipped by the elder Woodson instead. Woodson's grandfather was punished, but not too severely, because he had expressed some remorse.[4]

---

vanna cties., Va., in RG 29; Fluvanna Cty. Deedbooks, 1821–30, in Archives Division, Virginia State Library, Richmond; Land Tax Lists, Buckingham and Fluvanna cties., 1823–63, in Virginia State Library; Personal Property Tax Lists, Buckingham and Fluvanna cties., 1813–63, in Virginia State Library.

3. See Martin Boyd Coyner, "John Hartwell Cocke of Bremo: Agriculture and Slavery in the Ante-Bellum South" (Ph.D. dissertation, University of Virginia, 1961), and "John Hartwell Cocke: Southern Original," *Bulletin of the Fluvanna County Historical Society*, VI (1968), 3–13.

4. Woodson, "My Recollections of Veterans of the Civil War," *Negro History Bulletin*, VII (February, 1944), 103–104; John B. Cade, "Out of the Mouths of Ex-Slaves," *Journal of Negro History*, XX (1935), 319–20; Raymond B. Pinchback, *The Virginia Negro Artisan and Tradesman* (Richmond, 1926), 12–13, 32–33, 45–46, 64–65. On rebelliousness

Woodson's grandfather passed on his sense of rebelliousness to at least two of his sons. George, who worked as a field slave, was purported to have been an unruly and rebellious slave and was frequently punished, even after performing all of his duties. He grew tired of being punished and began to strike back. Like his father, he got into a fight with an overseer when he believed he was punished without cause. When Toney interceded, George apparently struck him as well and then escaped into the woods, stopping long enough, however, to induce other slaves to join him. Using bloodhounds to track him down, Toney caught George and had him beaten so severely that he bled profusely and had scars on almost every part of his body. After George had recovered sufficiently, Toney sent him to Richmond to be sold, and his family never saw him again. Woodson believed that his uncle was purchased by a large planter in Louisiana, where "he was driven to death in the land of cotton." [5]

To his son James Henry, Grandfather Woodson bequeathed not only his defiance but his carpentry skills as well. As a young child James Henry Woodson probably worked in the fields with his mother and his siblings while observing his father's handiwork on the Toney plantation. If he was like most slave carpenters, his father probably began teaching him the skill when he was between the ages of seven and ten, during the late 1840s. Like his father, James Henry Woodson also eventually was hired out and, at least some of the time, was allowed to make his own contracts. He probably was one of four male slaves in their twenties whom Toney hired out in 1860. We know for certain that the last person for whom he worked was James Stratton, because Woodson wrote about his father's experience with him. [6]

In 1860 Stratton was employed by the James River and Kanawha Canal Company to maintain a lock on his property, and it was probably

among hired slaves, see Herbert Aptheker, *American Negro Slave Revolts* (New York, 1943), 98–106, 121–32, 264–324.

5. Woodson, "History Made to Order," *Journal of Negro History*, XII (1927), 336; Harvey Wish, "Slave Disloyalty Under the Confederacy," *Journal of Negro History*, XXIII (1938), 435–50.

6. Woodson, "My Recollections of Veterans of the Civil War," 103–104; Eugene Maloney, *A History of Buckingham County* (Waynesboro, Va., 1976), 45–51; Ellen Miyagawa, "The James River and Kanawha Canal in Fluvanna," *Bulletin of the Fluvanna County Historical Society*, XXXIII (1982), 7–32; James H. Brewer, *The Confederate Negro: Virginia's Craftsmen and Military Laborers, 1861–1865* (Durham, 1969), 4–11, 17–21, 34–37, 47–78, 131–64.

during 1863 or early 1864 when he hired James Henry Woodson to help him. Woodson recalled that his father was "debased to the level of a ditch-digger," although he was able to use his carpentry skills, even if in a fashion more rudimentary than he was accustomed to. Toney apparently required James Henry Woodson to live on Stratton's property while he was hired out. Woodson's father had always used evenings and other leisure time to make fish traps and furniture, which he sold for pocket change to purchase personal items for himself and his family. He continued this practice while he worked for Stratton. Upset because he saw James Henry Woodson using his leisure time for his own advantage, Stratton tried to whip him.[7]

In the tradition of his rebellious father and brother, James Henry Woodson whipped Stratton, and then he rushed back to Toney's farm before Stratton could get there. Toney, however, would not listen to any explanation, reprimanded James Henry Woodson for his impertinence, and maintained that he acted as if he were free. Woodson recalled that his father retorted he did feel free, and then threatened Toney. Fearing consequences similar to those that had befallen his brother George, James Henry Woodson rushed to his cabin, grabbed his best suit of clothes and a white handkerchief, and fled to the woods, where he changed. Hired slaves had greater opportunity to learn of their physical and geographical surroundings and often were positioned to hear news of activities hundreds of miles away. Woodson noted that his father drew upon this knowledge when he escaped and joined up with Yankee troops; he carried the white handkerchief to flag them down.[8]

In the summer and fall of 1864, General Philip H. Sheridan was waging his Shenandoah Valley campaign. By September, Sheridan and his cavalry troops were in the vicinity of Fluvanna County, and it may have been at this point that James Henry Woodson made his successful escape, for purportedly he encountered a detachment of Union cavalry troops under Sheridan's command and told them his story. He led them back to Stratton's farm, where they apparently tied up Stratton and whipped him. James Henry Woodson then led the troops to mills and supply depots in the county, where they engaged in small skirmishes with Confederate troops who were guarding military supplies. The Union troops emerged victorious and loaded the confiscated provi-

7. Woodson, "My Recollections of Veterans of the Civil War," 103–104.

8. *Ibid.* On slave resistance in Virginia during the Civil War, see, for example, James L. Roark, *Masters Without Slaves: Planters in the Civil War and Reconstruction* (New York, 1977), 81–85, 99, 114.

sions, burning whatever they could not carry. Woodson's father told him that he served the rest of the war under Sheridan and General George A. Custer's command and participated in many of the battles of the Appomattox campaign that led to General Robert E. Lee's surrender in April, 1865. The rest of Woodson's family, including his maternal ancestors, were not as lucky. During the last months of the war they remained in bondage.[9]

On the eve of the Civil War, in 1860, Woodson's mother, Anne Eliza, and maternal grandmother, Susan Riddle, were slaves of Thomas Henry Hudgins, a struggling small farmer in Buckingham County, Virginia, which bordered the James River, just across from Fluvanna County. Susan and her husband, Henry Riddle, had an "abroad" marriage, Henry being owned by a more prosperous neighboring farmer, Watkins P. Riddle, who had inherited him from his father, Joseph Riddle. Woodson maintained that Henry was the son of Joseph Riddle and one of his female slaves, and it is possible that Woodson was correct. Although Woodson did not indicate that Susan Riddle and her children were owned by at least two different masters, neither Thomas Hudgins nor any other member of his household owned them in 1850. Because of his financial circumstances, it was unlikely that Hudgins would have been able to purchase slaves in the 1850s, especially since prices almost doubled then, and he probably inherited Susan Riddle and her children or acquired them through marriage.[10]

Despite their abroad marriage, the Riddles had six children: Nelson, born about 1843; Anne Eliza, born in 1848; a female child whose name Woodson never mentioned, born in 1852; and James Buchanan, Robert Henry, and John Morton, all born between 1855 and 1859. As soon as the children were old enough, at age six or seven, they probably joined their mother in the fields, growing wheat, corn, oats, and tobacco. In addition to working in the fields on Riddle's farm, Woodson's grand-

9. Woodson, "My Recollections of Veterans of the Civil War," 103–104.

10. Woodson to Jackson Davis, June 13, 1940, in Jackson Davis Papers, Alderman Library, University of Virginia; Woodson, Obituary of John Morton Riddle, in *Journal of Negro History*, XXVII (1942), 243–46; Woodson, Review of James G. Randall's *The Civil War and Reconstruction*, in *Journal of Negro History*, XXII (1937), 375–76; Population, Agricultural, and Slave Schedules, Censuses of 1850, 1860, Buckingham Cty., Va., in RG 29; Censuses of 1830, 1840, Buckingham Cty., Va., in RG 29; Personal Property Tax Lists, 1813–63, and Land Tax Lists, 1823–63, Buckingham and Fluvanna cties., in Virginia State Library.

father also may have been hired out as a skilled boatman. Woodson contended that for several months during the Civil War his grandfather hid Watkins Riddle from Confederate recruitment officers by ferrying him back and forth along the James and Willis rivers between Cartersville and Richmond. Like many slaves who were experienced boatmen, Henry Riddle would have been in considerable demand by Buckingham County farmers, who needed to transport their crops to markets in Richmond and Lynchburg.[11]

The income that Henry Riddle earned as a boatman may have improved his master's economic status during the 1850s, when the Riddles' total slave labor force increased. It was a different case for the Hudgins family, whose economic status declined. Hudgins' fortunes rose and fell during the 1850s; and late in 1860, continually pressed by creditors, overwhelmed with debt, and threatened with bankruptcy, he decided to sell some of his slaves.[12]

Hudgins was certainly not intent upon breaking up slave families. In fact, according to Woodson, "the poor and indebted slaveholders had tried to show compassion in trying not to sell" Susan Riddle and her two youngest sons, but were forced to in order to pay their bills. Further evidence suggesting the compassion of the Hudgins family lies in Woodson's recollection that his mother "was instructed until she could read in the first reader" by her young mistress, Francis Hudgins. Anne Eliza Riddle, then about thirteen or fourteen years old, persuaded Hudgins to sell her so that her mother would not be separated from the younger children, and Hudgins sent her to Richmond to be sold.[13]

Recounting in detail this terrifying experience that was indelibly etched upon her memory, Anne Eliza Riddle later told her son that she felt like an animal as she was carted from slave pen to auction block each day. While awaiting a buyer, Woodson's mother met another young woman, who had been forcibly separated from her children. This woman's grief further strengthened Anne Eliza Riddle's resolve to

11. Population, Agricultural, and Slave Schedules, Census of 1850, Buckingham Cty., Va., in RG 29; Woodson, Obituary of John Riddle, 243–46. On abroad marriages and interrelations among slave families, see, for example, Elizabeth Fox-Genovese, *Within the Plantation Household: Black and White Women of the Old South* (Chapel Hill, 1988), 294–98.

12. Population, Agricultural, and Slave Schedules, Censuses of 1850, 1860, Buckingham Cty., Va., in RG 29; Woodson, Obituary of John Riddle, 243–46.

13. Woodson, Obituary of John Riddle, 243–46; Woodson, *The Education of the Negro Prior to 1861* (1915; rpr. New York, 1968), 213; Cade, "Out of the Mouths of Ex-slaves," 306; Woodson, "My Recollections of Veterans of the Civil War," 104.

be sold in place of her mother, and day after day, as she stood in chains at the auction block in Richmond, she tried hard to impress a prospective buyer. But no one purchased her, and so Hudgins brought her back to Buckingham County and put her up for sale at the courthouse. He still was unable to sell her. Although Woodson's mother had just reached childbearing age, she was too young to command the $1,100 price Hudgins was asking. "As a last resort," Woodson recalled, Hudgins sold Susan Riddle and her two youngest sons. [14]

Woodson's grandmother was still able to bear children and the presence of her two young sons on the auction block with her was further proof of her fecundity. Hudgins apparently was unsuccessful in finding a local buyer, who would ensure Susan Riddle's proximity to her other children. Instead, desperate to raise needed cash, he sold the three slaves to a man named Barnett, who lived in the far western part of the state, for $2,300, which "brought relief" from his creditors. [15]

The Woodson family was among those thousands of freedmen and women who left their former masters in the winter of 1866 seeking employment elsewhere. Owning little and having only their labor to offer, they worked as sharecroppers in Buckingham County. It is uncertain where James Henry Woodson went or what he did in the first few months of freedom. Although there was a strong desire to get away from former masters, there was an equally strong desire to remain near family and kin, and James Henry Woodson may have returned to Fluvanna County to find his family on John Toney's farm before looking for work in Buckingham County. [16]

Despite his skill, James Henry Woodson was unable to earn a living

14. In "George Washington," New York *Age*, February 28, 1936, p. 6, Woodson recalled stories his mother had told him about her brush with slave traders. Also see Woodson, "My Recollections of Veterans of the Civil War," 104; Woodson, Obituary of John Riddle, 243–46; Cade, "Out of the Mouths of Ex-Slaves," 306.

15. In his Obituary of John Riddle (p. 244), Woodson said that his grandmother had been sold to a buyer in Botetourt County; in "My Recollections of Veterans of the Civil War" (p. 104), he said the buyer was from Buchanan County. In 1860 there were no Barnetts living in Botetourt County, but William Barnett, a forty-five-year-old slaveless farmer resided in Buchanan County. See Population and Slave Schedules, Census of 1860, Botetourt and Buchanan cties., Va., in RG 29.

16. On freedmen and the aftermath of the war, see, for example, Margaret Bayne Williams, *The Woods of Fluvanna County* (Norfolk, Va., 1984), 95–133; Armstead L. Robinson, "The Difference Freedom Made: The Emancipation of Afro-Americans," in *The State of Afro-American History*, ed. Darlene Clark Hine (Baton Rouge, 1986), 53–63.

as a carpenter and was forced into sharecropping. Every year from 1866 to 1869 he moved until he found suitable employment. Usually other family members moved with him, and he may have relied on an extensive network of kin to obtain work. He married Anne Eliza Riddle in 1867, and their first child was born the following year. From 1869 to 1872, when he left seeking work in West Virginia, he worked on Thomas Boatwright's land in Buckingham County. The family moved to West Virginia because James Henry Woodson hoped to earn enough money to buy land, as his father had been able to do in Virginia. [17]

Woodson's grandfather was one of the fortunate few blacks able to purchase land during the 1870s. While still a slave, Woodson's grandfather had married a second time, probably in 1863 or 1864. His second wife was at least thirty years younger than he, and the couple had two more children, Sherman, born about 1864, and Courtney, born about 1867. The younger children from his previous marriage also lived in the household. Having a large family to support and unable, at least initially, to use his carpentry skills, Woodson's grandfather was forced to work as a sharecropper, although he may have done small carpentry jobs for neighboring whites and the few blacks who could afford to pay him. After working for several different farmers, he moved rapidly from the status of a sharecropper to a share tenant and finally to a landowner in 1870. The elder Woodson was able to purchase his own "mechanic's tools" and farm implements, and by 1872 had purchased farm animals, household goods, and a small plot of land. [18]

Accustomed to working on someone else's land for more than fifty years, Woodson's grandfather understood that ownership of even a small plot of land meant freedom from white control. He purchased twenty-three acres of land of fairly good quality on Rocky Creek for four dollars per acre. Family ties and extended kin networks were among the most important factors affecting a decision to purchase land in a particular area, and Woodson's grandfather undoubtedly decided

17. Land Tax Records, 1866–72, Marshall District, Buckingham Cty., in Virginia State Library; Population and Agricultural Schedules, Census of 1870, and Population, Agricultural, and Slave Schedules, Census of 1860, Buckingham Cty., Va., in RG 29; Woodson, Obituary of John Riddle, 245; Woodson to Luther P. Jackson, February 23, 1946, in Luther P. Jackson Papers, Johnston Memorial Library, Virginia State University, Petersburg, Va.

18. Population Schedules, Census of 1870, Buckingham Cty., Va., in RG 29; Land Tax Lists, 1866–72, Marshall Dist., Buckingham Cty., and Personal Property Tax Lists, 1866–72, Buckingham Cty., in Virginia State Library. Also see Robinson, "The Difference Freedom Made," 53–63.

to buy land and remain in Buckingham County because his sons and their families lived nearby. Within this group, however, few others were as successful as Woodson's grandfather. Woodson's uncle Carter was never able to buy land. In 1870 he worked as a sharecropper, and was still sharecropping in 1880. James Henry Woodson was more successful and eventually purchased land, but he had to leave Buckingham County to earn the money.[19]

In 1872 James Henry and Anne Eliza Woodson and their three children, Robert Henry, William, and Cora, left Buckingham County because wages for agricultural work had been declining since 1866. Construction of the railroad in nearby West Virginia offered an escape from sharecropping and share tenancy and provided the opportunity to earn better wages. In just two years of working in West Virginia, James Henry Woodson had earned enough money to purchase twenty-one acres of land near his father's farm in New Canton. By the time historian Woodson was born, his father was a struggling landowning farmer with an income of $95 that barely remained stable each year. In 1880, when Woodson was five years old, the family's farm was valued at only $160 and their crops sold for a mere $100. Woodson recalled that his mother, with seven children to feed, often "had her breakfast and did not know where she would find her dinner." Frequently during the winter and early spring the family did not have sufficient food and "would leave the table hungry to go to the woods to pluck the persimmons which the birds had pierced with their beaks and left on the trees." Often Woodson "had to go to bed early on Saturday night," because he "had only one garment" and his mother had to "wash and iron it over night" so he "would have something clean to wear to Sunday school."[20]

Although they were poor, James Henry and Anne Eliza Woodson instilled in their children not only high morality and strong character through religious teachings but also a thirst for education. As the youngest boy and a frail child, Woodson purportedly was sheltered and his mother's favorite, perhaps because she had lost two children in infancy. The future historian was among the first generation of blacks

19. Land Tax Lists, 1872, 1889, Buckingham Cty., in Virginia State Library; Population and Agricultural Schedules, Census of 1880, Buckingham Cty., Va., in RG 29.

20. Population and Agricultural Schedules, Census of 1880, Buckingham Cty., Va., in RG 29; Personal Property Tax Lists, 1875–87, 1889–91 (list for 1888 is missing), Land Tax Lists, 1875–91, Buckingham Cty., in Virginia State Library; see Baltimore *Afro-American*, June 25, 1932, p. 15.

whose mothers did not have to curry favor with whites to provide an education for their children, and Anne Eliza Woodson, who was literate, expected her son to work hard to obtain an education. Like Woodson, many educated blacks who had come from humble roots credited their mothers with making the sacrifices necessary for them to attend school. Consequently, they expressed their admiration for black women in their scholarship.[21]

Woodson and his siblings helped on the family farm, but four months out of the year they also attended a one-room school, where their uncles John Morton and James Buchanan Riddle taught. Educated in schools established by the Freedmen's Bureau, the Riddle brothers undoubtedly were important role models for Woodson. Nevertheless, the historian credited his father, who remained illiterate all of his life, with teaching him his most important lessons. Despite his poverty, James Henry Woodson would not accept handouts from whites and "taught his children to be polite to everybody but to insist always on recognition as human beings; and if necessary to fight to the limit for it." He commanded his children to never accept insult from whites, compromise their principles, mislead their fellowmen, or betray their people.[22]

During the 1880s Woodson's two older brothers left the family and went back to Huntington, West Virginia, to work. Still too young to leave home, Woodson continued to work on the family farm. By 1890 he had hired himself out as a farm laborer in Buckingham County to supplement the family income. Woodson also took odd jobs and once drove a garbage truck in Buckingham County. Frustrated by his inability to earn a decent wage, and hearing stories from his brothers about the money that could be made in West Virginia, Woodson left Buckingham County for that state in 1892. For part of the year he laid

21. Francille Russan Wilson suggested the influence Woodson's parents exerted in a speech delivered on February 27, 1982, at the Carter G. Woodson Institute for African and African-American Studies, University of Virginia. Sister Mary Anthony Scally and Patricia Romero argue that Woodson was his mother's favorite child. See Sister Mary Anthony Scally, *Walking Proud* (Washington, D.C., 1983), 95, and *Carter G. Woodson: A Bio-Bibliography* (Westport, Conn., 1985), 3–19; Patricia W. Romero, "Carter G. Woodson: A Biography" (Ph.D. dissertation, Ohio State University, 1971), 29. The 1900 Census of Cabell Cty., W. Va., in RG 29, indicated that Anne Eliza Woodson had borne nine children, two of whom had died.

22. Woodson to Luther P. Jackson, February 23, 1946, in Jackson Papers; Woodson, Obituary of John Riddle, 243–46; Woodson, "Early History of Negro Education in West Virginia," *Journal of Negro History*, VII (1922), 23–63.

railroad ties near Charleston. Soon, however, he joined his brothers in Fayette County to work in the coal mines.[23]

The Woodson brothers were part of a large black migration who worked in the mines and other industries in West Virginia. It was the only southern state in which the black population increased from 1890 to 1910. Woodson later wrote about one of his most formative educational experiences while working in Fayette County as a coal miner. One of his coworkers was Civil War veteran Oliver Jones, who operated a tearoom for black miners out of his home. Woodson described Jones's establishment as a "godsend," since white coal operators owned most of the commissaries and charged inflated prices. Jones, who could neither read nor write but was well educated in Woodson's eyes, sold fruit and ice cream and provided a gathering place for blacks at the end of a hard day's work in the mines. When Jones learned that Woodson was literate, he engaged him to read the daily newspapers to the group in exchange for free fruit and ice cream.[24]

Woodson used to read Virginia newspapers to his father, although he could not afford to buy newspapers very often. Miners in West Virginia, on the other hand, had more money than they knew what to do with and subscribed to several black weeklies. Many also subscribed to several white daily papers, and occasionally Woodson read to the group from the Springfield *Republican*, the New York *Sun*, and the New York *Tribune*. Woodson maintained that by reading newspapers he learned "in an effective way most important phases of history and economics."[25]

Woodson recalled that Jones's home "was all but a reading room." Jones owned many volumes that described black history and achievements, including J. T. Wilson's *Black Phalanx*, W. J. Simmons' *Men of Mark*, and George Washington Williams' *Negro Troops in the War of Rebellion*. "Whenever a veteran of the Civil War came out as a candidate for office or achieved distinction," Woodson looked "him up in the books, inform[ed] [his] friends as to what battles he had fought, victories he had won and principles which he thereafter sustained." He read

23. Woodson, "My Recollections of Veterans of the Civil War," 115–16; Woodson to Jesse E. Moorland, May 22, 1920, in Jesse E. Moorland Papers, Moorland-Spingarn Research Center, Howard University.

24. Woodson, "My Recollections of Veterans of the Civil War," 115–16. Also see Joe W. Trotter, *Color, Class and Coal: Blacks in Southern West Virginia, 1915–1932* (Urbana, 1990).

25. Woodson, "My Recollections of Veterans of the Civil War," 115–16.

"speeches, lectures, and essays dealing with civil service reform, reduction of taxes, tariff for protection, tariff for revenue only, and free trade," and became knowledgeable about populist doctrines advocated by Tom Watson and William Jennings Bryan. Frequently Woodson discussed "the history of the race" with black miners at Jones's house, and his "interest in penetrating the past of [his] people was deepened and intensified."[26]

To further develop this interest, Woodson moved to Huntington in 1895, at the age of twenty, to live with his parents and attend high school. His parents and his uncles had returned to Huntington from Buckingham County in the early 1890s. He enrolled in Frederick Douglass High School, Huntington's only black high school, and his instructors included his uncles John Morton and James Buchanan Riddle and his cousin Carter Harrison Barnett, who had graduated from Denison University in Ohio and was currently serving as principal at Douglass High School. Inspired by these relatives, and perhaps believing that he needed to catch up, Woodson completed four years' worth of course work in two years and graduated in 1897. Desiring more education, he then enrolled in Berea College in Kentucky in the fall of 1897.[27]

Why Woodson chose to attend Berea is uncertain. Purportedly he read a magazine article on the college and was impressed with its system of interracial education. Physical proximity and his family's financial struggles also must have factored into Woodson's decision to attend Berea. The school was relatively close to Huntington, offered scholarships, and encouraged students to work on campus to defray their expenses. Established in 1855 by abolitionist John G. Fee on land donated by Cassius Clay, Berea was incorporated in 1866 and funded by the American Missionary Association. During and after the Civil War, blacks came in droves desiring admission. Every aspect of life at Berea was integrated—classrooms, dining halls, and dormitories, as well as extracurricular activities and entertainment.[28] However, by the time

26. *Ibid.*, 115–18. The Richmond *Planet, West Virginia Pioneer and Mountaineer*, Pittsburgh *Telegraph*, Toledo *Blade*, Cincinnati *Commercial Gazette*, and Louisville *Courier Journal* were among the newspapers from which he read.

27. Woodson, Obituary of John Riddle, 243–46, "My Recollections of Veterans of the Civil War," 103–104, and "Early History of Negro Education in W. Va.," 23–63.

28. Elizabeth S. Peck, *Berea's First Century, 1855–1955* (Lexington, Ky., 1955), 39–57; Joe M. Richardson, *Christian Reconstruction: The American Missionary Association and Southern Blacks, 1861–1890* (Athens, Ga., 1985), 78, 124, 227, 297. Rayford W. Logan, in "*Phylon* Profile VI: Carter G. Woodson," *Phylon*, VI (1945), 319, contends that Woodson attended Lincoln University in Pennsylvania for six months.

Woodson enrolled there, the commitment to interracial education had weakened. And in 1904, just a year after Woodson graduated, the Kentucky state legislature passed the Day Law, which was specifically directed at Berea in proscribing integration in higher education, and black students were no longer admitted. Instead, the college educated poor white Appalachians.[29]

Woodson's strict morality probably was reinforced at Berea. Before being admitted, applicants were required to present not only a high school diploma but also a testimonial of good character. Students selected an academic adviser who also served as a surrogate parent by providing advice on personal problems. The use of alcohol and tobacco was forbidden, and students were required to attend chapel every day except Tuesday and Saturday.[30]

When Woodson arrived at Berea, he was placed in the preparatory department at a level equivalent to the third year of high school, even though he had graduated from high school. He did, however, receive advanced credits by taking tests. Woodson was in residence for only two quarters in the 1897–1898 academic year, because he did not have the money for a full year's tuition. He attended Berea part-time from 1901 to 1903, and the University of Chicago during the summer of 1902. He earned enough credits to graduate in the spring of 1903.[31]

Woodson followed the prescribed program for a B.L. degree, taking courses in literature, rhetoric, science, sociology, economics, international law, and history. He received his first formal training in history under Howard Murray Jones, who also taught philosophy. Woodson studied general history and took advanced courses in British and Roman history. Jones used Philip Van Ness Myers' *A General History for Colleges and High Schools* as the text for the general course, and Myers' *Ancient History for Colleges and High Schools* and *Outlines of Medieval and Modern History* as texts for the advanced courses.[32]

While this first exposure to formal historical training at Berea probably did not influence Woodson's decision to become a historian or to

29. Peck, *Berea's First Century*, 40–50; Paul David Nelson, "Experiment in Interracial Education at Berea College, 1858–1908," *Journal of Negro History*, LIX (1974), 13–27; Charles T. Morgan, *The Fruit of This Tree* (Berea, Ky., 1946), 145–89; William G. Frost, "Berea College," in *From Servitude to Service*, ed. American Unitarian Association (Boston, 1905), 67–80.

30. Romero, "Carter G. Woodson," 23–25.

31. *Ibid.;* Maxine H. Sullivan, Registrar of the University of Chicago, to author, December 6, 1984.

32. Sullivan to author, December 6, 1984; *Berea College Quarterly*, II (April, 1903), 1–44; Romero, "Carter G. Woodson," 23–25.

study black history, his experiences there profoundly shaped his attitude toward race relations. Woodson was thrust into an educational and social milieu that forced him to deal emotionally and intellectually with the values, attitudes, and ideas of poor Appalachian whites, who were potentially, if not in fact, his social and academic equals. Woodson had had prior contact with this class of whites while growing up in post-Reconstruction Virginia and as a coal miner in West Virginia. But Berea provided him with daily, long-term interaction with whites, not only in the classroom, but also in the dining hall and dormitory. Although white students as a group may have expressed hostility toward black students, individual interracial friendships probably were formed, and Woodson may have had some white friends.[33]

Woodson and Berea president William Frost apparently had some interpersonal contact, which was unusual because of Berea's size. The school was just large enough so that the college president was not personally acquainted with many students. Moreover, Woodson did not remain in residence during his college years as most students did. Frost may have admired or been attracted to Woodson because he was an older student. Years after he graduated, Woodson asked Frost for letters of recommendation for several teaching jobs. Although he undoubtedly abhorred Frost's racial views—Frost believed that blacks were inferior—Woodson probably respected his administrative ability and his influence in the educational establishment. Frost's views on the ability of education to transform the lower classes of society—in this case, poor white Appalachians—shaped Woodson's ideas about the same possibilities for blacks. Like Frost, Woodson held a deep respect for the value of manual labor as a means of building character and preparing for life. Years later Woodson argued that a combination of classical and vocational training was best for blacks, training similar to that he had received at Berea, and he adopted outreach programs (adult education courses and a Lecture Bureau) for the Association for the Study of Negro Life and History similar to those Frost had created.[34]

Woodson's commitment to teaching was deepened both by his interaction with his teachers at Berea and through his friendships with other

33. The sympathy for poor Appalachian whites that Woodson expressed years later in his scholarship on the antebellum, Civil War, and Reconstruction periods was influenced by actual contact with this class.

34. Woodson to William G. Frost, March 21, June 18, 1908, in Presidents' Papers, College Archives, Berea College, Berea, Ky.; Frost, "Berea College," in *From Servitude to Service*, 48–80; Peck, *Berea's First Century*, 40–48; Morgan, *The Fruit of This Tree*, 145–89.

black students, most of whom also planned to teach. In return for all the practical lessons he had learned from ordinary blacks, Woodson decided to become a teacher in the black community.[35]

From 1898 to 1900 Woodson taught in Winona, West Virginia, in a school established by black miners for their children. He left Winona in 1900, searching for greater opportunity in Huntington. Just five years after he had graduated from Douglass High School, Woodson was hired there as history teacher and principal, replacing his cousin Carter Harrison Barnett, who had served since 1890. In 1903 the state legislature began to require teachers to be certified, but Woodson had already earned a state teaching certificate in 1901. The certification exam tested teachers in all subjects, not just their specialization; Woodson had been tested in drawing, music, science, and educational methods, as well as history. His average grade was 91 percent; his lowest, 82 percent. He earned a score of 90 percent in United States history, general history, and government, but his best grades were in Latin, arithmetic, and algebra. When Woodson assumed his new post, his salary more than doubled, from $30 to $65 per month.[36]

While he was in Huntington, Woodson lived with his parents, who owned their home by this time. His interest in history was stimulated further in this environment, where he still read to his father from a variety of newspapers and on Sunday mornings brought him breakfast at the railway shops where he worked. Woodson eagerly performed this task, for it allowed him to listen to conversations between his father and other black and white workers, many of whom also were Civil War veterans. He recalled years later that he learned "so much about the Civil War from the actual participants." These discussions inevitably aroused differences of opinion, and one Sunday, James Henry Woodson got into a fight with his foreman, a white Confederate veteran named Wysong. Wysong, who defended slavery and the Lost Cause, lost the fight, and in retaliation he unsuccessfully tried to fire James Henry Woodson.[37]

Woodson also became acquainted with Civil War veteran and minister George T. Prosser, who founded the first African Methodist Epis-

35. Woodson, "My Recollections of Veterans of the Civil War," 103–104, 115–18. On other black students at Berea, see Peck, *Berea's First Century*, 48; *Berea College Quarterly*, II (February, 1897), 22–25.
36. Census of 1900, Nuttall Dist., Fayette Cty., and City of Huntington, Cabell Cty., W. Va., in RG 29; Woodson, "Early History of Negro Education in W. Va.," 23–63; Copy of Woodson's certificate, in *Negro History Bulletin*, XII (May, 1950), 180.
37. Woodson, "My Recollections of Veterans of the Civil War," 117.

copal (AME) church in Huntington. Prosser had served in the Massachusetts Fifty-Fourth Regiment under Robert Gould Shaw and
frequently illustrated his Sunday sermons with stories about his Civil
War experiences. Taken prisoner in 1863 and held through the end of
the war, Prosser maintained that while white prisoners were treated
well, blacks' food, clothing, and medical care were inferior. Woodson
met many other veterans and was greatly impressed with their stories
about the war, and years later he noted that they had influenced his
views about history.[38]

In 1898 the Treaty of Paris ended the Spanish-American War and
brought the Philippines under American jurisdiction. Believing that
American troops not only would quash the local revolt but also would
bring political stability and economic prosperity to the country, the
wealthy white landowning class welcomed American military intervention. American military troops laid the foundation of civil government
on the islands, supervised elections of local officials, organized the legal
system, and built public health and educational facilities. Most American troops and military support staff were withdrawn by 1902, and political authority was transferred to a civil commission headed by William Howard Taft. Prior to the establishment of Taft's administration,
during military occupation in 1898, a superintendent of schools was
appointed and began to recruit American teachers, purportedly to train
the Filipinos to govern themselves.[39]

    Because of his belief in the uplifting power of education and because
of the opportunity to travel to another country to observe and experience the culture firsthand, Woodson decided to teach in the Philippines. He also undoubtedly was attracted to the high salary—$100 per
month—and may have hoped to save enough money to continue his
formal education. He arrived there on his twenty-eighth birthday and
further developed his beliefs regarding the ability of education to transform society.[40]

    To attract American teachers, the War Department had used seduc-

    38. *Ibid.*
    39. Willard B. Gatewood, Jr., *Black Americans and the White Man's Burden, 1898–
1903* (Urbana, 1975), 181–82; Vincent R. Catapang, *The Development and the Present
Status of Education in the Philippine Islands* (Boston, 1926), 64–97.
    40. Sister Mary Anthony Scally, "The Philippine Challenge," *Negro History Bulletin*,
XLIV (January-March, 1981), 16–18; Gatewood, *Black Americans and the White Man's
Burden*, 181–82.

tive advertising, promising adventure in a tropical paradise. In fact, these teachers faced extremely difficult conditions, especially in outlying provinces, as they tried to substitute sixteenth-century educational methods with twentieth-century ideas and systems. The tropical climate took its toll on the teaching force; 38 teachers left because of ill health, while 14 others died, most from disease. In 1902 the combined American and native teaching force was 4,227. By late 1903, when Woodson arrived, Americans had trained 3,400 native teachers.[41]

Woodson was not the only African-American teacher to go to the Philippines. Many others seized the opportunity and left the United States. In 1901, Booker T. Washington wrote to the War Department to inquire about placement of Tuskegee Institute graduates in the Philippines. During his tenure in the Philippines, Woodson had at least half a dozen black colleagues. He later wrote about one of the most successful, John Henry Manning Butler, who had taught high school and college courses at North Carolina Agricultural and Technical College before going to the Philippines in 1902. Butler stayed in the islands through 1933 and served as superintendent of schools in Isabella Province.[42]

Although Woodson passed the Civil Service exam in the winter of 1903, his appointment was delayed until the fall. In November he traveled on the Union Pacific Railroad from Chicago, where he had been enrolled in the University of Chicago, to San Francisco; there he boarded the SS *Korea* for Hong Kong. After a short layover, he boarded another steamship for the fifty-six hour voyage to Manila. During the trip to Manila, Woodson met a missionary en route to China, who advised him against trying to Americanize the Filipinos and suggested that he immerse himself in the language, culture, and history of the people. He also met a businessman who gave up his insurance business to teach in the Philippines.[43]

---

41. Catapang, *Development and Present Status of Education in the Philippine Islands*, 64–97; Helen P. Beattie, "American Teachers and the Filipinos," *Outlook*, LXXVIII (October 15, 1904), 419–26. Also see John Henry Manning Butler, "New Education in the Philippines," *Journal of Negro Education*, IV (1935), 257–68; *Report of the Secretary of Instruction of the Philippine Islands, October 1902* (Washington, D.C., 1902), 867–83.

42. Butler, "New Education in the Philippines," 257–68; Woodson, Obituary of John Henry Manning Butler, in *Journal of Negro History*, XXX (1945), 243–44.

43. David P. Barrows to Woodson, February 27, 1903, Woodson to Colonel C. R. Edwards, October 17, 1903, W. Leon Pepperman to Woodson, October 20, 1903, Edwards to Woodson, October 20, 1903, Woodson to Edwards, October 22, 1903, Edwards

Woodson arrived in the Philippines in the middle of the academic year and was assigned to a school in San Isidro, a small town near Manila, in the province of Nueva Ecija. Most of the land was owned by a few wealthy white aristocrats and was worked by small farmers, peasants, and sharecroppers. Since Woodson could not speak Spanish when he arrived, he had a difficult time communicating with his students; but he soon enrolled in correspondence courses in Spanish and French through the University of Chicago, and within a year was speaking fluent Spanish and French. Woodson taught English, health, and some agricultural skills, probably in a one-room bamboo hut. In June, 1904, he was promoted and transferred to the province of Pangasinan, where he served as supervisor of schools and was in charge of teacher-training.[44]

Woodson must have sent glowing reports of his experiences home to his family, since his brother Robert and sister Bessie wrote to the Civil Service Commission indicating that they also would like to go to the Philippines to teach. When Woodson's tour of duty concluded in December, 1905, he signed up for two more years. The following year, however, he asked for a leave of absence to return to the United States to visit his family, and when he became too ill to return to the Philippines, he reluctantly resigned from his post in February, 1907.[45]

After recovering at home, Woodson embarked on a six-month world tour, visiting Africa, Asia, and Europe. He traveled to Malaysia, India, Egypt, Palestine, Greece, Italy, and France, where he studied educational methods, visited libraries, and met many scholars whom he would later call upon to assist him in his research on black history. In Paris, Woodson conducted research in the Bibliothèque Nationale and spent one semester at the University of Paris studying European history and attending lectures given by professors François-Alphonse Aulard, Charles Diehl, and Henry Lemonnier.[46]

---

to Woodson, October 26, 1903, Woodson to Edwards, October 29, 1903, Edwards to Woodson, October 31, 1903, Woodson to Edwards, November 5, 1903, all in Record Group 350, Records of the Bureau of Insular Affairs, File 8898, NA; Woodson, *The Mis-Education of the Negro* (Washington, D.C., 1933), 151–54.

44. Woodson, *The Mis-Education of the Negro*, 151–54.

45. Bessie A. Woodson to the Bureau of Insular Affairs, August 30, 1904, Robert H. Woodson to Colonel C. R. Edwards, August 31, 1904, W. Leon Pepperman to Robert H. Woodson, September 6, 1904, Acting Bureau Chief to John C. Block, December 12, 1907, all in RG 350, File 8898.

46. Woodson to James R. Angell, October 12, 1920, in Carnegie Foundation Archives, Butler Library, Columbia University; Woodson to William G. Frost, March 21,

After that brief period of formal study under these eminent historians, Woodson apparently decided to pursue graduate work in history. By the fall of 1907 he was back in the United States, enrolled as a full-time student at the University of Chicago. Woodson intended to take graduate courses for a master's degree in history, but he was informed that he must take some undergraduate courses to earn another bachelor's degree. His degree from Berea College was considered inadequate preparation for entrance to the graduate program. Although discouraged, Woodson complied with the university's requirement and took undergraduate and graduate courses simultaneously.[47]

Woodson began graduate work in American history under the direction of Edwin Earle Sparks and Andrew McLaughlin, perhaps because he initially planned to write his master's thesis on the black church. In February, 1908, he wrote to Atlanta University professor W. E. B. Du Bois requesting statistics on the number of black churches in the United States and information on the training of black ministers. Du Bois sent him the Atlanta University study of the Negro church along with a bill. Sparks or McLaughlin may have disapproved of the topic, or Woodson may have had difficulty obtaining enough information that would enable him to write the thesis and complete his degree by the end of the summer. In any case, he ended up working with Ferdinand Schevill, an extraordinarily gifted teacher who gave generously of himself to students, ensuring that they received the best historical training. Interested in European history, Woodson had familiarized himself with French primary source materials while at the University of Paris. He decided to write his thesis on the French diplomatic policy toward Germany in the eighteenth century, covering the corrupt administration of Louis XV, French efforts to partition Austria during the War of the Austrian Succession, 1740–1748, and the origins of the French Revolution. In addition to secondary sources, Woodson used French diplomatic correspondence and the personal papers of Louis XV. The thesis was accepted in August, 1908, and Woodson received a master's degree in history and Romance languages and literature. He earlier had

---

1908, in Berea College Archives. He also told Louis Mehlinger about his travels. See Hubert E. Potter, "A Review of the Life and Work of Carter G. Woodson" (MS in Moorland-Spingarn Research Center) Appendix A, "Interview with Captain Louis Mehlinger," 56–57.

47. Sullivan to author, December 6, 1984; Woodson to Frost, March 21, 1908, in Berea College Archives.

completed requirements for the bachelor's degree and received it in March, 1908.[48]

Determining that Woodson was capable of advanced study, his professors at Chicago undoubtedly encouraged him to seek the Ph.D. degree and may have advised him to apply to Harvard University since he was interested in American history. Moreover, because Chicago was just beginning to award doctorates at the time Woodson was studying for his master's degree, Harvard was a better choice. Woodson also may have been attracted to Harvard because Du Bois, the only other professionally trained black historian, graduated from that university, and because he believed the history department faculty were liberal and racially enlightened. After Woodson began his course work, however, he found that some were not as liberal as he had hoped.[49]

After completing his master's thesis, Woodson remained in Chicago. Early in September, 1908, he wrote to Charles Haskins, dean of Harvard's Graduate School of Arts and Sciences, seeking admission. He was anxious to complete his course work and exams for the doctorate as soon as possible because of the expense he would incur if he remained in residence for more than a year, and he inquired about the residency requirement. Furthermore, Woodson hoped to return to the Philippines in the summer of 1909 and teach. He arrived at Cambridge in October, 1908. In December, the history department approved Woodson's plan of study but not his request to take the general and special examinations during the spring of 1909. Despite his intention to leave Harvard to return to the Philippines, Woodson applied for a fellowship that would provide him with the financial resources to remain in residence for a second year, but was turned down.[50]

While Woodson may not have been as academically well-prepared

48. Woodson to W. E. B. Du Bois, February 18, 1908, in W. E. B. Du Bois Papers, University of Massachusetts; Lawrence Reddick, "As I Remember Woodson," *Crisis*, LX (February, 1953), 75–80; Howard K. Beale, "The Professional Historian: His Theory and His Practice," *Pacific Historical Quarterly*, XXII (1953), 233; Woodson, "The German Policy of France in the War of Austrian Succession" (M.A. thesis, University of Chicago, 1908); and Sullivan to author, December 6, 1984.

49. The Ph.D. program at Chicago was established in 1901 by J. Franklin Jameson. See Robert Dallek, *Democrat and Diplomat: The Life of William E. Dodd* (New York, 1968), 50–58.

50. Woodson to Charles Haskins, September 12, 1908, Haskins to Woodson, September 18, November 24, 1908, Minutes of History Department Meetings, December 3, 1908, March 23, 1909, all in Records of the Department of History, Harvard University Archives, Pusey Library.

as his first-year counterparts, probably few others had traveled as much or experienced life in as many different cultures as Woodson had. While he was in Cambridge, Woodson lived in College Hall, a graduate dormitory, and although none of his classmates in the History and Government Program lived there, he made friends with at least two students in the program. He later corresponded with Arthur Howland Buffington, who graduated from and later taught at Williams College, and Orren Hormell, who became president of Bowdoin College.[51]

During the two semesters he spent in residence at Harvard, Woodson took seminars and reading courses in European and American history. Because official transcripts are available only to immediate relatives, it is uncertain which specific seminars Woodson took. However, by considering the seminars listed in the Harvard catalog for 1908–1909 in light of the subjects on which Woodson was examined, one can surmise that he took "The First Eight Christian Centuries" and "The Church in the Middle Ages" with Ephraim Emerton, "The History of England During the Tudor-Stuart Period" with Roger B. Merriman, "English History from the Revolution of 1688 to the Reform of Parliament" with Silas M. Mac Vane, reading courses in German and French history from Charles Gross and William B. Munro, and American history from Edward Channing. Seminars were offered in the morning, and Woodson had afternoons free for reading courses, research, and writing.[52]

Although Woodson had believed that Channing was liberal on racial issues, he later recalled that in seminar Channing not only belittled the Negro's role in American history but also argued that the Negro had no history. On one occasion Woodson maintained that when discussing the American Revolution, Channing "refer[ed] to the Boston Massacre in a most facetious fashion. He spoke of Crispus Attucks and his companions as idlers who happened to be among those who were throwing missiles at the British soldiers stationed in Boston." According to Woodson, Channing "laughed at the idea" that "the incident [was] an important contribution to the independence of this country." Thus, Woodson frequently challenged Channing's views and interpretation of American history, and Channing, in turn, challenged Woodson's views

51. Woodson was one of thirty-six students admitted in 1908 to the graduate programs in history and government, and political science, although one hundred students had applied for admission. See *Harvard University Catalog, 1908–1909* (Cambridge, 1909), 99–121.

52. *Ibid.*, 361–65.

and asserted that Woodson should undertake research to prove that the Negro had a history.[53]

Because of Channing's negative attitude toward blacks, Woodson asked Albert Bushnell Hart to serve as his dissertation adviser, even though he took no courses with Hart and Channing remained on his committee. Woodson soon found out, however, that Hart was just as conservative as Channing. Hart believed blacks to be an inferior race, although he maintained that they should be given an opportunity to improve themselves through education. Woodson was not the first black student Hart had supervised at Harvard; he also had served as Du Bois' dissertation adviser.[54]

While Woodson did not share many of Hart's views or his interpretation of American history, Hart probably did influence Woodson's philosophy of history. Both men thought that an accurate understanding of the past would enlighten the present generation and that the mere assembling of facts would lead to the truth. Hart wrote historical articles for numerous magazines and newspapers, believing, as did Woodson, that it was important to present history to the general public. In addition, Woodson shared Hart's view on the value of oral testimony as a supplement to documentary sources for historical research. In preparation for writing *Slavery and Abolition*, published in 1906, Hart traveled throughout the South and interviewed former slaves and their masters. Because Hart encouraged his students to write on subjects with which they were familiar, he may have influenced Woodson's decision to write his dissertation on the secession movement in western Virginia.[55]

First-year students in the American history seminar were encouraged to choose a dissertation topic and begin their research as soon as possible. Although Woodson initially hoped to complete all of his requirements during his first year at Harvard, it is unlikely that he made considerable progress on the dissertation. After he learned that he would not be permitted to take his exams in the spring, and that he would not receive a fellowship, Woodson decided to return to the Philippines and abandon hope of completing the Ph.D. He reasoned that

53. Woodson, "The George Washington Bicentennial Eliminates March 5th, Crispus Attucks Day," New York *Age*, January 6, 1932, p. 9. Merle Curti, a student in Channing's seminar in 1920–21, described his experiences in a letter to Davis D. Joyce, August 2, 1966, in Curti Papers, State Historical Society of Wisconsin, Madison.

54. Carol F. Baird, "Albert Bushnell Hart," in *The Social Sciences at Harvard, 1860–1920*, ed. Paul H. Buck (Cambridge, 1965), 129–74.

55. *Ibid.*

once he was settled in the Philippines he would be unable to conduct the necessary research to complete his dissertation and probably could not arrange to return to the United States to take his examinations.[56]

At the end of the spring term, Woodson began preparations to return to the Philippines. At the same time, however, he applied for a teaching position in the Washington, D.C., public schools and took the required examinations. If he were offered a job in Washington, he could complete his degree. In July, 1909, he left Cambridge to visit his family in Huntington, where he received word of a job offer in Washington at a salary comparable to what he would receive in the Philippines. On July 15, just five days before he was to leave Seattle and sail to the Philippines, Woodson wrote to the assistant chief of the Bureau of Insular Affairs claiming that he was too ill to accept the teaching post in the Philippines and including a letter from his cousin, physician Clinton Constantine Barnett, who certified that Woodson suffered from stomach trouble. It is possible the illness that had prompted Woodson to resign from his teaching post in the Philippines in 1907 had reappeared. However, in mid-May while Woodson was still in Cambridge, a physical examination he was required to undergo before he could sail to the Philippines had shown him to be in excellent health. Perhaps an ulcer or signs of other stomach disorders would not have appeared during this physical examination. Or perhaps once Woodson learned he had a job in Washington and therefore could complete his dissertation, he asked his cousin to help him out and provide him with an excuse. Clearly he wanted to complete the Ph.D., and he accepted the post with the Washington public schools.[57]

Once Woodson had settled into a daily routine of teaching high school, he continued to study for his Ph.D. examinations and worked on his dissertation at the Library of Congress. He was fortunate in that Louis Mehlinger, who worked as a stenographer in the Treasury De-

---

56. Haskins to Woodson, September 18, November 24, 1908, and Woodson to Haskins, February 15, 1909, in Dept. of History Records, Harvard University Archives.

57. Frank M. McIntyre to Woodson, December 29, 1908, Woodson to McIntyre, January 8, 1909, McIntyre to Woodson, April 5, 1909, Woodson to McIntyre, April 10, 1909, McIntyre to Woodson, April 13, 1909, "Record of Medical and Physical Examination," May 15, 1909, Woodson to McIntyre, July 2, 1909, McIntyre to Woodson, July 9, 1909, Woodson to McIntyre, July 9, 1909, July 15, 1909, and enclosed affidavit from Dr. C. C. Barnett, McIntyre to Woodson, July 19, 1909, all in RG 350, File 8898. Also see Minutes of Board of Education, July 1, 1909, in Records of Washington, D.C., Board of Education, Sumner School Archives Washington, D.C., which list Woodson as passing his examinations and certifying his eligibility for appointment to a teaching position.

partment, was interested in history and helped him do research at the Library of Congress. Mehlinger also provided clerical help. Woodson would dictate his chapters to Mehlinger, who wrote them in shorthand and then produced typed transcripts.[58]

In September, 1909, Woodson wrote to Haskins to inform him that he would be completing the requirements for the degree, and he began to make arrangements to take the general examination in European history. By November, Woodson felt well prepared for the general examination. He took it in early January and easily passed. Channing chaired a committee consisting of professors Emerton, Mac Vane, Merriman, and Munro, who examined Woodson in "Early and Modern British History," "German History," "Theory of the State," and "The History of the Church from the Fall of the Roman Empire to the Middle of the Fifteenth Century." By the spring of 1910, Woodson had completed a draft of the dissertation and submitted it to Haskins, Hart, and Channing.[59]

While Woodson always had encountered problems with Channing, he got along with Hart, initially at least, and may not have anticipated the trouble he would have getting his dissertation approved. Haskins was left with the unpleasant task of informing Woodson that Hart and Channing found his dissertation unacceptable. Not only was the literary composition "distinctly rough" but "important aspects of the subject [had] not been covered." Woodson "had not worked out the latter part of [his subject], . . . the decade or so preceding the Civil War." He had failed to cover "the growth of relations between Virginia and the Ohio Valley." According to Haskins, Hart and Channing believed that "the thesis also suffer[ed] to a certain extent from a lack of breadth in failing to take account of the general movements of American history in the period [Woodson was] considering." Haskins advised Woodson to seek more specific advice from Hart before he began his revisions. Since no copy of Woodson's dissertation in draft form is extant, it is uncertain whether Hart and Channing had just complaints. It is also uncertain whether Woodson took Haskins' advice and sought more de-

---

58. Potter, "A Review of the Life and Work of Carter G. Woodson," Appendix A, 56–57.

59. Woodson to Haskins, September 27, October 25, 1909, Haskins to Woodson, October 30, 1909, Woodson to Haskins, November 13, 1909, Haskins to Woodson, December 7, 1909, Woodson to Haskins, December 18, 1909, Haskins to Woodson, January 12, 1910, "Division of History and Political Science, Special Examinations for the Degree of Ph.D., 1909–1910," January 8, 1910, Minutes of History Dept. Meeting, March 10, 1911, all in Dept. of History Records, Harvard University Archives.

tailed criticisms from Hart, since no correspondence about this matter exists in Hart's papers.[60]

While he undoubtedly was discouraged by this setback, Woodson was determined to produce an acceptable dissertation and obtain his degree, even if it meant that he had to deal with Hart's and Channing's criticisms. By January, 1911, Woodson had produced a draft that he believed would be satisfactory. He wrote to Haskins and Hart stating that he had spent a year "rearranging and amplifying the thesis" and asking them to read the revised manuscript. If Hart did agree to read the draft, he probably was not satisfied, for the evidence suggests that he then asked Frederick Jackson Turner, who had joined Harvard's history department in the fall of 1910, to read the manuscript; the final version, which was accepted fifteen months later, greatly reflects Turner's influence and incorporates many of his ideas.[61]

Woodson faced an additional stumbling block on the way to earning his doctorate: he failed his special examination in American history. He had arranged to take the special examination as well as his language examinations in May, 1911. Hart chaired the examining committee, which also consisted of Channing, Turner, and Munro. It is unknown why Woodson failed, for the minutes of the history department only reflect the final decision, not the reasons for his failure, and he was the only student of sixteen who did not pass the special examination that year. Undoubtedly, Woodson's views on American history differed from those of his white professors. Hart, as chairman of the committee, may have influenced the final decision to fail Woodson; when Woodson took the examination again in April, 1912, Hart had been removed from the committee and replaced as chairman by Channing, and Woodson passed. His dissertation was approved and accepted by the graduate school shortly thereafter. Although Woodson did not acknowledge Hart as the chairman of his dissertation committee, Hart's signature appears first on the title page of Woodson's dissertation, followed by Turner's and Channing's.[62]

*   *   *

60. Haskins to Woodson, May 4, 1910, in Dept. of History Records, Harvard University Archives.

61. Woodson to Haskins, January 13, 1911, and Woodson to Hart, January 13, 1911, in Dept. of History Records, Harvard University Archives. Turner went to Harvard in the fall of 1910, but received the appointment in 1909. See J. Franklin Jameson to Frederick Jackson Turner, November 22, 1909, in J. Franklin Jameson Papers, Manuscript Division, Library of Congress.

62. Woodson to Haskins, February 20, 1911, "Division of History and Political Science, Examinations for the Degree of Ph.D., 1910–1911," May 6, 1911, "Division

Despite Woodson's later assertion that it took him twenty years to re-
cover from the education he received at Harvard, and his admission
that *he* was miseducated, it is clear that his bibliographic and research
skills were developed and his views on American history were influenced by the training he received there. Woodson was greatly influenced by Turner and must have read his work, and yet he cited neither
Turner nor Turner's student Charles Henry Ambler in his dissertation.
Turner almost certainly referred Woodson to Ambler's book, *Sectionalism in Virginia from 1776 to 1861*, which was published in 1910, but if
Woodson had read it, he did not acknowledge its existence. Ambler's
book was a revision of his 1908 University of Wisconsin doctoral dissertation and covered much of the same ground as Woodson's. The two
differed in important respects, however, for Ambler's emphasis was on
political, rather than economic, forces. Like Woodson, Ambler was influenced by Turner, and he emphasized sectional conflict, tracing the
roots of western Virginia's secessionist movement to the eve of the
revolutionary war. Yet Woodson's study went back even further in time,
to the early 1700s. Ambler devoted more attention to the formation of
political parties and to the struggles in the Virginia General Assembly.
Unlike Woodson, he was not as concerned with class conflict among
whites, or with slavery as an economic cause of the struggle between
the eastern aristocracy and the western frontiersmen.[63]

Woodson would insist later that he never published his dissertation
because he was preempted by the publication of Ambler's book in 1910.
Initially, however, he sought Turner's help in finding a publisher for
his manuscript. Shortly after receiving the Ph.D., Woodson began expanding and revising his dissertation, and in the spring of 1914 he asked
Turner to read the revised manuscript. While Woodson acknowledged
in his letter to Turner that Ambler's work was similar, he maintained
that he had made an additional contribution by presenting a different
emphasis and covering a longer period of time. Because Turner had

---

of History and Political Science, Examinations for the Degree of Ph.D., 1911–1912,"
April 11, 1912, Minutes of History Dept. Meeting, May 23, 1912, all in Dept. of History
Records, Harvard University Archives.

63. Woodson, "Twenty Years Wasted, Says D.C. Historian," *Negro World*, March 21,
1931, pp. 1, 8; Woodson, "The Disruption of Virginia" (Ph.D. dissertation, Harvard
University, 1912). On Turner's influence, see Turner to Jameson, May 27, 1916, in
Jameson Papers; Charles Henry Ambler, *Sectionalism in Virginia from 1776 to 1861* (Chicago, 1910).

helped Ambler get his thesis published and had been on Woodson's dissertation committee, Woodson felt that Turner also might help him find a publisher.[64]

Apparently Turner could not read the manuscript right away, and Woodson made further revisions before sending it to him in the winter of 1915. Turner replied two months later, indicating that he thought it would be difficult to publish the manuscript because it was too similar to Ambler's recent book. Turner tried to be encouraging as well as realistic and made a few stylistic suggestions. He expressed doubt that the history department would be willing to include it in the "Harvard Historical Studies," a series of published dissertations, or that Harvard University Press would be interested, but proposed that Woodson take a chance and send it to a publisher. He cautioned that Woodson might have to provide a subvention, since the book would probably not make money. He ended the letter by suggesting that Woodson ask "some Southern man" like Ulrich B. Phillips or Charles Ambler for advice.[65]

Woodson also had difficulty publishing *The Education of the Negro Prior to 1861*, which he completed at the time he was revising his dissertation. In early July, 1914, Woodson wrote to J. Franklin Jameson, the director of the Department of Historical Research for the Carnegie Institution of Washington and the editor of the *American Historical Review*, and asked him to read the manuscript. Jameson, who was interested in black history, replied that he wished he were able to comply with Woodson's request but countless other duties took up his time.[66]

A few weeks after receiving Jameson's response, Woodson wrote to Henry Holt and Company to inquire about the prospects of publication. He indicated that this was the first of a projected two-volume study and sent a chapter outline. Less than a week later, however, Woodson was turned down on the grounds that there would be no market for the manuscript. This time Woodson did not seek Turner's advice to secure a publisher; he had decided to provide G. P. Putnam's

64. Woodson to Turner, June 20, 1914, in Frederick Jackson Turner Papers, Huntington Library, San Marino, Calif.

65. Woodson to Turner, April 17, 1915, and Turner to Woodson, April 28, 1915, in Turner Papers. I examined both collections of U. B. Phillips Papers, in the Southern Historical Collection, University of North Carolina, Chapel Hill, and in Sterling Memorial Library, Yale University, and corresponded with the archivist at Wise Library, West Virginia University, where the Charles Henry Ambler Papers are; since I found no correspondence on this subject, it is uncertain whether Woodson took Turner's advice.

66. Woodson to Jameson, June 27, 1914, and Jameson to Woodson, July 2, 1914, in Jameson Papers.

Sons with a subvention, and they agreed to publish the manuscript. Woodson sent a copy of the book to Turner, who praised it by stating that Woodson had "made a substantial contribution to the subject." [67] The book was widely and favorably reviewed in the white popular press and in historical journals, and it is still cited by contemporary historians. Certainly Henry Holt and Company made a mistake by not publishing it. Because Woodson had to pay a publisher's subvention on a meager salary, perhaps he was limited to pursuing publication of either his dissertation or *The Education of the Negro*, and chose the latter as more important.

Charles Henry Ambler did not have the last word on the secession movement in western Virginia. In 1913, shortly after Woodson completed his dissertation, James C. McGregor finished a dissertation on the same subject at the University of Pennsylvania under the direction of John Bach McMaster. Like Woodson's work, it was titled "The Disruption of Virginia," and in 1922 it was published by the MacMillan Company. The book covered the period from Lincoln's election through the establishment of West Virginia, a much shorter time period than that treated in Woodson's dissertation. Woodson reviewed the book in the *Journal of Negro History*, describing it as more of a polemic than a historical account. He pointed out that McGregor's interpretation differed widely from his own and that of Charles Ambler, whose book he praised. Woodson conceded the fact that McGregor had found some new evidence but concluded that this was not enough to justify the book's publication. In 1934, Garrett and Massie Publishers of Richmond, Virginia, brought out Henry T. Shanks's *The Secession Movement in Virginia, 1847–1861*. Shanks's book was broader in coverage than McGregor's but narrower than Woodson's dissertation or Ambler's book. In 1964 the University of Pittsburgh Press published Richard Orr Curry's *House Divided: A Study of Statehood Politics and the Copperhead Movement in West Virginia*. Like McGregor's and Shanks's books, Curry's was a political history that began in the nineteenth century. To his credit, however, Curry was the only scholar writing on the subject to cite Woodson's 1912 dissertation. [68]

67. Woodson to Henry Holt Company, July 22, 1914, and R. Holt to Woodson, July 27, 1914, in Holt Company Archives, Firestone Library, Princeton University; Turner to Woodson, May 31, 1915, in Turner Papers.
68. Woodson, Review of James C. McGregor's *The Disruption of Virginia*, in *Journal of Negro History*, VIII (1923), 239–42. Allison Goodyear Freehling, in *Drift Towards Dissolution: The Virginia Slavery Debate of 1831–1832* (Baton Rouge, 1982), similarly gave

Although Woodson never published his dissertation, he incorporated large portions of it into articles that appeared in the *Journal of Negro History* and into the chapters of *The Negro in Our History*. He never appeared to be bitter because he was unable to get the manuscript published, and throughout his life he maintained that it was not published because of its similarity to Ambler's work. It is clear, however, that if Woodson had been able to obtain support from a prominent white historian, the manuscript might have been published.[69]

It was remarkable that Woodson completed his dissertation, revised it for publication, and researched, wrote, and published a monograph on black education all while holding down a full-time teaching job.[70] During his first few years in the District of Columbia public school system Woodson taught at several different schools. Initially he was assigned to teach eighth grade at Thaddeus Stevens School, but after only a month he was transferred to Armstrong Manual Training High School, where he remained until October, 1911. He then was transferred to M Street High School. Woodson apparently was dissatisfied by the frequent moves, for late in 1911, he took the Civil Service examination and had a physical, hoping to resume teaching in the Philippines. He wrote to the director of the Bureau of Education in Manila, enclosing favorable letters of recommendation and requesting a salary of $1,800 per year. Perhaps because Woodson's unexpected resignation in 1909 had caused the Bureau of Education some inconvenience, the acting director replied that he could give Woodson no assurance that his application for reinstatement would be given consideration in the near future. He also indicated that if Woodson were reinstated, his salary would be $1,200 per year, the same amount he had received almost ten years earlier. Apparently Woodson did not pursue the possibility of returning to the Philippines any further, perhaps because he was already earning almost $1,200 per year.[71]

---

great attention to slavery and to the economic and geographic causes of the secession movement.

69. Romero, "Carter G. Woodson," 4; Earl E. Thorpe, *The Central Theme of Black History* (Durham, 1969), 50.

70. Minutes of Board of Education, September 18, 19, 1909, July 1, November 2, 1910, October 1, 1911, in Records of D.C. Board of Education.

71. Woodson's Biographical Sketch and Examination Results, December 27, 1911, Letters of Recommendation from Willis M. Menard, Alonzo T. Brown, and William J.

From the fall of 1911 until the end of 1917, Woodson remained at M Street High School, where he taught American history, French, Spanish, and English. Although technically any black student could attend M Street High School, only the most financially secure and academically well-prepared students were admitted, because of space constraints and perhaps because students had to buy their own books. Most of the students came from Washington's growing black bourgeoisie, and the school was more like an elite black preparatory school than a public high school. More M Street High School students went on to attend college than did graduates of any other high school in the city, black or white.[72]

A gifted and dedicated teacher, Woodson inspired many students to study Negro history. Rayford W. Logan, who was a student at M Street High School when Woodson taught there, went on to earn a Ph.D. in history at Harvard and work as Woodson's research assistant. Montague Cobb and Jesse Holstock Roy became acquainted with Woodson when they were high school students, and later they wrote about their experiences. Roy, who wrote children's articles for the *Negro History Bulletin*, recalled that in 1910 Woodson was a very dignified, stern-looking new teacher at M Street High School. She noted, however, that he had a twinkle in his eye. Woodson monitored the study hall to which she was assigned, and while the students studied, Woodson usually was absorbed in his own work. Cobb became a physician, and during the 1930s he published a history of the National Medical Association with Woodson's assistance. Although Cobb was never a pupil of Woodson's, he recalled that Woodson used to stand outside his classroom between periods to ensure orderly passage in the hallways. "When Dr. Woodson stood so posed," Cobb noted, "the quiet, unsmiling dignity of his figure commanded good order." Logan similarly remembered that Woodson was serious and a strict disciplinarian.[73]

De Catur, and Acting Director of the Bureau of Education to Woodson, June 24, 1912, all in RG 350, File 8898.

72. On M Street High School, see Mary Gibson Hundley, *The Dunbar Story* (New York, 1965); M. Melinda Chateauvert, "The Third Step: Anna Julia Cooper and Black Education in the District of Columbia, 1910–1960," in Student Supplement to *Sage: A Scholarly Journal on Black Women* (1988), 7–13.

73. W. Montague Cobb, "Carter G. Woodson: The Father of Negro History," *Journal of the National Medical Association*, LXII (September, 1970), 385–92, 402; Jesse Holstock Roy, "Recollections," *Negro History Bulletin*, XXIX (November, 1965), 185; Rayford W. Logan, "Carter G. Woodson, Mirror and Molder of His Time," *Journal of Negro History*, LVIII (1973), 1–17.

Assistant Superintendent of Colored Schools Roscoe C. Bruce appreciated the importance of Negro history. While the basic curriculum for black students was established by the white superintendent and the board of education, Negro history was incorporated into the curriculum at all levels in black schools. In his 1915 report to the board of education, Bruce took special pains to point out Woodson's achievements, noting the publication of his book on Negro education. Knowledge of Negro history, Bruce asserted, "gives our children and youth a sense of pride in the stock from which they sprang, an honorable self-confidence, a faith in the future and its possibilities, to know what men and women of Negro blood have actually done."[74] That summer Woodson traveled to Chicago and founded the Association for the Study of Negro Life and History to further promote Negro history.

By 1915 this son of former slaves had come a long way. Working as a farm laborer, sharecropper, and coal miner, Woodson acquired an appreciation for both the black masses and black folk culture. During those formative years he recognized the importance of slave testimony and oral history, and formulated his most fundamental perceptions about the black past. From the time Woodson left his parents' home to attend Berea until the time he founded the Association for the Study of Negro Life and History eighteen years later, he underwent experiences that expanded and influenced his world view and shaped his ideas about the ways in which education could transform society and uplift the lower classes. The seeds of several programs that Woodson later founded through the auspices of the Association for the Study of Negro Life and History were planted during his early career as a student and secondary school teacher. Woodson's educational philosophy developed and became more inclusive as he recognized that both a rural agricultural black working class and an urban industrial black working class could better themselves through vocational training courses. He deemed the black bourgeoisie to be lacking in classical education, which needed to be supplemented with courses in black history. Woodson's commitment to the study of black history was intensified when he taught in Washington public schools, and there he prepared himself for his life's work.

74. Roscoe C. Bruce, "Report of the Assistant Superintendent in Charge of Colored Schools, 1914–1915," in *Report of the Board of Education* (Washington, D.C., 1915), 249.

BEGINNING LIFE'S WORK, 1915–1922

Woodson, who was almost forty years old when he founded the Association for the Study of Negro Life and History in 1915, may have been undergoing a midlife crisis at that time. Although he already had achieved a great deal, it is possible he began a period of intense reflection about his past accomplishments and plans for the future. Years later, Charles H. Wesley recalled that after Woodson had published *The Education of the Negro Prior to 1861*, he was obsessed with the idea of founding a new organization to educate blacks about Negro achievements and to promote Negro history. Woodson also may have been stimulated, albeit indirectly, by D. W. Griffith, for in 1915 *The Birth of a Nation* was released. Whites across the country eagerly packed movie houses to see the film, while blacks and some liberal whites mounted campaigns to prevent its showing.[1]

Woodson went to Chicago that summer to participate in the Exposition of Negro Progress, which was organized to commemorate the fiftieth anniversary of emancipation. There he displayed and sold Negro history books and photographs of historic black notables such as Frederick Douglass, Sojourner Truth, and Paul Laurence Dunbar. Woodson also hoped to conduct research and to write while in Chicago, and he brought suitcases full of notes and books. He arrived in Chicago at the end of June and took a room at the black YMCA, on Wabash Avenue.[2]

1. Charles H. Wesley, "Our Fiftieth Year: The Golden Anniversary, 1965," *Negro History Bulletin*, XXIX (November, 1965), 172–73, 195; Robert Brent Toplin, "From Slavery to Freedom: The View Through Film and TV Drama," in *The State of Afro-American History: Past, Present and Future*, ed. Darlene Clark Hine (Baton Rouge, 1986), 205–208; Thomas Cripps, *Slow Fade to Black: The Negro in American Film, 1900–1942* (New York, 1977), 41–69.

2. James E. Stamps, "Fifty Years Later: A Founding Associate Reminisces: The Beginning of the Association for the Study of Negro Life and History," *Negro History Bul-*

In an attempt to counter Griffith's racist depiction of blacks in *The Birth of a Nation*, University of Chicago sociologist Robert E. Park held a conference to interest southern whites in collecting black folklore. Park also invited Woodson, but Woodson declined to attend, explaining that he was not a folklorist and that he planned to start an organization devoted to the preservation and dissemination of historical and sociological information on the Negro race.[3]

Race relations, politics, and Negro history were the topics Woodson discussed with fellow boarders at the YMCA after returning each evening from a long day spent researching and writing. Monroe Nathan Work, Tuskegee's pioneer sociologist and compiler of *The Negro Year Book*, and William B. Hartgrove, a school teacher from Washington, D.C., whom Woodson knew, were also staying at the YMCA and participated in these nightly discussions. Frequently they were joined by George Cleveland Hall, personal physician to Booker T. Washington and a surgeon at Chicago's Provident Hospital, Alexander L. Jackson, recently appointed executive secretary of the YMCA, and James E. Stamps, a graduate student in economics at Yale University and assistant to Jackson that summer. Woodson had met Jackson in 1911 when Jackson was a sophomore at Harvard. After graduating in 1914, Jackson took a job as student secretary of the YMCA in Washington under the direction of Jesse Moorland, national executive secretary. While Jackson was in Washington, he frequently discussed Negro history with Woodson.[4]

In the course of these nightly discussions, Woodson was persuaded to form an organization that would promote Negro history. To garner additional support for its establishment, he met with black and white social workers and activists in the Chicago branches of the NAACP and the National Urban League. Among them were Jenkin Lloyd Jones, Celia Parker Wooley, who directed the Frederick Douglass Center,

---

letin, XXIX (November, 1965), 31–32; Wesley, "Our Fiftieth Year," 172–73, 195; Alexander L. Jackson, "Reminiscences, Greetings, Challenges," *Negro History Bulletin*, XXIX (November, 1965), 181–82.

3. Woodson, "Ten Years of Collecting and Publishing the Records of the Negro," *Journal of Negro History*, X (1925), 598–606; Wesley, "Our Fiftieth Year," 172–73, 195.

4. Stamps, "Fifty Years Later"; Wesley, "Our Fiftieth Year"; Jackson, "Reminiscences, Greetings, Challenges." On George Cleveland Hall, see Louis Harlan, *Booker T. Washington: The Wizard of Tuskegee* (New York, 1983), 140–42, and W. Montague Cobb, "Carter G. Woodson: The Father of Negro History," *Journal of the National Medical Association*, LXII (September, 1970), 385–92, 402.

Sophonisba Breckinridge, dean of the school of social work at the University of Chicago, and Park.[5]

Late in August, Woodson wrote to Jesse Moorland telling him of plans to form "The Historical Alliance." Woodson stated that everyone with whom he had consulted agreed that the records of the Negro race should be preserved. "The Historical Alliance" would raise funds to organize a "Bureau of Research" to collect and preserve historical sources and publish a "Quarterly Journal of Negro History." Woodson would serve as "Director of Research" and editor of the journal, and would rent and furnish an office in Washington. Park had agreed to subsidize part of the cost of publishing the journal. Woodson planned to ask Work, Richard R. Wright, Sr., president of Georgia State Industrial College, George Edmund Haynes, of Fisk University, Walter Dyson, of Howard University, J. A. Bigham, of Atlanta University, Benjamin Brawley, of Morehouse College, and Theophilus G. Steward, of Wilberforce College, to serve as associate editors of the journal, and invited Moorland to serve as secretary-treasurer of the new organization.[6]

While Moorland enthusiastically endorsed Woodson's plan for "The Historical Alliance" and agreed to serve as secretary-treasurer, he wanted Woodson to consider affiliating the organization with Howard University. Moorland had recently donated his collection of books to the university's library and believed that the collection would aid Woodson's research activities. He also saw an advantage in the new organization's being associated with an existing institution. Although Woodson told Moorland that he would consider the idea, he was determined to create something new and independent and desired no interference from anyone.[7]

The new organization, the Association for the Study of Negro Life and History, was founded on the evening of September 9, when Woodson, Hall, Stamps, and Jackson met in Jackson's office in the YMCA. Stamps recorded the minutes of this founding meeting, but later nei-

---

5. Woodson to Jesse E. Moorland, August 24, 1915, in Jesse E. Moorland Papers, Moorland-Spingarn Research Center, Howard University.

6. Woodson to Moorland, August 24, 1915, in Moorland Papers. George Haynes was studying at the University of Chicago when Woodson attended during the summer of 1907, and it is likely that the two men became acquainted there. Similarly, Woodson probably met Theophilus Steward in the Philippines in 1903, when Steward was government superintendent of schools for Luzon Province.

7. Moorland to Woodson, September 2, 1915, in Moorland Papers.

ther he nor Hartgrove took an official role in the organization. Hall agreed to serve as president, and Jackson as an executive council member. Also invited by Woodson to join the executive council were G. N. Gresham, of Kansas City, Breckinridge, Garnett C. Wilkinson, principal of Armstrong High School in Washington, and J. A. Bigham. Bigham, however, preferred participating as an associate editor of the journal. Woodson planned to ask Wright and Steward to serve as associate editors, but either he changed his mind and did not ask them, or they turned down the offer. Instead, Park and Kelly Miller, of Howard, were appointed, along with Haynes, Brawley, Dyson, and Work. Gresham agreed to provide financial assistance but declined to serve on the executive council. After returning to Washington, Woodson, Moorland, and Bigham went to the Recorder of Deeds Office and incorporated the association.[8]

By the end of October, Woodson had printed stationery bearing the names of his new organization and its official publication; it listed the names and addresses of officers, executive council members, and associate editors. Throughout the next few months he worked diligently putting together the first issue of the *Journal of Negro History*, borrowing $400 against his $2,000 life insurance policy from New England Mutual in December to pay for printing costs. Although Woodson initially wanted Robert L. Pendleton, a black printer in Washington, to print the *Journal*, Pendleton's bid was too high. Instead, a white firm in Lancaster, Pennsylvania, New Era Printers, which printed the *American Historical Review*, received the job.[9]

Just four months after the association was founded, the first issue of the *Journal* appeared. Some members of the executive council thought that Woodson should have obtained greater financial support for the

8. Stamps, "Fifty Years Later"; Wesley, "Our Fiftieth Year"; Jackson, "Reminiscences, Greetings, Challenges"; Woodson, "Ten Years of Collecting and Publishing," 598–606, and "An Accounting for Twenty-Five Years," *Journal of Negro History*, XXV (1940), 422–31; Certificate No. 13939, Articles of Incorporation for the Association for the Study of Negro Life and History, October 2, 1915, Corporate Records Office, Washington, D.C.

9. James A. Bigham to Moorland, October 9, 14, 1915, Alexander Jackson to Woodson, October 20, 21, 1915, Woodson to Moorland, November 2, 1915, Moorland to Caroline Chapman, November 6, 1915, Woodson to Moorland, November 24, December 26, 1915, Moorland to George Cleveland Hall, December 31, 1915, all in Moorland Papers. Also see Woodson, "Ten Years of Collecting and Publishing," 598–606; Patricia W. Romero, "Carter G. Woodson: A Biography" (Ph.D. dissertation, Ohio State University, 1971), 92–94.

new organization before launching the *Journal.* But Woodson would not delay publication, for he believed that fund-raising would be easier if potential subscribers and contributors could see the product of his labors. Yet Woodson did not know where he would obtain the money to publish successive issues. He sent sample copies of the *Journal* to the white press, and at the end of January, 1916, the Boston *Herald* and the Trenton *Times* announced its appearance and praised the first issue. To encourage libraries to subscribe, Park paid for one hundred copies to be sent to libraries across the country. By early February, there were one hundred paid subscribers.[10]

Woodson managed to scrape together enough money to bring out the second issue of the *Journal* in April, 1916, by sending several hundred extra copies of the January issue, along with a letter asking for donations and subscriptions, to two hundred black and white scholars and philanthropists. Among them were John Spencer Bassett, of Smith College, novelist George Washington Cable, Alexander A. Goldenweiser, of the New School for Social Research, Edward A. Ross, of the University of Wisconsin, and his former Harvard professors Channing and Munro. Woodson also sent copies to editors J. Franklin Jameson and Franz Boas, who mentioned the *Journal* in the *American Historical Review* and the *Journal of American Folklore* respectively.[11]

The *Journal* was only one of many vehicles for research and writing that Woodson hoped to promote through the association, and he solicited advice on funding sources from Jameson. Jameson, who in addition to editing the *American Historical Review* directed a very suc-

10. Woodson, "Ten Years of Collecting and Publishing," 598–606, and "An Accounting for Twenty-Five Years," 422–31; Woodson to Moorland, January 29, February 3, 1916, in Moorland Papers; Boston *Herald,* January 31, 1916, p. 8; and Darlene Clark Hine, "Carter G. Woodson, White Philanthropy, and Negro Historiography," *History Teacher,* XIX (1986), 405–25.
11. George Washington Cable to Woodson, December 19, 1915, Edward Channing to Woodson, January 31, 1916, A. A. Goldenweiser to Woodson, January 31, 1916, John Spencer Bassett to Woodson, December 14, 1916, all in Carter G. Woodson Collection, Manuscript Division, Library of Congress; Woodson to Moorland, April 8, 15, 1916, Moorland to Jameson, April 15, 1916, all in Moorland Papers; Woodson to Jameson, May 15, October 26, 1916, in Jameson Papers, MS Div., LC; Woodson to Franz Boas, October 17, 30, 1916, in Franz Boas Papers, American Philosophical Society Library, Philadelphia; Woodson to Edward A. Ross, November 11, 1916, and Ross to Woodson, November 18, 1916, in Edward A. Ross Papers, State Historical Society of Wisconsin, Madison; "Historical News," *American Historical Review,* XXI (1915–16), 643.

cessful historical research program for the Carnegie Institution of Washington, intended to compile a documentary history of the slave trade to the United States, and another of the legislation governing slavery during the colonial period. Since Woodson hoped to obtain funds from the Carnegie Foundation and did not want to duplicate Jameson's work, he wrote to Jameson in the spring of 1916 seeking suggestions for black history research topics that would attract support from white philanthropists.[12]

Even though Jameson endorsed the *Journal*, he wanted further assurance that Woodson could carry out a research program before he gave Woodson advice. Woodson later asserted that Jameson had considered asking him to join the research staff of the Department of Historical Research at the Carnegie Institution but was reluctant to risk condemnation by his white colleagues. Although there is no evidence to support Woodson's assertion, it is possible that Jameson may have entertained such an idea, for it seems unlikely that he would have bothered to verify Woodson's scholarly credentials before giving him advice about research projects and funding sources; he freely gave similar advice to countless other historians whom he did not know personally. Before answering Woodson's letter, Jameson wrote to Woodson's former Harvard professors Hart, Channing, and Turner to inquire about Woodson's graduate work. Satisfied by their assessments, Jameson urged Woodson to focus on the collection of black sources in local areas. Believing that Woodson would have the greatest chance for success in gathering information in the black community, Jameson advised him to conduct comparative studies of slaves and free blacks at the county level in different southern states.[13]

Woodson followed Jameson's advice and submitted funding proposals for local studies of slaves and free blacks to Abraham Flexner of the Rockefeller Foundation, but he was turned down. Jameson had discouraged him from applying to the Carnegie Foundation, indicating that the foundation would not be interested in Negro history. Although disappointed, Woodson believed he would eventually obtain the money

12. Woodson to Jameson, May 15, 1916, in Jameson Papers.
13. Jameson to Woodson, May 17, 1916, Woodson to Jameson, May 18, 1916, Edward Channing to Jameson, June 1, 1916, Jameson to Woodson, June 24, 1916, all in Jameson Papers; Woodson, Obituary of J. Franklin Jameson, in *Journal of Negro History*, XXIII (1938), 131–33. Jameson's authority as "head" of the historical profession was challenged in 1915 by a small group of southern and midwestern historians, and he may have been more cautious than usual.

to pursue these projects, and his immediate priority was to ensure financial stability for the *Journal*.[14]

Woodson began advertising the *Journal* in the NAACP's *Crisis* magazine sometime after January, 1916, and by the end of June, fifty members of the NAACP had become subscribers. He had postcards printed announcing the contents of the forthcoming July issue and sent them to several hundred potential subscribers. While Woodson received many subscriptions after these first solicitations, he raised $14 in contributions. But he refused to become discouraged.[15]

Woodson's spirits were buoyed after association president Hall and executive council members Jackson and Breckinridge persuaded Chicago philanthropists and businessmen Julius Rosenwald, Harold Swift, and Morton Hull to donate a total of $800 a year to fund the *Journal*. Other wealthy whites sympathetic to black causes contributed funds and advice on potential donors. William Jay Schieffelin, owner of the New York City Chemical Company, provided Woodson with a list of possible patrons, and Joel E. Spingarn, a civil rights and NAACP activist, wrote letters urging friends and business acquaintances to contribute to the *Journal*. Spingarn also distributed sample copies of the *Journal* to guests attending the Amenia Conference at his Troutbeck, New York, estate, in August, 1916, urging them to subscribe. Anson Phelps Stokes pledged $200 per year from the Phelps-Stokes Fund. By December, almost one thousand subscriptions had been obtained, and $1,400 in contributions raised.[16]

Still, Woodson had incurred an $1,100 deficit, and executive council members criticized his administration of funds. Declaring that at twenty-five cents per copy Woodson was practically giving the *Journal* away, Moorland urged Woodson to raise prices and economize on

14. Woodson to Abraham Flexner, June 23, 1916, Flexner to Woodson, June 26, 1916, E. C. Sage to Woodson, June 27, 1916, all in General Education Board Records, Rockefeller Archive Center, Tarrytown, N.Y.; Jameson to Woodson, May 17, 1916, in Jameson Papers.

15. Woodson to Moorland, June 10, 29, 1916, in Moorland Papers; Woodson, "Ten Years of Collecting and Publishing," 598–606, and "An Accounting for Twenty-Five Years," 422–31.

16. Alexander Jackson to Moorland, May 4, 1916, Jackson to Woodson, May 4, 1916, Woodson to Moorland, October 31, 1916, Anson Phelps Stokes to Moorland, December 16, 1916, Woodson to Moorland, December 28, 1916, Moorland to William Jay Schieffelin, February 24, 1917, all in Moorland Papers; Woodson to Joel E. Spingarn, May 23, August 21, 1916, and Conference Program, Amenia, August 14–26, 1916, in Joel E. Spingarn Papers, Moorland-Spingarn Research Center.

office space. Like Moorland, Woodson's former professor Channing thought the price of the *Journal* was too low. Chicago philanthropist Swift contended that Woodson should produce a cheaper product, maintaining that the printing and the paper stock of the *Journal* were of too high a quality for a pioneering venture. Although Woodson secured cheaper office space on U Street, in the heart of Washington's black business district, he countered the criticism of his executive council by accusing them of not helping enough to raise funds. Woodson said that he needed assistance in writing solicitation letters and also suggested that officers and executive council members become life members of the association.[17]

Membership in the association included a discount on a *Journal* subscription, and both the fee for a subscription and that for a membership were inexpensive to begin with. Woodson purposely kept rates low to encourage blacks to subscribe to the *Journal* and join the association. As an incentive for libraries to subscribe to the *Journal*, the rate for institutions was the same as that for individuals. Woodson was so eager to obtain lifetime members that the fee for that category of membership was extraordinarily low—$15—in comparison with that charged by other black organizations. Yielding to continuing pressure from his executive council, Woodson finally decided in 1917 to raise lifetime membership fees to $25. By the spring of 1917, Woodson felt financially secure enough to enter into a long-term contract with New Era Printers, thereby reducing printing costs.[18]

Throughout 1917 Woodson continued his letter-writing campaign and personal visits to wealthy whites. He persuaded Moorfield Storey,

17. Woodson to Moorland, May 20, 1916, Annie R. Sewell to Moorland, May 22, 1916, Woodson to Moorland, June 17, 1916, Moorland to Alexander L. Jackson, July 6, 1916, Moorland to Woodson, July 6, 1916, Woodson to Moorland, July 21, 1916, Jackson to Moorland, September 2, 1916, Moorland to Jackson, September 8, 1916, Woodson to Moorland, October 28, 31, November 2, 1916, Moorland to Woodson, November 2, 1916, Woodson to Moorland, November 8, 14, 17, December 2, 1916, Executive Council Resolution, December 6, 1916, all in Moorland Papers.

18. Woodson to Mary Church Terrell, February 16, 1917, in Mary Church Terrell Papers, MS Div., LC; Woodson to Moorland, December 27, 1916, Moorland to George Cleveland Hall, January 9, 1917, Woodson to Members of the Executive Council, February 3, 1917, Woodson to Moorland, February 10, 1917, Alexander L. Jackson to Moorland, February 15, 1917, Moorland to Woodson, February 20, 1917, Moorland to Hall, February 23, 1917, Moorland to Jackson, March 13, 1917, Woodson to Moorland, March 14, 1917, Moorland to Hall, March 19, 1917, Sophonisba Breckinridge to Moorland, March 20, 1917, all in Moorland Papers. Lifetime memberships were the same rate for institutions and individuals.

Boston attorney and NAACP activist, to contribute $50 per year; he also obtained a pledge of $25 per year from Oswald Garrison Villard, another NAACP activist. Storey, who believed that the NAACP should assist Woodson financially, persuaded Du Bois to offer Woodson an affiliation with the *Crisis*. Woodson would be provided with office space and a small salary, but the *Journal* would be published by the NAACP rather than the association. Briefly tempted by the offer, Woodson decided not to give up his autonomy and work under Du Bois' direction, even if it meant that he had to contribute his own money to sustain the *Journal*.[19]

By July, 1917, Woodson had contributed over $1,000 of his own money to finance the *Journal*. Increasingly disenchanted with what he perceived as a lack of support from the association's officers and executive council, and believing that most of them lacked contacts with wealthy whites, he decided to reorganize and expand the executive council so as to resemble the structure of the biracial governing boards of the NAACP and the National Urban League.[20] After inviting several wealthy whites and influential blacks to attend the first biennial meeting of the association in August, 1917, Woodson carefully selected his new appointees. Because he expected his new executive council members to contribute their own funds or use their influence to raise funds, only the rich or those with connections passed muster. Several were trustees of black colleges. Of the three new black appointees, two were ministers of high position in religious circles and the third was a physician. Among the white appointees were millionaire Julius Rosenwald, head of the newly established fund bearing his name, a banker, an attorney, and representatives from the Jeanes Fund and the Phelps-Stokes Fund. Hall resigned from the presidency because of ill health,

19. Woodson to Charles G. Dawes, January 20, 1917, Moorland to William Jay Schieffelin, February 24, 1917, Woodson to Moorland, April 13, 18, 1917, Robert R. Moton to Woodson, May 29, 1917, Woodson to Moorland, June 28, 1917, all in Moorland Papers. The *Crisis* had become self-supporting in five years and had an annual income of twenty-four thousand dollars in 1915. Over a million and a half copies circulated between 1911 and 1915, reaching every state, as well as countries in Europe, Africa, and Asia. See W. E. B. Du Bois, *Dusk of Dawn: An Essay Toward an Autobiography of a Race Concept* (1940; rpr. New York, 1971), 226.

20. Woodson to Moorland, June 28, 1917, Moorland to George Cleveland Hall, June 28, 1917, Moorland to Robert R. Moton, July 6, 1917, Woodson to Moorland, July 15, 1917, Moorland to Hall, July 27, 1917, all in Moorland Papers; Woodson to Robert E. Park, July 9, 1917, in Robert E. Park Papers, University of Chicago Library. Also see Romero, "Carter G. Woodson," 88.

and Park replaced him. Breckinridge, who previously had been the only white member of the executive council, resigned, but she continued to support the association. Bigham and Wilkinson also resigned. Jackson and Moorland remained as an executive council member and secretary-treasurer respectively. Most of these individuals were too busy to exercise any influence over the administration of the association, and that was just the way that Woodson wanted it. He appointed them merely to enhance the credibility of the association among wealthy white philanthropists.[21]

With the increased prestige of his executive council, Woodson was hopeful that he would attract financial support for the *Journal* and for scholarly research projects in black history. In November, 1917, he again wrote to Abraham Flexner of the Rockefeller Foundation and requested $5,000 for the *Journal.* While Flexner was impressed by the new executive council, he turned down the request. In December, Woodson submitted an extensive research proposal entitled "A Tentative Plan for the Establishment of the Rosenwald Foundation for the Study of the Negro" to the Julius Rosenwald Fund. Since Rosenwald was on the executive council and his sponsorship would be publicly acknowledged, Woodson believed he would fund the proposal, and Rosenwald did give it serious consideration. His personal secretary, William C. Graves, wrote to Jameson for an assessment of the proposal. Because Woodson proposed to conduct precisely the research—local studies of free blacks and slaves—that Jameson had suggested, Jameson

21. The new black executive council members included: John R. Hawkins, a minister in Washington and member of the boards of trustees of Howard University and Tuskegee Institute; Robert E. Jones, a minister in New Orleans and editor of the *Southwestern Christian Advocate;* and Charles Victor Roman, a Nashville physician. The other new white members included: James Hardy Dillard, director of the Jeanes Fund; Thomas Jesse Jones and J. G. Phelps Stokes, both of the Phelps-Stokes Fund; George Foster Peabody, a member of the boards of trustees of Hampton and Tuskegee institutes; Moorfield Storey; L. Hollingsworth Wood, an attorney and chairman of the board of trustees of Fisk University; and Sir Edmund Walker, president and chairman of the board of directors of the Canadian Bank of Commerce in Toronto. Woodson also invited Robert R. Moton, president of Tuskegee Institute, to join the executive council, but he declined because he was too busy. See Moorland to Moton, July 27, 1917, Moorland to Robert E. Jones, July 27, 1917, Moorland to Thomas Jesse Jones, July 27, 1917, Moorland to Woodson, July 30, 1917, Moorland to Rosenwald, July 30, 1917, Moorland to William C. Graves, July 30, 1917, Robert E. Jones to Moorland, August 1, 1917, Graves to Moorland, August 13, 1917, Hall to Moorland, August 15, 1917, Woodson to Moorland, August 15, 18, 27, 1917, all in Moorland Papers; Rosenwald to Woodson, August 27, 1917, in Woodson Collection, LC.

endorsed it. He believed, however, that a team of scholars should conduct the research so that several points of view would be represented. Yet Rosenwald did not fund the proposal.[22]

In the first two years of the association's existence, Woodson not only struggled to keep the *Journal* financially afloat, he also had to solicit enough articles and book reviews to fill its pages. Since most of the association's officers and executive council members were philanthropists and administrators rather than scholars, they were unable to assist in editorial matters; and associate editors, who were supposed to solicit articles, did not take this charge seriously. Most of the *Journal's* early contributors were Woodson's black colleagues and associates from the Washington public schools, Howard, and the organizations with which he was affiliated. At times when he lacked enough articles, Woodson may have written articles and signed his friends' names. He also wrote the majority of book reviews in early issues, sometimes leaving them unsigned or using pseudonyms. These editorial problems, however, were of small consequence compared with Woodson's continuing financial difficulties.[23]

In the early years of the association, when Woodson was just beginning to develop educational programs, he built up a popular constituency of supporters and raised funds for the association by traveling throughout the country lecturing to a variety of audiences. For example, in 1915, just after he founded the association, Woodson was invited by Booker T. Washington to speak to Tuskegee faculty and students. Through the content of his speeches and, more importantly, in the delivery of his message, he communicated to the audiences his ardent belief in promoting accurate knowledge of black history. Woodson overwhelmed his audiences with a wealth of information in his speeches, starting with African history and working his way through all of African-American history, and he frequently electrified them with his oratorical skills. Lawrence Reddick recalled that Woodson was a

22. Woodson to Abraham Flexner, November 23, 1917, Flexner to Woodson, November 28, 1917, Woodson to Flexner, November 30, 1917, Flexner to Woodson, December 3, 1917, Flexner to Woodson, December 6, 1917, all in General Education Board Records; Woodson, "A Tentative Plan for the Establishment of the Rosenwald Foundation for the Study of the Negro," n.d., *ca.* Fall, 1917, and William C. Graves to Woodson, February 14, 1917, in Julius Rosenwald Papers, University of Chicago Library; Graves to Jameson, December 12, 1917, and Jameson to Graves, December 20, 1917, in Jameson Papers.

23. Romero, "Carter G. Woodson," 98.

charismatic speaker who made every sentence count. Woodson presented a lecture to Reddick's elementary school class in Jacksonville, Florida, and Reddick maintained that he handled himself like a "skilled boxer: never hurried, never faltering, sparring skillfully for openings, driving home his blows deftly." In fact, at the time, Reddick found Woodson to be the most impressive speaker he had heard. Years later, he recalled that during a taxi ride to a lecture Woodson was to give to Reddick's college class, "Woodson talked so interestingly . . . that when we arrived at the college, the taxi driver said that he would park his cab, if he would be permitted to come inside the classroom and hear Dr. Woodson speak." After the mid-1920s, Woodson's calendar was so full of speaking engagements during some years that it is difficult to imagine how he was able to accomplish anything else.[24]

In addition to lectures, every other opportunity to raise funds was seized by Woodson, and he frequently developed socially relevant projects, hoping to appeal to wealthy whites. When the United States entered World War I, for example, Woodson proposed to compile a history of black soldiers and submitted requests for funds to several white philanthropists in the fall of 1918. At the same time, Du Bois convinced the NAACP to finance a similar project and invited Woodson to join him, George Haynes, and Emmett J. Scott as coeditors of a volume. Initially Woodson planned to cooperate, and he drew up a contract requesting $2,500—half in advance—for research and salary. Unwilling to accept this contract, Du Bois tried to persuade Woodson to compromise. Woodson, however, remained firm, maintaining that he could conduct the research himself and merely needed financial support from the NAACP.[25]

24. Booker T. Washington to Woodson, October 3, 1915, in Woodson Collection, LC; Lawrence Reddick, "As I Remember Woodson," *Crisis*, LX (February, 1953), 75–77. See Woodson's Annual Reports for the mid-1920s through the early 1930s, published in the *Journal of Negro History*.

25. Harold Swift to Woodson, January 12, 1918, Woodson to Colonel Charles Young, November 14, 1918, Young to Woodson, November 30, 1918, in Woodson Collection, LC; George Foster Peabody to Wallace Buttrick, February 15, 1918, and Buttrick to Peabody, February 18, 1915, in General Education Board Records; William Graves to Rosenwald, January 28, 1918, in Rosenwald Papers; Woodson to Carnegie Foundation, October 15, 1918, and Secretary of the Carnegie Foundation to Woodson, October 29, 1918, in Carnegie Foundation Archives, Butler Library, Columbia University; Woodson to W. E. B. Du Bois, October 28, 1918, Du Bois to Woodson, October 30, November 8, 1918, Woodson to Du Bois, November 9, 1918, Du Bois to Woodson, November 12, 1918, in W. E. B. Du Bois Papers, University of Massachusetts; Woodson

Early in 1919 Woodson launched a $20,000 fund-raising drive, and by March had raised $1,200, all of it contributed by whites. He appealed again to the Rockefeller Foundation to fund a $2,000 salary for a business agent to sell subscriptions to the *Journal*, but was turned down. Although Woodson relied primarily on whites to finance the *Journal*, he retained his independence. Many wealthy white contributors thought that blacks should give more to finance the *Journal*, and Woodson agreed, believing that as long as whites provided the majority of funds, there was a danger that they would try to influence editorial policy and interfere with his administration. To involve more blacks in the association, he invited several black scholars to present papers on blacks in World War I at the second biennial meeting of the association in June, 1919. His persistent efforts to convince black scholars to contribute funds to the association paid off, for eventually he received $25 per year from half a dozen black scholars.[26]

At the 1919 meeting Woodson made only slight personnel changes

to Arthur B. Spingarn, October 28, 1918, in Arthur B. Spingarn Papers, Moorland-Spingarn Research Center; Du Bois to Albert Bushnell Hart, November 14, 1918, and Hart to Du Bois, November 15, 1918, in Albert B. Hart Papers, Pusey Library, Harvard University; C. W. Weeks to Emmett J. Scott, September 24, 1918, Woodson to Robert E. Jones, October 14, 1918, Frank Parker Stockbridge to Scott, November 14, 29, 1918, Scott to Woodson, January 14, 1919, Scott to Lyman Beecher Stowe, March 7, 1919, Scott to Woodson, May 1, 19, 1919, L. M. Walter Company to Woodson, June 21, 1919, Woodson to Walter Co., June 21, 26, 1919, in Emmett J. Scott Papers, Soper Library, Morgan State University, Baltimore; Emmett J. Scott, *Scott's Official History of the Negro American in World War I* (New York, 1969), 9–14. Also see William B. Toll, *Resurgence of Race: Black Social Theory from Reconstruction to the Pan-African Conferences* (Philadelphia, 1979), 204–205.

26. Woodson to Wallace Buttrick, February 1, 1919, in General Education Board Records; Woodson to Colonel Charles Young, March 11, 1919, and Charles Banks to Woodson, June 14, 1919, in Woodson Collection, LC; Arthur B. Spingarn to Woodson, March 17, 1919, in Arthur B. Spingarn Papers, Moorland-Spingarn Research Center; Woodson to Archibald Grimké, May 8, 1919, and Program, Meeting of Association for the Study of Negro Life and History, June 17–18, 1919, enclosure in Woodson to Grimké, June 11, 1919, in Archibald Grimké Papers, Moorland-Spingarn Research Center; Woodson to Emmett J. Scott, March 8, 1919, Scott to Woodson, May 12, 1919, Woodson to Scott, June 21, 1919, Scott to H. E. Perry, September 18, 1919, Scott to Solomon C. Johnson, September 18, 1919, Scott to H. H. Pace, September 18, 1919, Woodson to Scott, October 11, 1919, all in Scott Papers. In addition to regular contributions from Rosenwald, Swift, Storey, Hull, and the Phelps-Stokes Fund, Woodson also received money from the Slater Fund, Jacob Schift, Cleveland Dodge, Henry Hornblower, and Katherine Du Bois.

in his executive council. Since fund-raising remained a priority, most of the wealthy whites who were appointed in 1917 agreed to stay on the council. J. G. Phelps Stokes and Edmund Walker resigned and were replaced by William G. Wilcox, an investment banker from New York City, and Irving Metcalf, president of Oberlin College. All the blacks previously appointed remained on the council, and they were joined by Scott, who was then secretary of Howard.[27]

Although he was newly appointed at Howard, Scott, who had worked with Woodson on the project to produce a history of blacks in World War I, commanded influence with the university's board of trustees. He may have persuaded Woodson to accept the position of dean of the university's School of Liberal Arts and director of the graduate program in history.[28] By the summer of 1919 Woodson had become increasingly frustrated with black and white administrators in the Washington public school system. Lack of funds, inadequate facilities and staff, declining enrollments, and the inability to correct these problems probably led to Woodson's decision to resign from his position as principal of Armstrong High School in July, 1919, and join the faculty at Howard.[29]

When the principalship of Armstrong High School became vacant in 1918, Roscoe Bruce appointed Woodson to the post and specifically

27. Emmett J. Scott to Woodson, May 12, 1919, in Scott Papers; William G. Wilcox to Woodson, May 16, 1919, in Woodson Collection, LC.

28. Two years earlier Woodson told Jesse Moorland that he had turned down the position of university librarian offered to him in 1916 by Kelly Miller, and maintained that the only job he would accept was that of university president, and only on the condition that he could clean up the institution. See Woodson to Moorland, April 9, 1917, in Moorland Papers. On Scott and Woodson's recruitment to Howard, see D. W. Woods to Scott, June 8, 1919, in Scott Papers; Arthur A. Schomburg to John Cromwell, July 28, 1919, in Cromwell Family Papers, Moorland-Spingarn Research Center; Emmett J. Scott, "The New Howard," *Competitor Magazine*, I (January, 1920), 10–11; Michael R. Winston, *The Howard University Department of History, 1913–1973* (Washington, D.C., 1973), 18–39.

29. When Arthur C. Newman left the principalship of Armstrong High School to serve in World War I, Roscoe C. Bruce initially appointed Robert I. Vaughn to take his place, but Vaughn quickly became frustrated and resigned after one year. See Roscoe C. Bruce, "Report of the Assistant Superintendent in Charge of Colored Schools, 1917–1918," in *Report of the Board of Education* (Washington, D.C., 1918), 297, and "Report of the Assistant Superintendent in Charge of Colored Schools, 1918–1919," in *Report of the Board of Education* (Washington, D.C., 1919), 237–38, 242; Minutes of Board of Education, June 1, 1918, in Records of Washington, D.C., Board of Education, Sumner School Archives, Washington, D.C.

charged him with the task of improving the quality of vocational subjects so as to equal that of the academic subjects. Bruce also hoped that Woodson would be able to bolster Armstrong's enrollment, which had dropped dramatically during World War I. When Woodson taught at the school in 1910, 877 students were enrolled. In 1918 less than half that number made up the enrollment, and each semester students withdrew to join the military or to obtain jobs in the war industries.[30]

Woodson assumed his administrative duties with enthusiasm and energy. Drawing upon the education he had received at Berea College and his experience as a master teacher in the Philippines, he made the connection between vocational and academic subjects more concrete and improved teaching methods. Because so many students desired to work as well as attend school, Woodson established an employment bureau at the school. Employers could secure part-time student help while students stayed in school and finished their education. Over one hundred students secured jobs at the Bureau of Engraving, the Government Printing Office, the Treasury Department, and the Post Office. Before a student could drop out of school, Woodson sent teachers to visit the parents of the student and urge them to reconsider their decision. During this period, Woodson also served as assistant director of adult education for black schools, and developed further his appreciation of the benefits adult education brought to working class blacks.[31]

Although Woodson had autonomy in making policy at Armstrong, he could not obtain more space and equipment, or the necessary staff for a first-rate vocational high school. Even though enrollment had declined, adequate space for students still was lacking. There was no library, and one room served as cafeteria, study hall, and auditorium. In his report to the board of education in 1919, Woodson complained about the poorly equipped and crowded facilities, pointing out that Armstrong was not able to compete with the more modern and better-equipped Dunbar High School (M Street High School was renamed after Paul Laurence Dunbar when a new building was erected 1915–

30. Woodson, "Report of the Principal of Armstrong Manual Training School," in *Report of the Board of Education* (Washington, D.C., 1918), 324–27; J. C. Wright, "Job Description of the Principal of Armstrong High School," November 21, 1901, in J. C. Wright Papers, Moorland-Spingarn Research Center; Bruce, "Report of the Assistant Superintendent in Charge of Colored Schools, 1917–1918," in *Report of Board of Education*, 297.

31. Woodson, "Report of the Principal of Armstrong Manual Training School," in *Report of Board of Education*, 325.

1916). Many students who had previously attended Armstrong transferred to Dunbar once it was opened. Woodson also indirectly criticized Bruce, who had recommended in 1912 that M Street High School offer many of the same vocational courses taught at Armstrong High School. "If the Armstrong Manual Training School is a technical school and the Dunbar High School an academic one," Woodson wrote, "each should be restricted to its particular sphere. The offering of courses in printing and domestic science at the Dunbar High School," he maintained, "makes it almost a cosmopolitan institution, offering girls every course given at Armstrong except domestic art and at the same time offering them courses in academic work, a field which Armstrong is not allowed to invade." Competition between the two schools was the greatest handicap Woodson faced, and he recommended "that the work in printing, domestic science, and all other manual arts, except drawing, in the colored high schools be restricted to the Armstrong Manual Training School."[32]

Woodson was not the only teacher to criticize Bruce. Garnett Wilkinson and others at the two schools also complained that the duplication of course offerings wasted funds. Estimating that it would take $450,000 to $500,000 to modernize Armstrong, Woodson suggested that the old M Street building be converted into an annex for an art department and auto repair shop. He also recommended the "establishment of a laundry and foundry to make our work articulate still more closely with the needs of the community." And he wanted funds to hire specialized vocational instructors who would offer courses in "household chemistry, applied electricity, pattern-making, and automobile engineering," arguing that such "courses not only have an educational value, but have a direct bearing on the movement to increase the efficiency of our youths."[33]

Armstrong never did receive the funding that Woodson believed was necessary to turn it into a first-rate technical training school. Just weeks after he submitted his report to the board of education, he resigned from the principalship to take the position at Howard. The new post meant a salary increase for Woodson, who could then contribute more to the association's treasury. He also hoped the position would enable him to train young black historians and recruit them to his cause of promoting black history. And he believed he would have more time for

32. *Ibid.*, 326.
33. *Ibid.*

his own research and writing. During the ten years he had spent in the Washington public schools, Woodson deepened his belief in the uplifting power of education for blacks, and long after his resignation, he maintained an interest in the public schools and a commitment to the importance of vocational and adult education for blacks.

Woodson's appointment to Howard was part of a major reorganization plan implemented by the university's new white president, J. Stanley Durkee. After consulting the board of trustees, faculty members, and administrators, Durkee recruited Scott, Woodson, and several other talented blacks; he also upgraded the curriculum, and increased course offerings. Woodson replaced Kelly Miller, whom Durkee had demoted to the position of dean of the junior college after his attempt to fire Miller had been overruled by the board of trustees.[34]

Prior to Woodson's appointment, no black history courses had been offered at Howard. In 1913, Miller did succeed in convincing the board of trustees to approve a lecture series on black history, and Woodson was among those invited to speak; he presented a paper on black education in the antebellum period, adapted from his forthcoming book. And in 1915, Alain Locke, of the philosophy department, developed a course in race relations, and Charles H. Wesley, who had been teaching history at Howard since 1913, developed courses in Negro history. But it was only after Woodson's appointment that the board of trustees approved course offerings in black history, perhaps because Woodson was the only faculty member to hold a doctorate in history.[35]

Upon Woodson's arrival at Howard, all faculty members teaching history courses were combined into one department within the school of liberal arts. Woodson expanded the number of history courses from four to twenty-two. Wesley, Walter Dyson, Charles Cook, and William Tunnell taught European, Latin American, and African history, while Woodson taught all the U.S. history courses. He offered a three-quarter sequence in American history from 1609 to the present, a two-quarter sequence in Constitutional history, a one-quarter survey of the Negro in American history, and a specialized research seminar—

34. Winston, *Howard University Department of History*, 18–22; Rayford W. Logan, *Howard University: The First Hundred Years, 1867–1967* (New York, 1969), 170–72. On Kelly Miller, see Larry McGruder, "Kelly Miller: The Life and Thought of a Black Intellectual, 1863–1939," (Ph.D. dissertation, Miami University, 1984), 52–53.

35. Winston, *Howard University Department of History*, 22–25.

selected topics in American history—open only to graduate students and seniors who had taken the three-quarter American survey.[36]

Woodson integrated the Negro's role in American history into all the courses he taught, covering the slave trade, slavery, abolitionism, free blacks, blacks' roles in the Revolution, Civil War, and Reconstruction. European history was a prerequisite for American history courses, and each student was expected to complete a thesis. Students who planned to attend law school were advised to take Woodson's Constitutional history courses but were required to take the American survey first. Woodson structured the research seminar to resemble those he had taken ten years earlier at Harvard with Hart and Channing. He began the seminar with lectures on historiography and techniques in historical research methods. In consultation with Woodson, each student selected a topic, conducted independent research in primary source materials, and presented a report to the class at the end of the term.[37]

Woodson developed the history department's first graduate program, which offered a master of arts degree in the history and culture of the Negro. He told the five students enrolled in the program in the fall of 1919 that they must be serious about their work and be willing to spend at least six hours a day in the library. Woodson required them to turn in a thesis by May 1 and maintain a B average. A demanding, no-nonsense, and at times humorless teacher, Woodson lost four of his graduate students after two quarters. By the end of the school year, the undergraduate students, poking fun at the mannerisms and personalities of their professors in their magazine, the *Howard University Record*, wrote about Woodson, "Just imagine Dean Carter Woodson without his sarcasm." Arnett Lindsay, the sole survivor in the master's program, stuck it out with Woodson because he admired and respected him. He later recalled that Woodson could lecture for hours without books or notes. Under Woodson's direction, Lindsay completed his masters' thesis, "Diplomatic Relations Between the United States and Great Britain Bearing on the Relation of Negro Slaves, 1733–1828," which Woodson published in the *Journal* in October, 1920.[38]

36. *Ibid.; Howard University Catalog, 1919–20*, pp. 157–61, in Howardiana Collection, Moorland-Spingarn Research Center.

37. Winston, *Howard University Department of History*, 22–25.

38. "Just Imagine" (Section on the Faculty), *Howard University Record*, XIV (June, 1920), 429; Arnett Lindsay, "Diplomatic Relations Between the United States and Great Britain Bearing on the Relation of Negro Slaves, 1733–1828," *Journal of Negro History*,

In addition to teaching history and carrying out administrative responsibilities, Woodson served on the curriculum committee, the university council, and the Committee for Student Organizations and Activities. He also continued to edit the *Journal* and made several trips to New York City to secure funding for the publication from the Carnegie Foundation and the Commonwealth Fund. In the spring of 1920, President Durkee asked him to monitor faculty attendance at daily chapel services. Although attendance was not required, Durkee wanted reports on the "faithful."[39]

Woodson's relations with Durkee had been strained since the winter of 1920, when Senator Reed Smoot, a Republican from Utah, objected to the availability of Elbert Rhys Williams' *Seventy-Six Questions on the Bolsheviks and Soviets* in the university library. Smoot threatened to cut federal appropriations to the university if the book was not removed from the library, and Durkee quickly complied with his request. In a letter published in the Washington *Star*, Woodson criticized Durkee's compliance with Smoot's request, saying it threatened academic freedom. Congress had no right to interfere with what students read or learned, Woodson contended, and Howard would be better off without government intervention in its affairs. Unnerved by Woodson's public display of disloyalty, Durkee ordered him to his office for a meeting. Years later, Woodson maintained that during their discussion, Durkee "pulled from his files a letter from A. Mitchell Palmer's Department of Injustice based on a report of one of its Secret Service Agents." It accused Woodson of having communist tendencies. Stunned by Durkee's attempt to use the letter to silence him and to compel him to spy on the faculty and report any lapses in chapel attendance, Woodson defended himself against the charges.[40] He also refused

V (1920), 391–419, and "Dr. Woodson as a Teacher," *Negro History Bulletin*, XII (May, 1950), 183–91.

39. *Howard University Catalog, 1919–20*, pp. 21, 23–25; Woodson to Scott, October 11, 1919, and Scott to Woodson, October 15, 1919, in Scott Papers; Moorland to Woodson, October 14, 1919, Woodson to Moorland, October 23, December 3, 9, 1919, February 17, March 10, 1920, all in Moorland Papers.

40. Francis J. Grimké, "Bolshevist Literature," Letter to the Editor, Washington *Star*, January 11, 1920, p. 4; Woodson, "The Capstone of Negro Education Becomes the Capstone of Negro Politics" (Press Release), April 29, 1931, in Claude H. Barnett Papers, Chicago Historical Society; Logan, *Howard University*, 187–244. Francis J. Grimké, pastor of the Fifteenth Street Presbyterian Church, praised Woodson for his outspoken courage in defending academic freedom. See Woodson to Francis J. Grimké, January 18,

to comply with Durkee's request, and further tested their relations by arranging without Durkee's permission a series of continuing education courses for Washington public school teachers. Lorenzo Dow Turner, Miller, and Woodson taught the classes, which were held at the Miner Normal School on Howard's campus. Furious because he was not consulted first, Durkee not only threatened to cancel the classes but also continued to harass Woodson for his refusal to monitor chapel attendance.[41]

Complaining about Durkee to Moorland, Woodson threatened to resign if Durkee continued to pressure him. While not unsympathetic to Woodson's complaints, Moorland, who believed that black scholars were needed to upgrade the curriculum at Howard, urged Woodson to rise above the controversy for the good of the faculty and students. By the end of April, although Woodson believed he should resign, he feared being without a job the next academic year and followed Moorland's advice. Woodson decided to ask for a meeting with Durkee and wrote a conciliatory letter offering to discuss their disagreements. The meeting did not settle their dispute, and in fact, after the meeting, Durkee wrote in his diary that he intended to fire Woodson. Woodson wrote to Moorland again, contending that Durkee was unable to distinguish the difference between educational administration and personal service, and enclosing the letter of resignation that he intended to send to Durkee. Moorland again tried to persuade Woodson not to resign, maintaining that he and Durkee did not get along because they had similar temperaments. He advised Woodson, "Think it all over, go to church, sing some of the good old hymns you used to sing, take a stroll in the park to try to forget the world." Woodson lashed out at Moorland, asserting that he was too trusting of whites who were unfit to administer black colleges.[42]

1920, and Grimké to Woodson, January 21, 1920, in Woodson, ed., *The Papers of Francis J. Grimké* (4 vols.; Washington, D.C., 1942), IV, 265–67.

41. Winston, *Howard University Department of History*, 38; Raymond Wolters, *The New Negro on Campus: Black College Rebellions of the 1920s* (Princeton, 1975), 86; Cobb, "Carter G. Woodson," 389–90; Woodson, Memorandum to Washington public school teachers, March 13, 1920, in Moorland Papers. Woodson, Miller, and Turner offered courses in sociology, mathematics, French, German, history, English, and economics.

42. Woodson to Moorland, April 23, 1920, Moorland to Woodson, April 24, 1920, Woodson to Durkee, April 29, 1920, Woodson to Moorland, May 3, 1920, Moorland to Woodson, May 4, 1920, and Woodson to Moorland, May 11, 1920, all in Moorland Papers; J. Stanley Durkee Diary, March 13, May 4, 1920, (J. Stanley Durkee Papers,

While Woodson did not object to a white presence at Howard, he did object to a white administrator who was less competent than a black one. Far ahead of his contemporaries in arguing for black control over black colleges, Woodson was eventually joined by numerous other critics, and a growing movement was underway by 1925. Durkee eventually would be ousted by this pressure.[43] Woodson was not the last black faculty member to tangle with Durkee. After Woodson's dismissal, Durkee had a public altercation with botanist Thomas W. Turner, threatened to dismiss zoologist Ernest Everett Just, fired philosophy professor Locke, and once again fired and rehired Miller. In 1925, prominent black alumni formed the Howard Welfare League, proclaiming that "Howard Must be Rescued from Its Exploiters: The Ideals of Its Founders Must Be Restored." In November, 1925, league president Arthur W. Mitchell, later a congressman from Chicago, invited Woodson to a meeting to discuss a strategy for removing Durkee from the presidency. Although Woodson undoubtedly felt vindicated, he refused to attend the meeting, claiming that no one would listen to his earlier contention that Durkee was unfit to be university president. (A month earlier Woodson had been invited to address a meeting of the Maryland State Teachers Association. Discovering that he would be sharing the platform with Durkee, Woodson refused to speak at the meeting.) By April, 1926, Durkee was forced to resign and Mordecai Johnson replaced him.[44]

Back in 1920, Durkee still retained the confidence of the Howard board of trustees, although the university community was beginning to believe that Durkee could not get along with well-educated and independent black scholars. In addition to Moorland, Woodson had other black supporters at Howard. For example, Scott told Durkee that Howard could not afford to lose Woodson and that if Woodson were fired,

---

Moorland-Spingarn Research Center); Moorland to Woodson, March 11, May 13, 1920, and Woodson to Moorland, May 15, 22, 1920, in Moorland Papers. On May 4, Durkee wrote of Woodson, "He must go!"

43. Woodson to Moorland, May 15, 1920, in Moorland Papers. Also see Winston, *Howard University Department of History*, 35–39.

44. Kenneth Manning, *Black Apollo of Science: The Life of Ernest Everett Just* (New York, 1983), 132–33, 152–53; W. E. B. Du Bois, "George William Cook," *Crisis*, XXX (September, 1925), 216–17, in which Du Bois criticized Durkee's treatment of Cook; Washington *Tribune*, November 14, 1925, pp. 1–2; Arthur W. Mitchell to Woodson, November 23, 1925, in Durkee Papers; Alain Locke to Franz Boas, December 14, 1925, in Boas Papers; Wolters, *New Negro on Campus*, 97–109, 129–30.

it would strengthen the perception that Durkee clashed with black scholars. Although Scott believed that Durkee would not fire Woodson but would demote him, as he had earlier done to Miller, he also knew that Woodson would not accept a demotion.[45]

In late spring, Woodson, anticipating that he would be leaving Howard and in need of another job, intensified his efforts to secure enough funding for the *Journal* to make the editorship a full-time job. He asked several leading white historians to write letters endorsing his work and used them in appeals to foundations. In desperation he asked the NAACP to take over the *Journal* and pay him a salary to edit it. This time the NAACP turned him down, since the organization was beginning to have its own financial problems. Woodson's earlier refusal to cooperate with Du Bois on the publication of a history of blacks in World War I also may have led to the decision not to take over the *Journal*.[46]

In early June, Woodson decided to make one further attempt to settle his differences with Durkee and wrote him an apologetic letter. Durkee, however, required Woodson to make a public apology before the board of trustees. Although greatly insulted by Durkee's demand, Woodson planned to comply. Before he could do so, however, Durkee had convinced the board of trustees to fire Woodson, and he was dismissed before commencement day. As soon as Woodson learned of his dismissal, he worked feverishly to obtain another job; he wrote to the president of Wilberforce College in Ohio and offered to serve as superintendent of the combined normal and institutional department. Near the end of June, John W. Davis, president of West Virginia Collegiate Institute, invited Woodson to become dean of the college de-

45. Woodson to Moorland, May 11, 1920, Moorland to Scott, May 14, 1920, Moorland to Woodson, May 29, 1920, all in Moorland Papers.

46. Woodson to Scott, March 1, 1920, and Scott to Woodson, March 3, 1920, in Scott Papers; Woodson to Oswald Garrison Villard, March 16, 1920, in Oswald Garrison Villard Papers, Houghton Library, Harvard University; Woodson to Edward Channing, March 26, 1920, and Channing to Woodson, March 30, 1920, in Arthur B. Spingarn Papers, MS Div., LC; Woodson to Franz Boas, March 27, 1920, and Boas to Woodson, March 29, 1920, in Boas Papers; Jameson to Max Farrand, April 2, 1920, and Farrand to Jameson, April 6, 1920, in Jameson Papers; Woodson to the NAACP Board of Directors, May 8, 1920, in NAACP Records, Group I, Series C, Box 80, MS Div., LC; Woodson to Moorland, May 26, 1920, in Moorland Papers; Minutes of NAACP Board of Directors Meetings, May, 1920, and June 14, 1920, in Archibald Grimké Papers. The NAACP's refusal may not have been due to financial reasons. Du Bois, in *Dusk of Dawn*, 258, says that 1916–19 were the best years for *Crisis*.

partment at an annual salary of $2,700. Woodson quickly accepted the offer and was grateful to have employment.[47]

Woodson had been offered the presidency of West Virginia Collegiate Institute in 1919, but he declined because the administrative duties required of a college president would have left him little time for research and writing, and he wanted to remain in Washington to direct the association. Instead, Woodson recommended his friend Davis, the thirty-one-year-old secretary of the Washington YMCA, for the position. Although Davis had no experience as an educational administrator, Woodson promised to give him advice and assistance, and Davis accepted the job.[48]

During Woodson's first year at the institute, enrollment grew from 297 to 445, and the college department's enrollment increased by 50. Fifty-five students received degrees in 1921. New courses were offered in psychology, economics, mathematics, natural sciences, English, Latin, Greek, history, political science, and philosophy. Students from urban areas, rural communities, and mining towns all took advantage of the new educational opportunities offered by the school. Many students from mining towns were middle-aged when they enrolled, and Woodson was particularly impressed with their thirst for education, undoubtedly because he too had been a latecomer to higher education. Although older students frequently struggled to keep up with younger students, many of them became successful teachers, lawyers, physicians, and ministers.[49]

Woodson worked at a breakneck pace during his two-year tenure at the institute. In addition to teaching and administering the college department, Woodson studied the history of Negro education in West Virginia. Assisted by David A. Lane, who taught English, and Alrutheus Ambush (A. A.) Taylor, who taught history, math, economics, and logic, Woodson sent out questionnaires to black educators, conducted in-

47. Woodson to Durkee, June 5, 1920, in Moorland Papers; Durkee Diary, June 3, 7, 9, 1920; Woodson to Moorland, June 5, 7, 9, 1920, all in Moorland Papers. On Woodson's invitation to West Virginia, see Romero, "Carter G. Woodson," 77–78, and Woodson, "Notes," *Journal of Negro History*, V (1920), 493. On Davis, see Angel P. Johnson, "A Study of the Life and Work of a Pioneer Black Educator: John W. Davis" (Ph.D. dissertation, Rutgers University, 1987).

48. Romero, "Carter G. Woodson," 77–78; and John W. Davis, "The Open Window of History," *Journal of Negro History*, LXVI (1981–82), 349–50.

49. *Ibid.* Also see Woodson, "Notes," V, 493, and "Anniversary Address," *West Virginia State College Bulletin*, 3d ser., No. 3 (1941), 21, cited in Charles Ambler, *A History of Education in West Virginia* (Huntington, W. Va., 1951), 263–64.

terviews with respondents, and in 1922 published the results in the *Journal,* which he continued to edit. By the end of his first year at the school, he also had established the Associated Publishers to publish books on black history, because white publishing firms usually were reluctant to publish works by and about blacks unless a subsidy was provided. Remembering the subvention he paid G. P. Putnam's Sons, to publish *The Education of the Negro Prior to 1861,* which sold well and made a profit, Woodson reasoned that if a black firm were established, it would not only provide black scholars with a medium to present their findings but also generate revenue to fund other association activities. Woodson began promoting the establishment of his own publishing arm in May, 1920, writing to fifty black scholars requesting $500 contributions.[50]

While many blacks supported Woodson's idea for a black publishing firm, few contributed the money he requested. By June, 1921, however, he believed he had raised enough money, and the Associated Publishers was incorporated in Washington, D.C., with Woodson as president, Davis as treasurer, and Louis Mehlinger as secretary. In hopes of inspiring other blacks to purchase shares, Woodson announced the firm's establishment in the July, 1921, issue of the *Journal,* asserting that $25,000 had been raised from subscribers. The firm's incorporation papers, filed in the Recorder of Deeds Office, however, indicate that only $2,500 worth of stock had been purchased. Woodson purchased the majority of shares in the new firm, and $700 was contributed by four other investors listed on the incorporation papers. Woodson undoubtedly exaggerated the amount he had raised through stock sales, not only to obtain more black subscribers but also to impress white philanthropists. Although the Associated Publishers produced many books by black scholars that white firms would not publish, it did not, as Woodson hoped, provide much additional revenue for other association programs.[51]

50. Woodson, "Early History of Negro Education in West Virginia," *Journal of Negro History,* VII (1922), 23–63; Woodson to Moorland, May 26, 1920, in Moorland Papers.

51. Certificate No. 16170, Articles of Incorporation for the Associated Publishers, May 28, 1920, in Corporate Records Office; Woodson, "Notes," *Journal of Negro History,* VI (1921), 380–81. Among the subscribers listed in the *Journal* article were Davis, Mehlinger, Mordecai Johnson, who was then pastor of a church in Charleston, W. Va., Don Speed Smith Goodloe, president of Maryland Normal and Industrial School for Colored Students, and Byrd Prillerman and C. E. Mitchell, from Institute, W. Va. Those listed

Out of necessity Woodson continued his fund-raising activities while he was in West Virginia. By the fall of 1920 he had become increasingly annoyed with the blacks on his executive council, contending that most were neither assisting with fund-raising nor contributing much of their own money. Especially angry with Moorland, Woodson maintained that in the five years of Moorland's affiliation with the association, he had contributed a mere $25. D. F. Merritt, a wealthy white philanthropist, offered to contribute $1,000 if Woodson could raise an equal amount from each of nine others; Woodson wrote to George Foster Peabody and Arthur B. Spingarn, asking for names of potential contributors, but they offered no suggestions. In October, Woodson submitted a request to the Carnegie Foundation for $25,000 over a period of five years. Because Woodson had very good recommendations from white historians, James R. Angell, president of the Carnegie Foundation, seriously considered the proposal. About the time Woodson submitted his proposal to the Carnegie Foundation, Robert Russa Moton and Monroe Work asked for funds to conduct black research projects at Tuskegee, and Eugene K. Jones, of the National Urban League, also requested research funds. Initially Woodson was unaware that he was in competition with Tuskegee and the National Urban League; when he was informed and invited to cooperate with them on a joint project, he declined.[52]

Angell, who was especially impressed with Jameson's endorsement of Woodson's work, was more favorably disposed to fund a joint project that would combine various aspects of research proposed by Woodson, Work, and Jones. Aware that Jones and Work had submitted competing proposals, Moorland and association president Park hoped that Woodson would agree to participate in a cooperative project. But Woodson would not compromise, telling Moorland that he would

---

on the incorporation papers were Johnson, Mehlinger, Davis, and Alethe Smith, Woodson's secretary. Also see Romero, "Carter G. Woodson," 127–31.

52. See D. F. Merritt to Woodson, June 29, 1920, Woodson to George Foster Peabody, July 19, 1920, Peabody to Woodson, July 23, 1920, all in George Foster Peabody Papers, MS Div., LC; Woodson to Emmett J. Scott, June 14, 1920, in Scott Papers; Woodson to Arthur B. Spingarn, July 26, 1920, in Arthur Spingarn Papers, LC; Edward Channing to Jameson, September 28, 1920, in Jameson Papers; Woodson to Moorland, October 6, 1920, in Moorland Papers; Woodson to James R. Angell, October 12, 1920, Angell to Woodson, October 15, 1920, Angell, Memorandum on Tuskegee Institute Proposal, November 22, 1920, Robert R. Moton to Angell, November 27, 1920, all in Carnegie Foundation Archives.

never agree to cooperate with such "jackasses as Moton and Work." Woodson then worked behind the scenes, offering little information about his Carnegie Foundation proposal to the officers and executive council, fearing that they would interfere. Because of their earlier disagreements over the financial administration of the association and the conflicts with Durkee at Howard University, Woodson especially distrusted Moorland.[53]

Although Moorland believed that a compromise with Work and Jones could be reached, Park was not convinced. Reluctant to interfere or use his influence as president of the association to persuade executive council members to pressure Woodson, Park hoped that all three men would obtain funds from the Carnegie Foundation for their separate projects. As secretary-treasurer of the association, Moorland was naturally concerned with its financial condition and continued to urge Woodson to cooperate with Tuskegee and the National Urban League. Believing that the Carnegie Foundation would fund only a joint research project, Moorland also urged Moton and Work to continue negotiating with Woodson. In a sharply worded letter, Woodson told Moorland that he was too trusting of whites and of black race leaders, and characterized Moorland's efforts to persuade him to compromise as meddlesome interference. After this incident, their relationship was permanently damaged.[54]

Park became increasingly discouraged about Woodson's chances for success, and believed a new president was needed to administer association affairs. During his four-year term, Park never attended any of the meetings of the executive council and conducted all association business through correspondence. It was because Park hesitated to interfere in the administration of the association that he was exactly the kind of person Woodson wanted in the presidency. Park offered his resignation in May, 1921, and Woodson reluctantly accepted it. A new president would be elected in October at the next meeting of the association, so

53. Woodson to Moorland, December 6, 1920, in Moorland Papers; Monroe Work to Angell, December 4, 1920, in Carnegie Corporation Archives; Moorland to Woodson, December 4, 14, 1920, Park to Moorland, December 30, 1920, all in Moorland Papers.

54. Moorland to Park, January 7, 1921, Park to Moorland, January 12, 1921, Moorland to Park, January 17, 1921, Park to Moorland, January 19, 1921, Park to Moton, January 19, 1921, Moorland to Park, January 24, 1921, Park to Moorland, January 27, 1921, Moorland to Park, February 7, 1921; Park to Moorland, February 14, 1921, Moorland to Woodson, March 17, 1921, Moorland to Park, March 18, 1921, all in Moorland Papers; Moton to Angell, March 19, 1921, in Carnegie Corporation Archives; Woodson to Moorland, February 24, 1921, in Moorland Papers.

Park continued to try to work out a compromise between Woodson, Tuskegee, and the National Urban League.[55]

Although Angell was uncomfortable with the prospect of presenting three separate proposals for similar research projects to the Carnegie board, he finally gave up the notion that a compromise could be reached and awarded funds to Woodson, Jones, and Work in May, 1921. While no conditions were placed on the funds awarded to Tuskegee and the National Urban League, Woodson, who was to receive $5,000 a year for five years, would be paid in semiannual installments, with the money being administered by Jameson. Woodson was required to submit reports and budgets to Jameson every six months; when Jameson approved them, funds would be released. The Carnegie Foundation also required Woodson to hire a business manager and an agent to sell subscriptions to the *Journal*, memberships in the association, and books.[56]

Complying with the Carnegie Foundation's request to hire a business manager, Woodson selected Victor R. Daly, a graduate of Cornell University who had held a similar position with the *Messenger*, the radical magazine published by socialists Chandler Owen and A. Philip Randolph. In June, 1921, Woodson received a check for $2,500 from the Carnegie Foundation and submitted a detailed plan of research and a budget. He then informed Angell that the executive council had decided that he should be employed full-time as director of research and editor of the *Journal* at an annual salary of $3,000. When writing to the executive council members to announce receipt of the Carnegie grant, he told them that the foundation wanted him to devote all his time to the association and had suggested that he receive an annual salary of $3,000. Prior to this time, Woodson had not been paid a salary and had contributed much of his own money to the association. Thus his drawing a salary was not unreasonable, even if the way he obtained it was deceitful. He had agreed to remain at West Virginia Collegiate Institute for another academic year, however, and would be unable to devote himself full-time to the association until the summer of 1922.[57]

55. Park to Woodson, May 2, 5, 1921, Moorland to Park, May 11, 1921, Park to Moorland, May 16, 1921, Moorland to Park, May 19, 1921, all in Moorland Papers.

56. James R. Angell to Jameson, April 14, 1921, Jameson to Angell, April 15, 1921, Angell, Memorandum on the Association for the Study of Negro Life and History, May 2, 1921, Angell to Moton, May 24, 1921, Angell to Jameson, May 31, 1921, Woodson to Angell, June 7, 1921, all in Carnegie Corporation Archives.

57. Beardsley Ruml to Woodson, June 20, 1921, and Woodson to Moorland, June 25, 1921, in Moorland Papers; Woodson to George Foster Peabody, June 27, 1921, Pea-

Although Woodson had attained a measure of financial security for the association, he was about to incur the wrath of some white philanthropists because he made personnel changes in the association's governing body. At the October meeting of the association, five new black executive council members, a new black president, and a new black secretary-treasurer were appointed. While Park had willingly given up the presidency and was replaced by John R. Hawkins, who had previously been on the council, Moorland was removed without notice and replaced by Samuel W. Rutherford, secretary-treasurer of the Washington-based National Mutual Benefit Life Insurance Company. Moorland had moved to New York and did not attend the October meeting, and Woodson contended that Moorland's distance from Washington made it difficult to transact financial business. In fact, he removed Moorland because of their earlier disagreements. Hurt and surprised by the action, Moorland wanted further explanation and asked to see a copy of the minutes of the meeting. Woodson, however, refused to send the minutes or comment further. In spite of this rebuff, Moorland continued to support the association and Woodson, albeit in an unofficial capacity.[58]

Unlike Moorland, Thomas Jesse Jones, who was similarly removed from the association's governing body, refused to withdraw gracefully. In fact, over the next few years, Jones did everything he could to sabotage Woodson's fund-raising efforts. Although the Phelps-Stokes Fund had contributed $200 annually to the association for several years and Jones was a member of its board, Woodson wanted Jones removed. Since the publication in 1917 of *Negro Education*, his report on black education in which he called for increased funds for black vocational institutions and less money for black liberal arts colleges, Jones had been subjected to mounting criticism from the black community. As a member of the Phelps-Stokes African Educational Commission, Jones

body to Angell, June 29, 1921, Peabody to Woodson, June 29, 1921, all in Peabody Papers.

58. Woodson to Moorland, October 12, 1921, Moorland to Woodson, October 21, November 12, 1921, Woodson to Moorland, November 19, 1921, Moorland to Woodson, December 15, 1921, Woodson to Moorland, December 18, 1921, all in Moorland Papers. The new black executive council members were Robert A. Carter, AME bishop from Chicago, Robert R. Church, Tennessee millionaire and father of Mary Church Terrell, John Davis, Clement C. Richardson, president of Lincoln Institute in Missouri, and Robert C. Woods, of Virginia Theological Seminary in Lynchburg. Those who remained on the executive council were Dillard, John Hurst, Jackson, Robert Jones, Peabody, Rosenwald, Storey, and Hart.

traveled to Africa in 1920 to survey educational activities of missionary boards and advocated that vocational education was best for Africans too. Woodson, like Du Bois and numerous other blacks, was openly critical of Jones's views on black education in the United States and Africa. After Woodson successfully convinced other executive council members that Jones's views hampered fund-raising efforts among blacks, Jones was removed from that body.[59]

After receiving a grant from the Carnegie Foundation, Woodson believed he would be successful in securing additional support. By this time he had begun several research projects on slavery, free blacks in the antebellum period, the black Baptist church, and blacks in Reconstruction, and he had started to collect black family papers. Because his duties at West Virginia Collegiate Institute prevented him from devoting enough time to these projects, he sought funds to hire research assistants. In the fall of 1921 he submitted a proposal to the Commonwealth Fund, requesting eight thousand dollars. His request was denied, and he then began negotiations with the Rockefeller family foundations for $25,000 over five years from the Laura Spelman Rockefeller Memorial Fund.[60]

Woodson outlined a detailed plan of research in his proposal and included several letters of recommendation from prominent white historians. W. S. Richardson, executive secretary of the foundation, was impressed by Woodson's request and believed it should be given serious consideration. In February, 1922, the board of the Laura Spelman Rockefeller Foundation awarded Woodson $25,000. The only stipulation on the grant, which was to be paid in installments of $5,000, was that funds would be used to pursue the research projects outlined in Woodson's proposal and could not be used for operating expenses of the association or the *Journal.* Overjoyed at the prospect of leaving his position at West Virginia Collegiate Institute to work full-time on research for the association, Woodson notified his executive council of

59. Jones to Moorland, March 2, 1922, Du Bois to Moorland, May 19, 1921, Moorland to Du Bois, May 20, 1921, all in Moorland Papers.

60. Woodson to W. S. Richardson, September 9, 1921, Richardson, Memorandum on the Association for the Study of Negro Life and History, September 14, 1921, and Outline of the Request of the Association for the Study of Negro Life and History to the Laura Spelman Rockefeller Memorial Fund, January 28, 1922, in Laura Spelman Rockefeller Memorial Fund Records, Rockefeller Archive Center; Edward Channing to Max Farrand, October 14, 1920, in Edward Channing Papers, Pusey Library; Woodson to Wallace E. Buttrick, October 14, 1921, and Buttrick to Woodson, October 17, 1921, in General Education Board Records; "Appeals Declined Consideration," May 20, 1922, in Commonwealth Fund Records, Rockefeller Archive Center.

the receipt of the Rockefeller funds and sent each member a detailed budget and plan of research. He expected to hire several black graduate students to assist with research projects, and wrote to black and white scholars to solicit candidates.[61]

Not all executive council members approved of Woodson's budget and plans for research. Hart, Woodson's former mentor who had been appointed to the council in November, 1920, raised serious questions about the research Woodson proposed and maintained that funds from white foundations should be used for fellowships to assist black graduate students. In a conciliatory letter, Woodson suggested that Hart was welcome to raise questions about the proposed research projects at the next executive council meeting. He explained that while he intended to hire black graduate students as research assistants, he could not provide them with fellowships for graduate education because the Rockefeller grant restricted the use of funds to research projects. He maintained further that the executive council had approved his plans before they were submitted to the foundations (although this had been done through correspondence) and only the truly discerning members gave them serious attention.[62]

Unsatisfied with Woodson's explanations, Hart asserted that as "long as all the funds were collected on your solicitation and there was not much to do with, nobody objected to your carrying it on as in the sense of a personal enterprise." Hart did not recall being consulted and believed that other executive council members also were unaware of Woodson's research plans. He wrote, "Now that you have $10,000 a year from two foundations, now that you have brought together an executive committee and it brings you before the public, the conditions are different." Hart also objected to the $3,000 budgeted to pay Woodson's annual salary, since he was already employed by West Virginia Collegiate Institute. "More and more persons," Hart wrote, "ought to be drawn in than have been drawn in by your method [of] starting a plan without any details and asking members by correspondence to assent, for that is what the process really is."[63]

61. Richardson to Woodson, February 16, 1922, Woodson to Richardson, February 18, 1922, Richardson to Woodson, February 20, 1922, all in Laura Spelman Rockefeller Memorial Fund Records; Woodson to Albert B. Hart, March 29, 1922, in Hart Papers; Woodson to James Weldon Johnson, March 18, 1922, in NAACP Records, Group I, Series C, Box 80.

62. Hart to Woodson, February 25, 1922, and Woodson to Hart, March 29, 1922, in Hart Papers.

63. Hart to Woodson, April 4, 1922, in Hart Papers. Also see Woodson to Hart, March 30, 1922, and Hart to Woodson, March 31, 1922, in Hart Papers.

Although Hart probably was upset more about not having been consulted than about Woodson's proposed research projects, he was encouraged by Thomas Jesse Jones to continue his complaints about Woodson's methods of administration. Jones was angered not only by his removal from the executive council but also by Woodson's criticism of him in *The History of the Negro Church*, published in 1921. Just after Woodson had received the Rockefeller grant, Jones wrote to Moorland inquiring why he and Park had been removed from the association's governing board. Asserting that Woodson had replaced moderates like himself, Park, and Moorland with radical officers, Jones told Moorland that the Phelps-Stokes Fund would not make additional contributions to Woodson as long as radicals were in control of the association. Although Moorland assured Jones that Woodson's new officers were not radicals, and explained that Park had wanted to resign and it was more convenient for the secretary-treasurer to be based in Washington, Jones continued to raise questions about Woodson's personnel and administration.[64]

Unaware initially that Jones also was raising questions about his administration, Woodson again wrote to Hart. He assured Hart that he planned to resign from his administrative position at West Virginia Collegiate Institute on July 1 and would not receive a salary until he began full-time work directing the research projects outlined in the grant proposals. Woodson also asked Hart to suggest qualified black graduate students whom he could hire as research assistants. Still unsatisfied, Hart wrote to each member of the executive council stating his objections to Woodson's plan and notifying them of his intent to resign from the council. He also sent copies of these letters to officials of the Laura Spelman Rockefeller Memorial Foundation and the Carnegie Foundation, and to Jameson.[65]

Once again Woodson wrote to Hart urging him not to resign and maintaining that Jameson not only had endorsed his proposal for research but also had agreed it was unwise to provide black students with

64. Woodson, *The History of the Negro Church* (Washington, D.C., 1921), 310–11; Jones to Moorland, March 2, 1922, and Moorland to Jones, March 15, 1922, in Moorland Papers. Woodson also was critical of Jones in *The Negro in Our History* (9th ed.; Washington, D.C., 1947), 565.

65. Woodson to Hart, April 5, 1922, Hart to Members of the Executive Committee, April 12, 1922, Hart to Secretary of the Rockefeller Foundation, April 14, 1922, all in Hart Papers; Woodson to Wallace Buttrick, April 10, 1922, in General Education Board Records.

fellowships for graduate training. Woodson offered to modify the budget if Hart would give him specific recommendations beyond those he had made earlier. However, Hart was determined to resign from the executive council. He persuaded Peabody and Storey to complain also about Woodson's budget and research plans, and they in turn contended that they had not been consulted by Woodson and believed the salaries budgeted for research assistants to be too high. Peabody especially objected to Woodson's criticism of Jones, and both he and Storey resigned from the executive council.[66]

Undoubtedly, Peabody and Storey were encouraged also by Jones, who had written to the Rockefeller Foundation officials and to Rosenwald informing them of Hart's complaints about Woodson's budget and administration. Jones asserted that the changes in the association's governing board were indicative that Woodson no longer would cooperate with white racial moderates and that the white members who remained on the executive council were too busy to oversee or restrain Woodson. Jones charged further that Woodson had moved from scientific studies of Negro history to propaganda promotion and that Woodson was making objectionable statements about race relations in his publications. Although both Rosenwald and the Rockefeller Foundation investigated Jones's allegations, they determined that the charges were false. William Graves, Rosenwald's secretary, obtained an independent opinion from Scott, who assured him that while Woodson was a difficult person, he was a serious scholar and certainly was not a radical. Scott maintained that whites were too quick to condemn and characterize as a radical any black who defended black rights. When Woodson learned of Jones's letters to Rosenwald and the Rockefeller Foundation, he wrote to foundation officials to refute Jones's contentions and convince them that Jones made these accusations because he had been removed from the executive council.[67]

Two black members of the executive council—Jackson and Clement C. Richardson—were disturbed by the disagreements between Woodson and Hart, and believed that Hart's resignation would damage the reputation of the association with white philanthropists. Jackson, a for-

66. Woodson to Hart, April 13, 1922, Hart to Jameson, April 14, 1922, Moorfield Story to Hart, April 14, 1922, all in Hart Papers.
67. Jones to William C. Graves, April 22, 1922, and enclosures, Hart to Jones, April 12, 1922, Peabody to Hart, April 18, 1922, Scott to Graves, April 22, 1922, Woodson to Graves, May 4, 1922, all in Rosenwald Papers; Woodson to W. S. Richardson, April 25, 1922, in Laura Spelman Rockefeller Memorial Fund Records.

mer student of Hart's at Harvard, urged Hart to reconsider his decision to resign from the executive council. While he acknowledged Hart's position and the fact that Woodson was stubborn and difficult, he nevertheless believed that Hart should continue to try to compromise with Woodson. Richardson, who had been a student in Hart's Constitutional history class in 1907, similarly urged Hart to stay on the council and work with the black members to persuade Woodson to reorganize his research plans. He wrote that he knew "from experience that it is the easiest thing in the world to blast the life and service of any colored man by whisperings and misgivings about money matters. The report would no sooner be circulated that you were resigning over a financial question than the hasty public would conclude that Dr. Woodson, or any other colored man similarly situated, had been making away with funds." Hart, however, could not be persuaded to remain on the executive council. He told Richardson that while he did not believe Woodson was mishandling funds, he objected to the use of funds for research assistants and thought that Woodson's salary was too high. Convinced that Hart would not work with him to compromise on the budget, Woodson finally accepted his resignation late in April, 1922.[68]

Woodson was disturbed by the criticism and resignations of white council members, and in May he wrote to his remaining council members to inform them of the complaints about his budget and $3,000 salary. Justifying his salary on the basis of his research and writing experience, Woodson proposed that the best way to settle the matter was to let officials of the Laura Spelman Rockefeller Foundation decide whether it was too high. They, of course, did not object, and Woodson received no further complaints from his executive council. To fill the vacancies left by the resignations of Hart, Peabody, and Storey, Woodson appointed three other whites, William E. Dodd, of the University of Chicago, Carl Russell Fish, of the University of Wisconsin, and Henry Churchill King, of Oberlin College. In June he asked Dodd and Fish to help him select black graduate students whom he could hire as research assistants.[69]

Since Woodson had succeeded in obtaining enough money from white philanthropists to work full-time on his research and writing, he

68. Alexander L. Jackson to Hart, April 22, 1922, Clement Richardson to Hart, April 18, 1922, Hart to Richardson, April 22, 1922, Hart to Jackson, April 24, 1922, Woodson to Hart, April 24, 1922, all in Hart Papers.
69. Woodson to Emmett J. Scott, May 5, 1922, in Scott Papers; Woodson to William E. Dodd, June 13, 1922, in William E. Dodd Papers, MS Div., LC.

resigned from West Virginia Collegiate Institute in June, 1922. Disappointed by Woodson's decision, Davis, nevertheless, understood that Woodson needed to devote more time to promoting black history and accepted Woodson's resignation.[70]

Woodson had had his fill of administrative positions in higher education. He had expected to accomplish more research and writing than he did in the three years he served at Howard and West Virginia Collegiate Institute, and he actually had more leisure time while teaching high school. Thus he was greatly relieved when he was able to return to Washington in the summer of 1922 and was eager to devote full time to his life's work. He had acquired a thirst for greater knowledge and would devote the rest of his career to ensuring that the truth about the black past be told.

70. Woodson recounted his difficulties in working in black colleges in a letter to Sydnor Walker, June 24, 1929, in Rockefeller Foundation Archives, Rockefeller Archive Center.

THREE

THE FLOWERING OF THE ASSOCIATION
1922−1933

While in West Virginia, Woodson had continued to rent office space on U Street in the heart of Washington's black business district. But after returning to Washington in June, 1922, one of the first tasks he assumed was securing a permanent headquarters for the association. He spent the summer searching for a suitable facility, and early in September, he purchased a three-story row house on Ninth Street in Washington's Shaw neighborhood. Woodson obtained a loan for the $2,750 house, using the assets of the Associated Publishers as collateral, and he made a modest down-payment of only $10. Not only did this property serve as a base of operations for the association and increase its assets, it also provided Woodson with a home, for he used the third floor of the row house as his living quarters.[1]

In the summer and fall of 1922, Woodson also resumed work on two scholarly projects he had begun the year before: the research on free blacks in the antebellum period and a study of blacks during Reconstruction. He continued to survey and interview black Baptists and former slaves and their masters, and to collect black folklore and family papers. In addition, he assumed much of the clerical work necessary to promote the association, having fired Daly, his business manager, and employing only two secretaries for assistance. By the spring of 1922, Woodson had become increasingly disappointed with Daly's inability to solicit memberships for the association and subscriptions to the *Journal*. The Associated Publishers also was struggling financially, because, Woodson believed, Daly failed to promote its books. According

1. Transfer of title and deed for property at 1538 9th Street, N.W., from Ida J. Herberger to Woodson, September 6, 1922, Logbook 4734, p. 290, Office of the Recorder of Deeds, Washington, D.C.

to Daly, however, Woodson expected results that were unattainable and wanted him to recruit members and subscribers among poor southern blacks who could barely afford life's necessities. When Daly suggested that books published by the Associated Publishers be marketed to black doctors, lawyers, and other members of the black bourgeoisie, Woodson balked, contending that these individuals did not comprise the audience he most wanted to reach. After Daly asked for a raise in April, 1922, Woodson fired him. Consequently Woodson assumed promotional duties in addition to his scholarly activities.[2]

Engaged in historical and sociological research on all aspects of the black experience in the United States from the colonial period through the 1920s, Woodson also investigated black culture in the West Indies, Latin America, and Africa, although his interest in Africa would not peak until the 1930s. Prior to 1933, when white philanthropists desisted in contributing funds, Woodson and his assistants not only produced scholarly monographs and textbooks for elementary, high school, and college students, but also collected and published primary research materials that other scholars could use. Woodson realized that he could not correct the historical record alone and believed that black scholars had a major responsibility to preserve historical as well as contemporary documentation on the black experience for future generations of scholars. Indeed, the sociological studies that Woodson conducted during this period have served as historical sources for contemporary scholars researching the black experience of the 1920s and early 1930s.[3]

The major objective of Woodson's research program was to correct the racist bias in the work published by white scholars. To accomplish this goal Woodson and his assistants uncovered previously unknown source materials, asked different questions of source materials used by white scholars, and developed new historical and sociological research methods. By using new sources and methods, Woodson and his assistants pioneered in writing the social history of black Americans and moved away from interpreting blacks solely as victims of white oppression and racism. Instead, blacks were viewed as major actors in American history.[4]

In the spring of 1922, Woodson tried to recruit Sadie Tanner Mos-

2. Patricia W. Romero, "Carter G. Woodson: A Biography" (Ph.D. dissertation, Ohio State University, 1971), 132–38.

3. See my "Carter G. Woodson and the Collection of Source Materials for Afro-American History," *American Archivist*, XLVIII (Summer, 1985), 261–71.

4. See my "Countering White Racist Scholarship: Carter G. Woodson and the *Journal of Negro History*," *Journal of Negro History*, LXVIII (1983), 355–75.

sell, a graduate of the University of Pennsylvania with degrees in history and economics, to join his staff as a research assistant. But Mossell, who was the first black woman to receive a Ph.D. in economics, decided to attend law school. Woodson also failed to convince Charles Wesley to quit his Howard teaching job to work full-time as a research assistant. Wesley did collaborate with Woodson on a number of projects, however.[5]

In the summer of 1922, A. A. Taylor, a native of Washington, D.C., became the first young black scholar to join Woodson's research staff. Woodson recruited Taylor from West Virginia Collegiate Institute to study blacks during Reconstruction. Perhaps Woodson took seriously Hart's admonishment that he should assist young black scholars with graduate education, for he encouraged Taylor to seek advanced training in history at Harvard University and provided him with the funds to obtain both a master's degree and a doctorate in American history. Because Taylor had begun researching the Reconstruction period before he went to Harvard, he selected as a dissertation topic blacks in South Carolina during Reconstruction, thus furthering Woodson's research at the same time. Taylor met Hosea B. Campbell, another black doctoral student in history at Harvard, and convinced him to work for Woodson. Woodson also assisted Campbell financially in exchange for research on the black Reconstruction project. Since the association was subsidizing the education of these two young black scholars, Woodson took a proprietary interest in their progress and corresponded regularly with their Harvard professors. When Campbell's work for Woodson fell below par and his grades simultaneously dropped, Woodson ceased his financial support. Campbell never finished his degree at Harvard.[6]

Taylor's association with Woodson continued for several years after he received his Ph.D. Once the project on blacks in South Carolina during Reconstruction was completed, Taylor conducted a similar study on Virginia. Woodson published both studies in the *Journal* and again as monographs of the Associated Publishers. Taylor also assisted Woodson with research to update *The Negro in Our History* and compiled data on free blacks using the 1830 census.[7]

5. Woodson to Herman V. Ames, March 14, 1922, in Carter G. Woodson Collection, Manuscript Division, Library of Congress; Janette Houston Harris, "Charles Harris Wesley: Educator and Historian, 1891–1947" (Ph.D. dissertation, Howard University, 1975), 131.

6. Romero, "Carter G. Woodson," 139–40.

7. A. A. Taylor, "The Negro in South Carolina During Reconstruction," *Journal of Negro History*, IX (1924), 241–364, 381–569, and "The Negro in the Reconstruction of

The first edition of *The Negro in Our History* appeared in March, 1922, and was sold out in less than a year. The second edition was published in March, 1923, and it also sold quickly. With Taylor's assistance Woodson expanded and updated the third edition of the textbook, incorporating information he had been gathering for several years from the oral histories and surveys of former slaves and their masters, and from black Baptists. Woodson hoped to eventually publish separate monographs on black Baptists and on former slaves and their masters, but he never received funding to complete these studies.[8]

Encouraged by Jameson to investigate the status of free blacks in the antebellum period, Woodson chose the manuscript of the 1830 census as a means of doing so. He believed that it was important to capture the experience of free blacks at this moment in history, because by that date they had achieved their greatest status as a distinct class in the South. After the Nat Turner rebellion in Virginia in 1831, southern slaveholders perceived free blacks as an increasing threat to the slave system. Fewer slaveowners freed their slaves or allowed them to earn money to purchase themselves. And southern legislatures began to pass laws restricting their rights. In response, southern free blacks began migrating to the North. In 1924 Taylor and Woodson published in the *Journal* extracts of two lists they had compiled from the census: free blacks who owned slaves, and absentee owners of slaves. In the majority of these cases, Woodson contended, the owners and slaves were members of the same family. Work on this project continued through 1925, when Woodson published the complete lists in book form. The black poet and writer Langston Hughes, hired to assist Woodson and Taylor, had had the arduous and tedious task of alphabetizing the lists of names of free blacks in each southern state.[9]

Virginia," *Journal of Negro History*, XI (1926), 243–415, 425–37. Also see Woodson's Annual Reports in the *Journal of Negro History* for the years 1922 to 1926.

8. Romero, "Carter G. Woodson," 135; Advertisement for *Negro in Our History*, in *Crisis*, XXIII (August, 1922), 186; Woodson to Archibald H. Grimké, July 12, 1922, in Archibald Grimké Papers, Moorland-Spingarn Research Center, Howard University; Woodson to Wallace Buttrick, July 13, 1922, and Buttrick to Woodson, July 14, 1922, in General Education Board Records, Rockefeller Archive Center, Tarrytown, N.Y.; Woodson to L. V. Bryant, January 16, 1922, Woodson to Joseph A. Booker, June 14, 1922, Woodson to George Washington Carver, November 15, 1923, all in Woodson Collection, LC. Press runs of other books published by the Associated Publishers were one thousand copies, and so it is likely that these first two editions were also.

9. Woodson, "Free Negro Owners of Slaves in the United States in 1830," *Journal of Negro History*, IX (1924), 41–86, "Absentee Ownership of Slaves in the United States

In June, 1926, the NAACP presented Woodson with its highest honor, the prestigious Spingarn Medal, in recognition of his achievements. At the award ceremony, John Haynes Holmes, a minister and interracial activist, cited Woodson's indefatigable labors to promote the truth about Negro history. *Time* magazine carried a story on Woodson along with a photograph of him. Having secured a regular income for himself and a firm financial base for the association, Woodson reached his peak in scholarly output during the 1920s, when he churned out articles, book reviews, and monographs. Yet these administrative and scholarly achievements did not come without cost; they took their toll on his psychological and physical health. A month after receiving the NAACP honor, he was forced to take a two-month vacation.[10]

Receipt of the Spingarn medal and the development of his illness reminded Woodson of how much more work he needed to accomplish to promote Negro history. Preoccupied with his own mortality, he wrote a poignant letter to Rosenwald late in 1926, explaining that although he was fifty years old and in good health, he wanted to establish an endowment of half a million dollars for the association "[so] that the work to which I have devoted the best ten years of my life may be continued when I am gone." Pleading for funds, Woodson noted that if "this work is to be perpetuated . . . it must have an assured income." While there were "many Negroes qualified to succeed" him, Woodson wrote, "the next to hold this position will be a hired man. . . . [If] there is nothing on hand to hire him, the work may perish with me."[11] Throughout the fall of 1926, despite his forced respite from work, Woodson struggled to raise additional funds, pursued over a

---

in 1830," *Journal of Negro History*, IX (1924), 196–232, and *Free Negro Heads of Families in the United States* (Washington, D.C., 1925). Also see Langston Hughes, *The Big Sea* (New York, 1940), 210–11.

10. John Haynes Holmes, "On Presenting the Spingarn Medal," *Crisis*, XXXII (September, 1926), 231–34; Memorandum to Spingarn Medal Award Committee, May 1, 1925, in NAACP Records, Group I, Series C, Box 210, MS Div., LC; J. Franklin Jameson to Mary White Ovington, May 25, 1925, "Recommendations for Spingarn Medal," June 1, 1925, Archibald and Francis J. Grimké to John Hurst, April 6, 1926, "Recommendations for Spingarn Medal," June 1, 1926, Walter White to Woodson, June 11, 15, 1926, Henry Luce to White, July 16, 1926, all in NAACP Records, Group I, Series C, Box 211; "National Affairs" column, *Time*, July 12, 1926, p. 9.

11. Woodson to Julius Rosenwald, December 3, 1926, in Julius Rosenwald Papers, University of Chicago Library. Woodson mentioned his illness in Woodson to Allen Johnson, October 8, 1926, in American Council of Learned Societies Records, MS Div., LC.

dozen research projects, trained a coterie of young black scholars, and worked at a breakneck pace to continue to build the Negro history movement.

In the fall of 1928 Woodson decided to undertake a study of free blacks listed in the 1860 census. After the 1830 study was published, scholars realized that a vast potential for social history research lay in census manuscripts. Woodson assumed that the data on free southern blacks in 1860 would be equal in significance to, although different from, the 1830 data. On the eve of the Civil War, the absolute number of free blacks would be smaller, as would the ratio of free blacks to slaves. Also revealing, Woodson believed, would be an analysis of those free blacks who remained in the South, and he hoped to provide comparative data on their property holdings between the two periods. Before undertaking the project, however, Woodson asked leading white scholars of slavery and southern history to assess the value of the 1830 lists he had published and to provide him with an estimate of the research potential of a compilation based on the 1860 census.[12]

The scholars who responded to Woodson's inquiry enthusiastically supported the new project and recounted the uses that they had made of the 1830 lists. Ulrich Phillips, of the University of Michigan, contended that the "publication pertaining to 1830 has been useful to sundry students here, including myself. A similar one for 1860 is desirable."[13] Charles Sydnor, of the University of Mississippi, also endorsed the 1860 study, maintaining that he had used the 1830 lists to teach graduate students. He wrote, "I have used your work for 1830 in an article in the July 1927 American Historical Review (Free Negro in Mississippi Before the Civil War) and found it valuable." Other white scholars—E. M. Coulter, of the University of Georgia, Philip Hamer, of the University of Tennessee, Homer C. Hockett, of Ohio State University, Arthur M. Schlesinger, of Harvard, and St. George L. Sioussat, of the University of Pennsylvania—urged Woodson to go ahead with

12. Woodson to Jameson, September 25, 1928, in J. Franklin Jameson Papers, MS Div., LC; Woodson to Evarts B. Greene, September 25, 1928, and Woodson to U. B. Phillips, September 25, 1928, in Julius Rosenwald Fund Records, Fisk University, Nashville, Tenn.

13. Phillips to Woodson, September 27, 1928, in Rosenwald Fund Records. Also see Loren Schweninger, "Prosperous Blacks in the South, 1790–1880," *American Historical Review*, XCV (1990), 31–56, and *Black Property Owners in the South, 1790–1915* (Urbana, 1990). Schweninger relies on Woodson's work in the 1830 census.

the 1860 study. In spite of these enthusiastic endorsements, Woodson was unable to persuade white philanthropists to provide him with the funds necessary to hire research assistants to undertake the project.[14]

Woodson did execute several other research projects on the black experience during the antebellum period. Among them was the study of miscegenation between blacks, Indians, and whites in Virginia, which Woodson hired James Hugo Johnston to research and write in 1926. Woodson also hired Zora Neale Hurston, a Florida native and anthropology graduate student of Franz Boas' at Columbia, to collect black folklore and interview former slaves in Florida and Alabama. He published Hurston's article, "Cudjo's Own Story of the Last African Slaver," in the *Journal* in 1927.[15]

Hurston's research project was cosponsored by the association, the American Folklore Society, and the National Urban League; and folklorist Elsie Clews Parsons also contributed funds. Since 1923, Boas and fellow anthropologist Melville J. Herskovits had been urging Woodson to join them in finding young black scholars whom together they could train to become anthropologists. Initially Woodson was wary of cooperating with the National Urban League, fearing that the organization might exert too much control over the research project and the student investigator. But because he had had a successful relationship with Taylor, Woodson agreed to cooperate in the joint venture in 1926 and corresponded with several black and white scholars to identify deserving young blacks. Before Hurston's selection, Boas and Herskovits suggested many candidates and were frequently exasperated when Woodson concluded that they were unsuitable.[16]

14. Charles Sydnor to Woodson, September 26, 1928, E. M. Coulter to Woodson, September 28, 1928, Philip Hamer to Woodson, October 20, 1928, Homer C. Hockett to Woodson, October 30, 1928, Arthur M. Schlesinger to Woodson, September 26, 1928, St. George L. Sioussat to Woodson, October 8, 1926, all in Rosenwald Fund Records. Also see Jameson to Helen T. Catterall, April 4, 1923, and Jameson to Woodson, October 6, 1928, in Jameson Papers; Robert M. Lester to Woodson, February 14, 1929, in Carnegie Foundation Archives, Butler Library, Columbia University.

15. Woodson, "Annual Report for 1926–1927," in the *Journal of Negro History*, XII (1927), 567–76, and "Annual Report for 1927–1928," XIII (1928), 403–412; Zora Neale Hurston, "Cudjo's Own Story of the Last African Slaver," *Journal of Negro History*, XII (1927), 648–63. Robert E. Hemenway contends that Hurston plagiarized this article from Emma Langdon Roche, *Historic Sketches of the Old South* (New York, 1914). See Robert E. Hemenway, *Zora Neale Hurston: A Literary Biography* (Urbana, 1978), 95–103.

16. Woodson to Franz Boas, March 30, 1923, Boas to Woodson, April 2, 30, 1923, Woodson to Boas, May 7, 1923, Boas to Woodson, May 14, 1923, Woodson to Boas,

Although Woodson could be a demanding taskmaster, numerous young black scholars continued to assist him with research projects. In addition to Taylor's ongoing work on Reconstruction, Woodson began several studies of black labor and the black working class in the post–Civil War period, hoping to uncover the economic and social conditions faced in a variety of occupations. Beginning with the time just after emancipation, Woodson sought to determine whether the number of freedmen "increased or decreased in various occupations and to account for whatever changes may have taken place in the respective pursuits." He hired Iva R. Marshall, Lorenzo Johnston Greene, and Charles Wesley to assist with the research. While studying black laborers, Greene and Wesley began their long collaboration with Woodson.[17]

In 1928 Greene and Woodson conducted research on the experiences of blacks in the rural South during the twentieth century, a project begun in 1925. Woodson had hoped to publish a biography of Julius Rosenwald, which would include a history of the Rosenwald Fund, and Rosenwald had given him access to correspondence and reports published by the fund. Since the major initiative of the Rosenwald Fund had been to finance schools and libraries for rural southern blacks, the files contained rich documentation on education, sanitation, medical facilities, recreation, employment, and religion for virtually every community where Rosenwald had built a library and school. Woodson completed the biography in 1927, but Rosenwald would not finance its publication, preferring instead to compensate Woodson with $500 for his effort. Unwilling to discard the fruits of his research, Woodson used the data he had collected as the core materials for a larger project on blacks in the rural South and hired three other black scholars, Glenn C. Carrington, John T. McKinley, and Robert C. Woods, to join him and Greene. To supplement the documentary sources culled from the Rosenwald files, Woodson and his assistants traveled throughout

---

May 15, October 13, 1923, May 15, 1924, Boas to Woodson, May 20, 1924, Woodson to Boas, November 13, 23, 1926, Boas to Woodson, December 7, 1926, Boas to Elsie Clews Parsons, December 7, 1926, Woodson to Boas, February 17, 1927, all in Franz Boas Papers, American Philosophical Society Library, Philadelphia; Woodson to Melville J. Herskovits, February 11, 1924, Alain Locke to Herskovits, February 23, 1924, Locke to Herskovits, April 14, 1924, Herskovits to L. H. Wood, May 15, 22, 1924, all in Melville J. Herskovits Papers, University Archives, Northwestern University.
    17. Woodson, "Annual Report for 1926–1927," pp. 567–76.

the rural South interviewing teachers, doctors and other health professionals, ministers, and common black folk. In 1930 the Associated Publishers brought out *The Rural Negro*.[18]

Greene also assisted Woodson and Wesley with research on the contemporary black church. The New York City–based Institute of Social
and Religious Research recognized Woodson's interest and scholarship
in black religion by awarding him a $16,000 grant in February, 1928.
Woodson intended to put the grant, which was one of the few that he
did not solicit, to good use. He proposed to conduct a comparative
study of black urban and rural churches using Baltimore, Maryland, and
Suffolk, Virginia, as case studies. Woodson hired Wesley, who was then
an ordained AME minister as well as the chairman of the Howard history department, to direct the project, and he hired Greene to assist
Wesley. Greene was to conduct the research on Baltimore, and Wesley
would study Suffolk. In each community they would use surveys and
interviews to examine the number of churches and their denominations, the credentials and education of the ministers and their philosophy of religion, and the social support services offered.[19]

Eager to begin work on the project, Wesley arranged a leave from
his teaching duties at Howard, although he still attended to his administrative responsibilities as department chairman. He received half of
his regular salary in addition to $250 per month from Woodson's grant.
By midspring, 1928, Wesley had managed to complete a draft of his
study on Suffolk and turned it over to Woodson, who found it to be
unsatisfactory and termed it "worthless." Wesley shrugged off Woodson's caustic criticism and began to rewrite the section. In June, he was
chosen as a presiding elder of the AME church in Washington, D.C.,
and accepted the position.[20]

Months earlier, when the project began, Woodson had urged Wesley

18. Carter G. Woodson, *The Rural Negro* (Washington, D.C., 1930); Alfred K. Stern
to Woodson, November 3, 1926, Stern to William E. Dodd, April 15, 1927, Stern to
Woodson, September 15, 1927, all in Rosenwald Fund Records; Woodson, "Annual Re-
port for 1927–1928," pp. 403–12. Also see Lorenzo J. Greene, *Working with Carter G.
Woodson, the Father of Black History: A Diary, 1928–1930*, ed. Arvarh E. Strickland (Baton
Rouge, 1989), 11–194.

19. Woodson, "Annual Report for 1927–1928," pp. 403–12; Harris, "Charles Harris
Wesley," 134–44; Woodson to Leonard Outhwaite, February 24, 1928, in Laura Spel-
man Rockefeller Memorial Fund Records, Rockefeller Archive Center. Also see Greene,
Working with Carter G. Woodson, 11–194.

20. Harris, "Charles Harris Wesley," 133–44; Greene, *Working with Carter G. Woodson*, 11–194.

to take a leave of absence from Howard so that he could devote all of his time to the project. In June, Woodson fired Wesley, declaring Wesley had no business assuming additional responsibilities. Woodson maintained that Wesley's objectivity would be further compromised, and that he already was too influenced by the AME church. In a last-minute effort to hire a replacement, Woodson fired off a telegram to E. Franklin Frazier, offering him the research position. Frazier apparently did not accept the offer, and Woodson reluctantly returned the grant to the Institute of Social and Religious Research. In his annual report for 1928, Woodson announced receipt of the grant for the project but asserted that he had to abandon the study and return the funds because the "head investigator failed to give it all of his time." [21]

Although Wesley's relations with Woodson were temporarily soured after 1928, Greene continued to work with him on several important sociological projects. In addition to the study of rural blacks, Greene served as the major investigator on a study of black wage earners, a study of black professionals and businessmen, and a project to survey black unemployment in the District of Columbia during the depression. Assisted by black professionals and scholars, Greene and Woodson conducted interviews and surveys. For the study of black businessmen and professionals, they received research assistance from attorney Charles Hamilton Houston, of Howard University Law School, physician M. B. Jackson, also of Howard, Robert Moton, still at Tuskegee and also head of the National Negro Business League, Samuel Rutherford, of the National Mutual Benefit Life Insurance Company, and Charles C. Spaulding, of the North Carolina Mutual Insurance Company. Woodson hired two black women—Myra Colson Callis and Laura C. Glenn—to aid Greene with the black unemployment survey, which was cosponsored by the Committee for Improving Industrial Conditions Among Negroes in the District of Columbia. Greene also worked on several research projects during the late 1920s and early 1930s that remained unpublished because funding was lacking; included among them were a comparative study of black workers in Bal-

21. Woodson to E. Franklin Frazier, June 10, 1928, in E. Franklin Frazier Papers, Moorland-Spingarn Research Center. The Institute for Social and Religious Research then awarded the grant to Benjamin E. Mays and Joseph Nicholson and published their study, *The Negro Church*, in 1933, which was a national comparative study on rural and urban churches. Wesley and Greene completed a manuscript, which is available at Howard University. See Omnium-Gatherum, in Miscellaneous Collections, Moorland-Spingarn Research Center.

timore and the District of Columbia, a study of black fraternal organizations, and a study of "near great Negroes," which was a social history of common black folk, maids, mechanics, and farmers.[22]

It was also during the 1920s that Woodson initiated a number of projects on Africa and the Caribbean. He began collecting historical and contemporary documents on Africa, gathering folktales and stories, and corresponding with scholars Herskovits, Monroe Work, and Maurice Delafosse, who were researching the African past. The Associated Publishers brought out an English translation of Delafosse's *Les Noirs de l'Afrique*, as well as Woodson's *African Myths Together with Proverbs*. Woodson provided Alain Locke with funds for a two-year project of preparing a monograph on African art as a manifestation of African culture. He also supervised H. T. Richards, a student at Frelinghuysen University in Washington, in writing a master's thesis on the influence of black West Indians on black culture in the United States. African contributions to the language, religion, folklore, and customs of blacks in Haiti and Cuba were explored in several projects, and Woodson traveled to Cuba in 1928 to gather source materials.[23]

Since the collection of source materials was an essential component

22. Woodson's Annual Reports for 1926–1934, in the *Journal of Negro History;* Woodson, *The Rural Negro,* Woodson, *The Negro Wage Earner* (Washington, D.C., 1930); Lorenzo J. Greene and Myra Colson Callis, *The Employment of Negroes in the District of Columbia* (Washington, D.C., 1931); Woodson, Memorandum in Regard to the Situation in Baltimore, n.d., and Woodson to Beardsley Ruml, April 30, 1929, in Laura Spelman Rockefeller Memorial Fund Records. In *Black History and the Historical Profession, 1915–1980* (Urbana, 1986), 81, August Meier and Elliott Rudwick contend that Greene actually wrote all of *The Negro Wage Earner.*

23. Anna J. Cooper to H. Barrett Learned, May 21, 1931, in Records of Washington, D.C., Board of Education, Sumner School Archives, Washington, D.C.; Woodson's Annual Reports for the 1920s, in the *Journal of Negro History;* Maurice Delafosse, *The Negroes of Africa,* trans. Frieda Fligeman (Washington, D.C., 1931); Woodson, ed., *African Myths Together with Proverbs* (Washington, D.C., 1928); Irene Wright to Jeannette Thurber Connor, May 5, 1923, in Irene Wright Papers, MS Div., LC; Woodson to Herskovits, February 11, 1924, June 8, 1927, Herskovits to Woodson, June 10, 1927, Woodson to Herskovits, June 11, 1927, Herskovits to Woodson, June 15, 1927, all in Herskovits Papers; Woodson to the Phelps-Stokes Fund, September 11, 1926, in Phelps-Stokes Fund Records, Schomburg Center for Research in Black Culture, New York Public Library; Woodson to Franz Boas, November 16, 1926, Boas to Woodson, November 18, 1926, Woodson to Boas, November 18, 1926, Boas to Woodson, November 22, 1926, all in Boas Papers; Monroe Work to Woodson, July 13, 1927, in Monroe Work Papers, Tuskegee Institute Archives; Woodson, "Notes," *Journal of Negro History,* XIII (1928), 222–23. For the announcement of a prize Woodson offered for the best collection of West Indian folklore, see *Crisis,* XXV (April, 1923), 272.

of Woodson's research program, he seized every opportunity to educate the general public and the scholarly community about the need to preserve and collect sources that accurately reflected the feelings, thoughts, and experiences of African Americans. Many significant documents were published in the *Journal*—both those collected by Woodson and the numerous researchers he hired to comb through newspapers and archives in the United States and Europe, and those uncovered by black and white scholars in their research and sent to Woodson. William K. Boyd, of Duke University, provided materials on the religious instruction of slaves; Arthur H. Buffington, of Williams College and a former Harvard classmate of Woodson, sent him sources on black West Indian slaves in the eighteenth century; and N. Andrew Cleven, of the University of Pittsburgh, forwarded European diplomatic records pertaining to runaway slaves. Frank Klingberg, of the University of California at Los Angeles, and Annie Abel-Henderson, formerly of Smith College, discovered in British archives letters written by the Tappan brothers to abolitionists in England. Woodson published extracts of the letters in the *Journal* and brought out a separate volume edited by Klingberg and Abel-Henderson through the Associated Publishers. Fred Landon, of the Ontario Public Library, and William Renwick Riddell, justice of the Supreme Court of Ontario, sent letters of runaway slaves who had escaped to Canada. Waldemar Westergaard, of the University of California at Los Angeles, submitted maps and documents detailing a slave revolt in the Danish West Indies.[24]

With assistance from Jameson, Woodson engaged the services of George Francis Dow, Ruth Anna Fisher, and Irene Wright, who were

24. Woodson to William K. Boyd, November 3, 1927, in William K. Boyd Papers, University Archives, Perkins Library, Duke University; Arthur H. Buffington to Woodson, May 2, 1924, in Woodson Collection, LC; Woodson to Frank Klingberg, April 30, 1926, in Jameson Papers; Frank Klingberg and Annie Abel-Henderson, eds., "Correspondence of Lewis Tappan and Others with the British and Foreign Anti-Slavery Society," *Journal of Negro History*, XII (1927), 179–329, 389–554, and *A Side-Light on Anglo-American Relations* (Washington, D.C., 1927); "Notes on Negro Slavery in Canada Collected by Mr. Justice Riddell of the Supreme Court of Ontario," *Journal of Negro History*, IV (1919), 396–411; Fred Landon, "Records Illustrating the Condition of Refugees from Slavery in Upper Canada Before 1860," *Journal of Negro History*, XIII (1928), 199–209; N. Andrew Cleven, "The Convention Between Spain and Holland Regulating the Return of Deserters and Fugitive Slaves in Their American Colonies," *Journal of Negro History*, XIV (1929), 341–44; Waldemar Westergaard to Woodson, October 27, 1925, in Woodson Collection, LC.

conducting research for Elizabeth Donnan's *Documentary History of the Slave Trade*, Helen T. Catterall's volumes of legal cases, and other documentary editing projects sponsored by the Carnegie Institution's Department of Historical Research. Dow searched colonial New England newspapers for advertisements of runaway slaves; Fisher culled materials on slavery and abolition in colonial America and the West Indies from records in the British Museum and the Public Record Office; and Wright gathered sources documenting the experiences of slaves in Spanish Florida, Cuba, and Latin America from Spanish archives. Similarly, Donnan and Catterall forwarded to Jameson documents that would interest Woodson.[25]

By 1925 the *Journal* devoted at least one quarter of its space to the publication of transcripts of primary source materials and thereby encouraged their use by scholars who otherwise would not have known about them. Assisted by black scholars G. D. Houston, Luther Porter Jackson, James Hugo Johnston, Lorenzo Dow Turner, and others, Woodson collected materials on well-known and obscure nineteenth-century blacks. The speeches, writings, petitions, and letters documenting their experiences were published in the *Journal*, and in collections edited and published separately by Woodson through the Associated Publishers, such as *The Mind of the Negro Reflected in Letters Written During the Crisis*, and *Negro Orators and Their Orations*. To aid future scholars, Woodson placed the documents in context by providing appropriate biographical and introductory material.[26]

Through his own efforts and the good will of black and white scholars, Woodson had amassed a sizeable collection. Although many of these documents were published, they remained unknown to most white scholars, few of whom read the *Journal* or purchased the volumes brought out by the Associated Publishers. Thus, in 1928, Woodson decided to place his collection in the Library of Congress, where Jameson had been installed as chief of the Manuscript Division. He applied for and received a one-year grant of $4,000 from the Social Science

25. Jameson to Elizabeth Donnan, August 29, September 26, 1922, Jameson to George Francis Dow, September 26, 1922, Dow to Jameson, September 30, 1922, Irene Wright to Jameson, January 22, 1923, Jameson to Helen T. Catterall, April 4, 1923, Jameson to Woodson, September 21, 1923, Woodson to Jameson, September 24, 1923, all in Jameson Papers.

26. Woodson, ed., *The Mind of the Negro Reflected in Letters Written During the Crisis* (Washington, D.C., 1926), and *Negro Orators and Their Orations* (Washington, D.C., 1925); James Hugo Johnston to Woodson, August 6, 1925, and Luther P. Jackson to Woodson, August 8, 1926, in Woodson Collection, LC.

Research Council (SSRC) to build the collection and undertake a more systematic search for manuscripts. Although Woodson succeeded in collecting over twenty-five hundred manuscripts in 1929, the Social Science Research Council would not renew the grant. Further attempts to solicit funds from other foundations also failed, but Woodson continued to build the collection through the voluntary support of black and white scholars and the general public.[27]

Woodson had succeeded in obtaining funds from the SSRC probably because he had been appointed to its subcommittee on interracial affairs, for which he served as secretary from 1927 to 1928. Woodson knew several white scholars on the subcommittee, and was well acquainted with some of the white scholars and philanthropists on the executive board of the SSRC.[28] Three other black scholars served on the subcommittee with Woodson: Charles S. Johnson, of Fisk University and former editor of the National Urban League's magazine, *Opportunity;* Ernest Just, of Howard; and Work, of Tuskegee.

The interracial affairs subcommittee, one of seven special subcommittees of the SSRC, evaluated research proposals on race relations and was charged "to work out plans for discovering promising colored students for the research," and to assist them "in getting training."[29] In practice, however, the subcommittee funded projects undertaken by black and white scholars who were either on the subcommittee or who were members of the same institutions as subcommittee members. In addition to the grant Woodson received for his collecting project, funds

27. Woodson, "Annual Report for 1928–1929," *Journal of Negro History,* XIV (1929), 361–70; Jameson to Arthur M. Schlesinger, December 4, 1928, Herbert Putnam to Woodson, December 5, 1928, Woodson to Jameson, December 6, 1928, April 4, 1929, Jameson to Woodson, April 19, 1928, Woodson to Jameson, June 25, 1929, Jameson to Woodson, June 26, 1929, Woodson to Jameson, January 7, April 19, 1930, Jameson to Woodson, April 22, 1930, all in Library of Congress Archives, MS Div., LC; Woodson to Jesse E. Moorland, June 18, 1929, in Jesse E. Moorland Papers, Moorland-Spingarn Research Center; Woodson to George Foster Peabody, June 24, 1929, in George Foster Peabody Papers, MS Div., LC; Frederick P. Keppel to Woodson, December 26, 1929, Woodson to Keppel, November 25, 1930, Keppel to Woodson, December 4, 1930, January 16, 1931, all in Carnegie Foundation Archives; "Report on the Exploratory Effort to Collect Manuscript Materials Among Negroes," n.d., in Rosenwald Papers; Woodson to Jameson, March 20, 24, 1930, Jameson to John D. Rockefeller, April 1, 1930, Jameson to Woodson, April 17, 1930, all in Jameson Papers.

28. Woodson, "Annual Report for 1928–1929," pp. 361–70; *The Social Science Research Council: Decennial Report, 1923–1933* (New York, 1934), 51–53.

29. Will Alexander to Monroe N. Work, May 24, 1927, in Work Papers. Also see, John H. Stanfield, *Philanthropy and Jim Crow in American Social Science* (Westport, Conn., 1985), 3–15, 53–124, 140–42, 152–54, 185–99.

were awarded to fellow subcommittee members Charles Johnson, Howard Odum, and Thomas J. Woofter for a series of projects on the employment, culture, and religion of blacks on St. Helena Island. And Woodson influenced subcommittee members to fund projects proposed by his scholarly collaborators: a study on mental abilities of rural blacks, by Boas; an investigation of the black family, by Frazier; research on free blacks in antebellum Virginia, by Luther Porter Jackson; and the project on African art, by Locke. Woodson was merely perpetuating a practice initiated by white philanthropists since the establishment of the major foundations, and was not the only one to exert his influence to fund projects undertaken by his colleagues.[30]

The racial exclusivity of the major foundations ensured that controversial black proposals would not be funded and that the most conservative black social scientists would be rewarded with research money; black nationalists, Marxists, and ardent integrationists had little chance of receiving grants. Not surprisingly, black applicants were judged by different standards than those used for their white counterparts. Creativity and originality were not valued when assessing the merits of black research proposals. Rather, black applicants were judged on the facts they presented, their previous research and writing experience, and their politics.[31]

Research projects that promoted interracial cooperation and racial accommodation received backing, and usually the most conservative black institutions—Fisk, Tuskegee, the National Urban League, and the National Negro Business League, for example—won the lion's share of funds. Money was provided for studies on subjects such as methods to enhance business opportunities for blacks, black migration, urban conditions, and crime in the black community. Although Woodson received most of the funds that the Laura Spelman Rockefeller Memorial Fund allocated to blacks for historical research, he was urged to train black scholars for interdisciplinary research in anthropology, folklore, and sociology, and to deemphasize the documentation of black history.[32]

30. Also receiving funds were Moton, for intelligence tests among black children, and Sterling Spero, for a study of blacks in industry. See *Social Science Research Council*, 52–53. Also see Herskovits to Spero, November 10, 1926, in Herskovits Papers.

31. See Stanfield, *Philanthropy and Jim Crow*, 53–124, 140–42, 185–99.

32. Meier and Rudwick, *Black History and the Historical Profession*, 48–71. Also see Walter Jackson, *Gunnar Myrdal and America's Conscience: Social Engineering and Racial Liberalism, 1938–1987* (Chapel Hill, 1990), and "The Making of a Social Science Classic:

It was the Rosenwald Fund, however, that did the most to advance black social science and education, especially after Edwin Embree joined the staff. Embree was particularly liberal toward minorities and invited blacks to serve on his advisory board. He was an outcast among his peers in the foundation world because of his liberalism. In addition to funding the construction of black schools and libraries in the rural South, the Rosenwald Fund also financed social science research projects initiated by Charles Johnson at Fisk, Moton at Tuskegee, and Woodson at the association.[33]

Woodson made good use of the funds he received from white philanthropists, but by the early 1930s, he could no longer depend on their financial support. He refused to affiliate the association with a major black college, a move stipulated by the Laura Spelman Rockefeller Memorial Fund, the Rockefeller Foundation, and the General Education Board. Woodson also was unrelenting in his criticism of Thomas Jesse Jones; thus he continued to fuel Jones's vendetta against him and as a result lost additional white financial support.[34]

After Woodson removed him from the executive board in 1922, Jones orchestrated a letter-writing campaign to white foundation administrators. He made it increasingly difficult for Woodson both to renew the grants he had received earlier and to raise additional funds from other foundations. Although he was receiving $10,000 each year from the Carnegie Foundation and the Laura Spelman Rockefeller Memorial Fund, Woodson maintained that he needed an annual budget of $50,000 to conduct and publish research in black history and soci-

Gunnar Myrdal's *An American Dilemma,*" *Perspectives in American History,* II (1985), 221–67.

33. Stanfield, *Philanthropy and Jim Crow,* 3–15, 53–124, 140–42, 152–54, 185–89. Charles Houston and Charles Johnson were on the board.

34. Guy Stanton Ford to Woodson, January 27, 1925, Sydnor Walker to Woodson, June 18, 1929, Woodson to Walker, June 24, 1929, Walker to Woodson, June 27, 1929, all in Laura Spelman Rockefeller Memorial Fund Records; Walker to Woodson, March 21, April 23, 1930, Walker to Edwin Embree, April 24, 1930, Woodson to Walker, April 26, 1930, Walker to Woodson, January 22, 1931, all in Rockefeller Foundation Records, Rockefeller Archive Center; L. A. Roy to Woodson, April 18, 1924, and Stokes to Woodson, January 8, 1932, in Phelps-Stokes Fund Records; Anson Phelps Stokes to James Hardy Dillard, June 11, 1924, Stokes to Dillard, September 8, 1924, Stokes to Woodson, September 8, 1924, Dillard to Stokes, September 11, 1924, Stokes to Woodson, February 16, 1931, Thomas Jesse Jones to Stokes, August 5, 1932, all in Anson Phelps Stokes Papers, Sterling Memorial Library, Yale University; Woodson to W. E. B. Du Bois, January 7, 1932, in W. E. B. Du Bois Papers, University of Massachusetts.

ology, and he sought assistance from other white foundations. In 1923 Woodson wrote to the General Education Board, the sister institution of the Laura Spelman Rockefeller Memorial Fund, requesting $3,000 a year for five years to hire researchers. However, this and all subsequent appeals he made to the General Education Board were denied. Undoubtedly, it was Jones's letter writing that caused officials of the Rosenwald Fund to become suspicious of Woodson's financial administration in 1923. The Rosenwald Fund had been contributing to the association since its foundation, and Julius Rosenwald, although inactive, remained on Woodson's executive council. Still, foundation officials sought information on Woodson's credit rating from the National Information Bureau, which issued a report endorsing the association but noting that Woodson "had decided viewpoints" and was "somewhat difficult to work with."[35]

While Woodson suspected that Jones was responsible for his recent financial difficulties, he had no real proof. In an article solicited by the Indianapolis *Freeman* in 1924, Woodson denounced Jones, claiming that "we have lost this year probably as much as $2,000 as a result of his ham-stringing the Association."[36] Woodson's suspicion that Jones was writing letters to white philanthropists asking them to withdraw their support from the association is corroborated in a letter that James Hardy Dillard, who remained on Woodson's executive council, wrote to Anson Phelps Stokes of the Phelps-Stokes Fund after the article in the *Freeman* appeared. In support of Jones, the Phelps-Stokes Fund planned to release a statement countering Woodson's charges unless Woodson would publish a retraction in the *Freeman*. Anson Phelps Stokes circulated the statement to several whites for comment, and Dillard was among the respondents. While Dillard believed that Woodson should share more information about his financial affairs with his executive council, he had "no reason to believe" and did "not believe that there has been crookedness," and presumed that "Dr. Woodson interprets the attitude of Dr. Jones as practically making this accusation." Unfortunately, Dillard feared, "the letter or letters written against giv-

35. Woodson to E. C. Sage, February 27, 1923, Sage to Woodson, March 15, 1923, Woodson to Sage, July 15, 1925, all in General Education Board Records; Winifred C. Putnam to William C. Graves, October 20, 1923, in Rosenwald Papers.

36. Woodson quoted in Anson Phelps Stokes to James Dillard, June 11, 1924, and enclosure, Confidential Memorandum for the Trustees of the Phelps-Stokes Fund Regarding Dr. Carter G. Woodson's Attacks on Thomas Jesse Jones, which contains Woodson to Indianapolis *Freeman*, April 12, 1924; *Freeman* to Woodson, March 12, 1924, all in Stokes Papers.

ing financial support to Dr. Woodson's work will continue to be a basis of hostility." [37]

Other blacks besides Woodson felt hostility toward Jones. American Negro Academy members Arthur A. Schomburg and John W. Cromwell sympathized with Woodson, concurring that his courage in speaking out against Jones cost the association white financial support. Du Bois, who also long had been critical of Jones, wrote to Anson Phelps Stokes in 1924 supporting Woodson. "If you expect to work with black people and cooperate with them," Du Bois told Stokes, "the cooperation is going to be real; they are going to have the power to say what they think whether you like it or not and they will not submit to the dictation of men like Thomas Jesse Jones." [38]

In 1925 Woodson's request for renewal of the Carnegie grant was denied, despite support from Jameson, who closely supervised the first grant, and other white scholars, who wrote to the foundation on Woodson's behalf. Jones had convinced white officials not only that Woodson was an inept financial administrator but also that he was carrying out a research program that advanced radical interpretations of black history. During the time the Carnegie Foundation was considering renewal of the grant, Woodson met with Frederick Keppel of the foundation to make a personal appeal. When Keppel indicated that the grant would not be renewed, Woodson then asked John C. Merriam, Jameson's supervisor and the Director of the Carnegie Institution of Washington, to speak to Keppel on his behalf. "Inasmuch as the Carnegie Corporation was the first foundation to give substantial assistance to the Association," Woodson wrote Merriam, "its failure to continue this support would make upon other boards the impression that the Association has been tried and found wanting, when as a matter of fact, every person well informed as to the progress of the work thus prosecuted will testify that this society is now in the midst of its greatest achievements." Although Merriam did speak with Keppel, his intercession did not counter the damage done by Jones, and the Carnegie Foundation did not fund any other projects that Woodson proposed in subsequent years. [39]

37. Dillard to Stokes, September 11, 1924, and Confidential Memorandum, in Stokes Papers.

38. Schomburg to John Cromwell, April 6, 1924, in Cromwell Family Papers, Moorland-Spingarn Research Center; Du Bois to Stokes, December 13, 1924, in Stokes Papers.

39. Woodson to John C. Merriam, March 9, 1925, and Merriam to Woodson, March 25, 1925, in John C. Merriam Papers, MS Div., LC; Woodson to Morse Adams Cartwright, January 24, 1925, Woodson to Keppel, March 31, 1925, Keppel to Woodson,

Woodson was determined to raise funds from within the black community in order to make up the deficit, and in 1926 he initiated a campaign to establish a permanent endowment of $250,000. He told James Weldon Johnson of the NAACP, "It is much better to obtain one dollar from each of 20,000 persons than $20,000 from one." Woodson wrote letters to hundreds of blacks and to major black organizations asking for contributions, and dunned them for money throughout the rest of the 1920s. Woodson also mended fences with a few prominent whites who had contributed to the association in its early years, and received assurance of a contribution of $50 per year from former executive council member Storey. When Woodson launched the annual celebration of Negro History Week in 1926, he did so not only to increase awareness of and interest in black history among the black masses, but also with the hope that the newly initiated members would become contributors to his organization.[40]

Many of Woodson's contemporaries contended that the establishment of Negro History Week was Woodson's most impressive achievement. In *Dusk of Dawn*, published in 1940, Du Bois stated that it was the greatest single accomplishment to arise from the artistic movement of blacks during the 1920s. Similarly, Rayford Logan maintained that Negro History Week helped blacks overcome their inferiority complex and instilled racial pride and optimism. Impressed by the large following Marcus Garvey had attracted among northern urban blacks, many of whom were recent migrants from the South, Woodson hoped that an annual celebration of black achievements and contributions to history would do the same for his cause and subsequently generate funds for association programs and publications. Woodson also was capitalizing on the Harlem Renaissance of the 1920s, a movement among black intellectuals and artists seeking to produce a more accurate representation of black life and culture in literature and the arts.[41]

April 7, 1925, all in Carnegie Foundation Archives; Waldo G. Leland to Woodson, April 14, 1924, in American Council of Learned Societies Records.

40. Woodson to James Weldon Johnson, February 17, 1926, Woodson to William Pickens, December 19, 1925, Woodson to Robert W. Bagnell, December 19, 1925, Woodson to Pickens, January 7, 1926, Woodson to James Weldon Johnson, February 17, 1926, all in NAACP Records, Group I, Series C, Box 80; Moorfield Storey to Woodson, March 16, 1926, in Moorfield Storey Papers, MS Div., LC; Woodson to Jesse Moorland, April 26, 1926, in Moorland Papers; Woodson to Frederic Bancroft, September 12, 1927, in Frederic Bancroft Papers, Butler Library; Woodson to Archibald Grimké, September 12, 1927, in Archibald Grimké Papers.

41. W. E. B. Du Bois, *Dusk of Dawn: An Essay Toward an Autobiography of a Race Con-*

Woodson chose the second week of February for the annual event, to commemorate the birthdays of Frederick Douglass and Abraham Lincoln. Months before the first celebration, he sent out promotional brochures and pamphlets to state boards of education, elementary and secondary schools, colleges, women's clubs, black newspapers and periodicals, and white scholarly journals. In that literature, Woodson emphasized the importance of recognizing black achievements and contributions, and suggested ways to celebrate Negro History Week.[42]

Each year the association published a variety of books and other materials designed for use during the annual celebration to educate the black community. By 1929 the association was offering for sale reproductions of 160 photographs of significant blacks, and Woodson hoped to obtain funding to publish a pictorial history of blacks in Africa and America. He also produced specialized pamphlets that included bibliographies on various aspects of Negro history and prepared a "Table of 152 Important Events and Dates in Negro History," which sold for fifty cents by the early 1930s.[43]

Negro History Week generally included parades with costumed participants portraying famous blacks, breakfasts, banquets, speeches, poetry readings, lectures on Negro history, exhibits, and special presentations. One of Woodson's more successful programs was held in 1930, when he invited all former black congressmen and Oscar DePriest, then the only black member of Congress, to speak at a banquet. More than two thousand people attended, and Woodson raised a substantial amount of money, which enabled him to produce additional promotional materials for future celebrations.[44]

From the 1920s through the 1940s Woodson spent much time traveling throughout the country. He gave lectures to black congregations of all denominations and to interracial reform and peace organizations that were sponsored by religious groups. He frequently spoke before black and white teachers associations, the faculty and students of black col-

cept (1940; rpr. New York, 1971), 203; Rayford W. Logan, "*Phylon* Profile VI: Carter G. Woodson," *Phylon*, VI (1945), 317. Omega Psi Phi fraternity first began the celebration of Negro achievements during the month of February.

42. Woodson, "Annual Report for 1925–1926," *Journal of Negro History*, XI (1926), 547–55.

43. Woodson, "Annual Report for 1928–1929," p. 370; Advertisement, "Excellent Photographs of Eleven Distinguished Negroes," *Journal of Negro History*, XIV (1929).

44. Greene, *Working with Carter G. Woodson*, 436–64.

leges, and black fraternal, social welfare, and cultural groups. Representative of the last category were Washington's Mu-So-Lit Club and National Negro Music Center, Boston's League for Women in Community Service, and the Philadelphia branch of Alpha Phi Alpha fraternity during its annual "Go to High School, Go to College" campaign.[45]

In 1926, realizing that successful fund-raising needed to be organized among a group of prominent friends, Woodson assembled the Committee of 100. Headed by James E. Shepard, a professor at North Carolina College for Negroes, the committee was composed of middle- and upper-class blacks and included businessmen, ministers, newspaper editors, secondary school teachers and administrators, additional college professors, and community activists. Each member of the Committee of 100 was given the task of raising or contributing $500.[46]

Frederic Bancroft, an old friend of Woodson's, had planned to endow a "Bancroft Prize" for articles and book reviews published in the *Journal.* But Woodson wrote a letter to Bancroft insisting, "We need funds to train Negroes for such work rather than prizes for the few now qualified to compete in such a contest." And he enclosed a proposal to establish a $20,000 endowment for a fellowship in memory of Bancroft's brother, Edgar Addison Bancroft, to be titled "Negro College Graduates Specializing in History and Correlated Subjects in Accredited Universities."[47] Bancroft apparently rejected Woodson's idea, since the prizes were in existence in the 1930s and 1940s.

The need to accomplish as much as possible with meager funds led Woodson in 1927 to organize an "Extension Division," which included

45. See, for example, J. C. Burrells to Emmett J. Scott, February 8, 1924, in Emmett J. Scott Papers, Soper Library, Morgan State University, Baltimore; Vincent P. Franklin, "In Pursuit of Freedom: The Educational Activities of Black Social Organizations in Philadelphia, 1900–1930," in *New Perspectives on Black Educational History,* ed. Vincent P. Franklin and James Anderson, (Boston, 1978), 90–95; "Dr. Carter G. Woodson at First Baptist Church," in Bulletin of First Baptist Church, Charleston, W.Va., May 28, 1922, supplied by Joe M. Trotter of Carnegie Mellon University; Gloria T. Hull, ed., *Give Us Each Day: The Diary of Alice Dunbar Nelson* (New York, 1984), 337, 431; Nannie H. Burroughs to J. Raymond Henderson, September 2, 1931, in Nannie H. Burroughs Papers, MS Div., LC; Harriett Gibbs Marshall to Woodson, October 21, 1940, in Washington Conservatory of Music Records, Moorland-Spingarn Research Center.

46. See James E. Shepard to W. E. B. Du Bois, May 28, 1926, and Shepard to Du Bois, August 27, 1926, in Du Bois Papers.

47. Woodson to Frederic Bancroft, November 26, 1927, in Bancroft Papers.

a "Lecture Bureau" and a "Home Study Department," as a means of coordinating educational activities so as to benefit the greatest number of people. Woodson was in great demand as a lecturer, and the Lecture Bureau enabled him to schedule his speaking engagements for efficiency. Because Woodson believed that most black teachers in the public school systems lacked the necessary training to teach Negro history, he offered correspondence courses in Negro history, literature, philosophy, sociology, and art through the Home Study Department. In promotional literature for these courses, Woodson asserted that few black colleges and universities offered the kind of training that he was able to provide. He urged teachers to enroll in his courses so that they would be able to combat white prejudice and racism by teaching their students about blacks' contributions to history. Despite Woodson's efforts, only a few teachers took advantage of the home study courses. However, Woodson's efforts did stimulate black colleges and universities to offer Negro history courses through adult education programs, and in larger cities branches of the association also began to offer extension courses in Negro history.[48]

By the end of 1925 the association's funds were so low that Woodson's activities were limited to preparing previously compiled research data for publication. Several studies had been completed, but there was no money to publish them. It was imperative for Woodson to persuade the Laura Spelman Rockefeller Memorial Fund to renew its grant; and he asked for triple the amount previously awarded, $10,000 per year for research and $5,000 per year for publication for a period of five years, to expand his research and publications programs. To bolster his chances for renewal, Woodson once again called on white scholars to write letters of support. William Munro, his former professor at Harvard, wrote that "A proper understanding of the Negro problem, and the best means for ameliorating it, can only be had through the same careful research that is being given to other problems." Franz Boas expressed some reservations, noting that, "It is rather difficult to cooperate with him, but his work is credible." Charles M. Andrews, of Yale, Edward Channing, his former professor at Harvard, Evarts B. Greene, of Columbia, and Earnest A. Hooton, the Harvard anthropologist, also wrote supportive letters. And Woodson asked Waldo G. Leland, who had conducted a survey of learned societies for the Ameri-

48. Woodson, "Home Study Department," *Journal of Negro History*, XIII (1928), 115–19.

can Council of Learned Societies, to send his report to the foundation. Leland, Jameson, and Thomas Walter Page, of the American Economic Association, had evaluated the association in 1924 and given it favorable marks.[49]

In 1926 the Laura Spelman Rockefeller Fund renewed and increased Woodson's grant, although not to the level he had proposed. He received $7,600 per year for research and $5,000 per year for publication for a period of three years. The terms of the previous grant had required Woodson to submit annual reports of his expenditures. Under the renewal, foundation officials wanted Woodson to report his expenditures semiannually and in greater detail. They also urged him to find more permanent means of financial support and suggested that he consider affiliating his association with one of the black colleges. Woodson did not follow that suggestion, although he did try to persuade John D. Rockefeller, Jr., to permanently endow the association with his personal funds.[50]

In 1929 foundation officials began to put increasing pressure on Woodson to economize, work more efficiently, and secure other financial support. "While the Association is continuing to do scholarly and methodical research work in history," Leonard Outhwaite wrote to his board, "its utilization of the publication fund and in general its method of publication could be improved." Outhwaite also doubted that "an organization of this character in so specialized a field can be indefinitely sustained as an individual organization." When the grant came up for renewal that year, Woodson again asked foundation officials to increase the amount of funds awarded. By this time, the Laura Spelman Rockefeller Memorial Fund had merged with the Rockefeller Foundation, and Woodson had to confront a new group of white bureaucrats. He maintained that the prior grant of $12,600 per year was insufficient to support his research and publication programs. Contending that each

49. Woodson to Laura Spelman Rockefeller Memorial Fund, March 22, 1926, William B. Munro to Laura Spelman Rockefeller Memorial Fund, March 24, 1926, Franz Boas to Beardsley Ruml, March 8, 1926, Charles M. Andrews to Ruml, March 15, 1926, Edward Channing to Ruml, March 17, 1926, Evarts B. Greene to Ruml, March 23, 1926, Earnest Hooton to Ruml, March 13, 1926, Leland to Ruml, March 8, 1926, all in Laura Spelman Rockefeller Memorial Fund Records; Leland to Page, April 10, 1925, Leland to Woodson, April 14, 1925, Woodson to Leland, April 14, 1925, all in American Council of Learned Societies Records.

50. Leonard Outhwaite, Memorandum of Interview with Carter G. Woodson, June 7, 1926, and Ruml to Woodson, June 10, 1926, in Laura Spelman Rockefeller Memorial Fund Records.

monograph cost at least $1,000 to $3,000 to publish, Woodson requested $17,500 per year for research and publication for a period of three years.[51]

Since foundation officials already were wary of making continued financial contributions to Woodson, they hoped that white scholars would provide them with ammunition to justify their cutting off Woodson's funds. Their hopes, however, were not realized, for although some of the most conservative white scholars—Dodd, Phillips, Woofter, Joseph G. de Roulhac Hamilton, and Walter L. Fleming—were asked to provide assessments of Woodson's work, they argued that Woodson deserved continued financial support. The consensus of the group was that while Woodson's work was biased and amateurish, it deserved financial support.[52]

While these scholars disagreed with Woodson's interpretations, contending that he was trying to accomplish too much too quickly, they insisted that it was unfair to compare the work of black scholars with that of their white counterparts. Phillips maintained that the association was worthy in purpose and prospect rather than in actual accomplishment, and that much of Woodson's work was difficult to read, too detailed, and trivial. Fleming stated that Woodson's publications were "quite as good as were written by white people in the 1880's on similar subjects," noting that "the standards of the *American Historical Review* should not be applied to the *Journal of Negro History*." Hamilton asserted that "anything which throws light on negro history is distinctly worthwhile." Dodd, who served on Woodson's executive council and would continue to support him over the next several years by speaking personally with white foundation officials and writing letters on his behalf, gave the most positive assessment, declaring that "the money which has been appropriated to this purpose has been better spent than any other money I know. . . . The result has been the appearance at this [University of Chicago] and other universities of a higher type of negro

51. Leonard Outhwaite, Report on previous Appropriations, n.d., Woodson to Ruml, April 30, 1929, Woodson to George E. Vincent, May 5, 1929, Sydnor Walker to Woodson, May 3, 1929, all in Laura Spelman Rockefeller Memorial Fund Records; Woodson, Report on Publications, July 1, 1926 to April 30, 1929, in Carter G. Woodson Collection, Moorland Spingarn Research Center; Woodson to Edmund E. Day, April 30, 1929, in Rockefeller Foundation Archives.

52. Sydnor Walker to Thomas Jefferson Woofter, May 7, 1929, in Laura Spelman Rockefeller Memorial Fund Records. The same letter was sent to Fleming, Dodd, Hamilton, and Phillips.

student than we have ever had before, and at the same time a better sense in these students of the realities with which they have to deal." After learning that Rockefeller officials had solicited assessments of his work, Woodson asked Carl Fish, Evarts Greene, Jameson, and Schlesinger to write letters on his behalf, and their testimonies were more favorable.[53]

Still unconvinced that the grant should be renewed or increased, Rockefeller Foundation officials asked Woodson to provide them with additional financial information, including expenditures for research and publication already completed with Rockefeller funds. Woodson was certain that his original request for $17,500 per year would not be granted, so he reduced it to $7,500, the amount that he believed was necessary to publish those monograph manuscripts that were finished. In June, 1929, he was awarded $10,000 for one year; renewal was conditional upon Woodson's ability to obtain additional financial support elsewhere. Foundation officials also reiterated their earlier suggestion that Woodson develop a plan to affiliate with one of the black colleges.[54]

Although grateful for renewal of the grant, Woodson was adamant about not affiliating with a black college. Outlining in a lengthy letter the reasons why such an affiliation was impractical, he argued that "none of the so-called Negro universities has carried out a research program or produced through their professors any work appraised as scientifically valuable." While Woodson expressed hope that affiliation might be possible in the future, for the present, he wrote, "there is such little interest in the work at any one institution that . . . all of it can be better taken care of through one national organization than when superimposed where few persons have developed sufficiently to understand what it means." In part, Woodson's refusal to affiliate with a black college stemmed from his earlier difficulties at Howard, and from his belief that whites still controlled black institutions of higher education.

53. Walter L. Fleming to Walker, May 9, 1929, U. B. Phillips to Walker, May 9, 1929, J. G. de Roulhac Hamilton to Walker, May 10, 1929, Dodd to Walker, May 10, 1929, all in Laura Spelman Rockefeller Memorial Fund Records; Carl Russell Fish to Edmund E. Day, May 14, 1929, in Carl Russell Fish Papers, State Historical Society of Wisconsin, Madison; Jameson to Day, May 13, 1929, in Jameson Papers; Schlesinger to Day, May 16, 1929, in Laura Spelman Rockefeller Memorial Fund Records.

54. Woodson to Walker, June 6, 1929, and Woodson to George E. Vincent, June 15, 1929, in Laura Spelman Rockefeller Memorial Fund Records; Woodson to Dodd, June 7, 1929, in Woodson Collection, Moorland-Spingarn Research Center.

While black control over black colleges had increased by 1929, whites continued to command a great deal of power and influence in financial matters. And Woodson would not relinquish his autonomy in directing the association to anyone, black or white.[55]

When the Rockefeller Foundation turned down Woodson's initial request and awarded him a one-year grant of $10,000 instead, he hoped that the Rosenwald Fund would make up the deficit. He asked for $81,000 to undertake more than half a dozen new research projects, and Dodd, among other white scholars, wrote a letter supporting Woodson's request. The Rosenwald Fund would not consider this proposal and even contemplated reducing its annual gift from $400 to $200, but fortunately, Julius Rosenwald was not convinced that this appropriation should be reduced. Buoyed by that decision and undeterred by the rejection of his appeal for $81,000, in 1930 Woodson requested $10,000 from the Rosenwald Fund, maintaining that the Rockefeller Foundation would match the award. Embree promised to consult with the Rockefeller Foundation before making a final decision but asserted that "there seems to me little advantage in one foundation matching the gift of another." In the end, the Rosenwald Fund denied Woodson any grant money.[56]

When the Rockefeller Foundation grant came up for renewal in 1930, Woodson requested $20,000 to be paid in five annual installments of $4,000 per year. While foundation officials were unhappy with Woodson's refusal to affiliate with a black college, they nevertheless believed his reasons were valid. "If Mr. Woodson were a different type of man it would seem simpler to work out an affiliation at the present time," Sydnor Walker stated, "but everyone seems to agree that neither Howard, nor Fisk, nor Atlanta University is carrying out graduate work which would enrich the research program of the Association." To assist Woodson in building a more permanent base of financial support, the

---

55. Woodson to Walker, June 24, 1929, Walker to Woodson, June 18, 27, 1929, all in Laura Spelman Rockefeller Memorial Fund Records. On black higher education, see Raymond Wolters, *The New Negro on Campus: Black College Rebellions of the 1920s* (Princeton, 1975).

56. Woodson to Embree, March 18, 1930, and Embree to Rosenwald, July 11, 1930, in Rosenwald Fund Records; Dodd to Woodson, June 7, 19, July 1, 1929, in William E. Dodd Papers, MS Div., LC; Woodson to Walker, March 18, 1930, Walker to Embree, March 21, 1930, Woodson to Walker, March 22, 1930, Walker to Embree, April 24, 1930, all in Rockefeller Foundation Archives; Embree to Woodson, March 20, 1930, in Rosenwald Fund Records.

Rockefeller Foundation in May, 1930, awarded Woodson a three-year matching grant of $22,500.[57]

Although Woodson received more money than he had solicited, he faced the difficult task of raising $7,500 per year to match the Rockefeller funds. Over the next three years whites and white foundations contributed the largest single sums of money, while blacks provided smaller contributions. In 1931, probably at Jameson's suggestion, Woodson apparently tried to obtain funds from Edward Harkness, benefactor of the Commonwealth Fund, and from Adolph Ochs, owner of the New York *Times* and financier of the *Dictionary of American Biography*; but he was unsuccessful. To raise the necessary matching funds, Woodson donated much of his own salary and then reported that this money was given by individuals who wished to remain anonymous. While it was a struggle each year, Woodson managed to raise enough to match the Rockefeller grant.[58]

In 1932 Woodson asked the Rockefeller Foundation and the General Education Board for $12,600 for three years to hire a field worker to assist with teacher education in black history. Included in the proposal was a list of ninety-five individuals and institutions who had asked the association for reference and bibliographical assistance; among them were six scholars who had received funds from the General Education Board. Both the Rockefeller Foundation and the General Education Board turned down the request. Jackson Davis, of the General Education Board, again recommended that the association affiliate with a black college, advising his board that he had "made it clear to Dr. Woodson that the Board had invested large sums of money in these institutions and that . . . the opportunity and responsibility of the Board was in helping them to become centers of study and research rather than to build up independent agencies without institutional connec-

57. Woodson to Walker, March 18, 1930, Walker to Woodson, March 21, 1930, Woodson to Walker, March 22, 1930, Walker to Embree, April 24, 1930, Walker to Woodson, April 23, 1930, Woodson to Walker, April 26, 1930, Walker to Woodson, May 8, 1930, Woodson to Walker, May 10, 1930, all in Rockefeller Foundation Archives.

58. Woodson to Schlesinger, April 1, 1931, in Arthur M. Schlesinger Papers, Pusey Library, Harvard University. Also see Embree to Rosenwald, July 11, 1930, in Rosenwald Papers; George S. Beal to Woodson, September 11, 1930, Woodson to Rockefeller Foundation, June 2, 1932, Beal to Woodson, June 30, 1932, Woodson to Rockefeller Foundation, October 24, 1932, January 21, 1933, Beal to Woodson, May 9, 1933, all in Rockefeller Foundation Archives; Woodson to N. Penrose Hallowell, October 11, 1930, in Phelps-Stokes Fund Records; Woodson to Frederic Bancroft, November 5, 1931, in Bancroft Papers.

tions."[59] It is likely that the cause of the foundation's rejection was Woodson's insistence in maintaining his autonomy and independence, and his continuing feud with Jones, rather than the merits of his proposal.

When the Rockefeller grant came up for renewal in 1933, Woodson requested matching funds rather than an outright grant, hoping that this strategy would convince foundation officials of his willingness to assume a major burden of the fund-raising to support his programs. Again, several white scholars wrote to the foundation on his behalf. But because Woodson had not taken steps to affiliate the association with a black college and had not obtained any other permanent financial support, his request was denied. For these reasons, foundation officials suggested that Woodson apply again to their sister foundation, the General Education Board, and in November, 1933, Woodson requested $10,000 from the General Education Board. Jackson Davis replied that the General Education Board had "deferred consideration of [his] request" and indicated that Woodson must consider "working out with a group of higher institutions, some plan of cooperative support, the Association playing the part of a coordinating agency and publishing *The Journal of Negro History*." Davis then asked association officials James Dillard and John Hope to try to persuade Woodson to affiliate the *Journal* with one of the black colleges. But Dillard, while he believed that Woodson should leave research and publication to the black colleges, recommended that Woodson retain control of the *Journal* and suggested that the General Education Board provide at least $5,000 per year to finance it. Hope, on the other hand, who was then the president of the association, tried to convince Woodson to let Atlanta University provide facilities and financial support for the *Journal*. Hope had made this offer twice before, and each time, Woodson declined.[60]

59. Jackson Davis, Memorandum of Interview with Carter G. Woodson, May 13, 1932, Trevor Arnett to Jackson Davis, April 18, 1932, Woodson to Davis, April 21, 1932, Davis, Memorandum to Board of Directors, April 21, 1932, Davis to W. W. Brierly, April 23, 1932, all in General Education Board Records.

60. Jackson Davis to Woodson, November 6, 1933, in General Education Board Records; Sydnor Walker to Woodson, June 5, 1933, Schlesinger to Walker, June 7, 1933, Walker to Schlesinger, June 9, 1933, Rockefeller Report on funds granted to Carter G. Woodson, June 30, 1933, all in Rockefeller Foundation Archives; Jackson Davis, Memorandum of Interview with Carter G. Woodson, October 26, 1933, and Davis to Walker, October 30, 1933, in General Education Board Records; Davis to John Hope, November 6, 1933, Rockefeller Foundation Archives; Davis to Sydnor Walker, January 11, 1934, in General Education Board Records.

Angered by what he perceived to be interference in association affairs, Woodson would consider neither publishing the *Journal* elsewhere nor leaving research and writing to those in black colleges. He told Davis that his executive council voted against the proposal, but a vote was probably never taken. Even if the council had considered the proposal, Woodson undoubtedly would have aired his objections, and since he was the director of the association and editor of the *Journal*, the members probably would have gone along with his wishes. Displeased with Woodson's continued determination to remain independent and to not affiliate with a black college, the General Education Board did not award any funds.[61]

After 1933 no white foundations made substantial contributions to the association, and Woodson was forced to depend almost totally on the black community for the financial support necessary to continue his campaign to promote Negro history. Rather than give up his autonomy, Woodson preferred to struggle financially. Indeed, the 1930s would prove to be a struggle. Yet, these financial challenges were met by economizing, increasing administrative efficiency, and planning creatively. At the same time, Woodson further extended his reach to the masses of black Americans, and in doing so, broadened the base of his movement and heightened the black community's racial pride and cultural consciousness. To ease his physical and mental stress during the troublesome depression decade, he spent several summers in Europe, taking extended vacations for the first time in his life.

61. Woodson to John Hope, November 8, 1933, in John Hope Papers, Trevor Arnett Library, Atlanta University; Davis, Memorandum of meeting with John Hope and Trevor Arnett, November 15, 1933, Woodson to Davis, January 6, 1934, Davis to Woodson, January 13, 1934, Woodson to Davis, January 13, 1934, all in General Education Board Records.

Anne Eliza Riddle Woodson.
Carter G. Woodson Collection, Box 118-1, Folder 22, Moorland-Spingarn Research Center, Howard University.

Young Woodson, early 1900s.
Reprinted with the permission of the Afro-American Newspapers Archives & Research Center, Inc., Baltimore, Md.

Headquarters of the association and the Associated Publishers, 1538 Ninth St., N.W., Washington, D.C.
Reprinted with the permission of the Afro-American Newspapers Archives & Research Center, Inc., Baltimore, Md.

Mary Church Terrell.
Courtesy of the Library of Congress.

Charles H. Wesley.
Courtesy of the Library of Congress.

Alrutheus Ambush (A. A.) Taylor.
Courtesy of Fisk University Library, Special Collections.

Lorenzo Johnston Greene.
Lorenzo and Thomasina (Talley) Greene, Collection (Accession 4981), Western Historical Manuscript Collection, Columbia, Mo.

Julius Rosenwald.
Courtesy of the Library of Congress.

Nannie Burroughs.
Courtesy of the Library of Congress.

Luther Porter Jackson.
Special Collections, Johnston Memorial Library, Virginia State University.

Melville J. Herskovits.
Courtesy of University Archives, Northwestern University Library.

John Hope, president of Morehouse College and Atlanta University.
Photo courtesy Atlanta University Center, R. W. Woodruff Library, Special Collections, Atlanta University Archives, Atlanta, Ga.

Woodson working on the *Negro History Bulletin*, 1948.
Reprinted with the permission of the Afro-American Newspapers Archives & Research Center, Inc., Baltimore, Md.

Holding Steady: The Association During the Depression, New Deal, and World War II

From the early 1930s until after World War II, Woodson reached out to the black community to obtain the necessary financial support for the association. At times the association was so financially hard pressed that bills went unpaid and Woodson was hounded by creditors. Yet somehow he managed to keep the *Journal* and the association afloat and even began several new research projects and publishing ventures, including the *Negro History Bulletin*. Increasingly during this period, however, the association functioned as a clearinghouse, providing research assistance in black history to scholars and the general public.

Believing that he had to accomplish more with less money, Woodson put in even longer work days—sixteen to eighteen hours in length. Charles Johnson noted in 1933, "Woodson seems tremendously rushed these late days to encompass the full impact of the title of the Association for the Study of Negro Life and History." He mentioned that Woodson was investigating "economic and sociological and even literary questions as well as historical subjects."[1] With only a skeletal office staff, Woodson undertook along with scholarly tasks menial chores like wrapping and mailing books and cleaning his office. He refused to allow the young black scholar, Lorenzo Greene, who worked closely with him during the 1930s, to assume these duties, contending that he had not hired Greene to be a janitor. Greene believed that Woodson's ex-

---

1. Charles S. Johnson to Robert E. Park, March 13, 1933, in Robert E. Park Papers, University of Chicago Library.

periences as a coal miner gave him physical and emotional strength and prepared him for the arduous struggles he faced during these years.[2]

While Greene accurately assessed Woodson's constitution, for Woodson continued to toil long and hard to promote black history, he could not foresee the extent to which Woodson's personality and temperament would be adversely affected by the struggles he confronted. Woodson became increasingly possessive of the association and distant from his associates, internalizing his problems. Mary McLeod Bethune, who served as president of the association from 1935 through 1950, was the only person who called him by his first name. In 1936, Arthur Schomburg told Woodson that he had become "difficult to approach," seeming to demand "all the formalities of a Secretary of State, like William Du Bois used to be at the *Crisis* office."[3]

Even as Woodson advanced in years, he would not relinquish any administrative control over the association. Although he had always been obstinate, desiring to take over any activity in which he participated, Woodson became even more difficult to work with as he grew older, perhaps because he perceived himself to be the "Father of Black History." While he depended on younger black scholars to keep the association going and often sought their advice and guidance, Woodson usually did what he wanted. Once he made up his mind, few of his associates or adversaries could persuade him to change it. A stern and demanding taskmaster, he expected those under his tutelage to toil as long and hard as he did and required absolute loyalty to his cause.

Woodson took steps in the early 1930s to train Rayford Logan in administrative tasks, and he may have been grooming Logan to succeed him. In 1931, when Logan was at Harvard, he corresponded with Woodson about joining the staff after he received his degree, in exchange for financial help during graduate school. Woodson confided to Embree, of the Rosenwald Fund, that he wanted to write a multivolume history of black Americans. "If the Association could increase its in-

2. Patricia W. Romero, "Carter G. Woodson: A Biography," (Ph.D. dissertation, Ohio State University, 1971), 189–90; Lorenzo J. Greene, *Working with Carter G. Woodson, the Father of Black History: A Diary, 1928–1930*, ed. Arvarh E. Strickland (Baton Rouge, 1989), 297, 317, 376.

3. Lorenzo J. Greene, Remarks made at the inauguration of the Carter G. Woodson Institute for African and African-American Studies at the University of Virginia, February 27, 1982; Arthur A. Schomburg to Woodson, January 16, 1936, in Arthur A. Schomburg Papers, Schomburg Center for Research in Black Culture, New York Public Library.

come sufficiently to hire an additional competent assistant," he reasoned, he could "easily accomplish this task in a few years." He was
becoming "more and more apprehensive about the loss which may be
sustained" if he were to carry to his "grave the vast amount of information [he had] collected during the last generation."[4] Although Embree might have been personally moved by Woodson's plea, the Rosenwald Fund did not award any money.

Since Woodson's physical health had been in jeopardy in the past,
some in the black community were concerned about his proclivity to
dominate all aspects of the association and wanted assurances that the
organization would endure if Woodson became incapacitated. Writing
in 1935, Charles H. Thompson, editor of the *Journal of Negro Education*, maintained that Woodson was so busy building up the association
that he had no time to train his successor. "If Dr. Woodson died to-
morrow," Thompson asserted, "in all probability the Association would
die with him." Thompson pleaded with Woodson to find a successor
"so that he can profit by the experience and enthusiasm of the man who
has guided its destinies so successfully for the past twenty years." Although Woodson told Thompson that whenever he had taken steps to
train a younger black scholar to succeed him some other institution
hired him away, in fact Woodson allowed only a few young black scholars to work with him—and only those with the thickest skins could
remain under his direction. Writing ten years after Thompson, Logan,
who had joined Woodson's staff and remained loyal until 1936 when
Woodson fired him, asserted that Woodson had "alienated the friendship of his most loyal supporters." According to Logan, one of Woodson's greatest failings was his "inability to attach himself to a young
scholar who loves the work as much as Dr. Woodson does and who
would dedicate himself to perpetuating it as the greatest monument to
his magnificent achievements."[5]

It was not only with younger black scholars but also with those of his

4. Ruth Logan to Rayford Logan, postmarked November 13, 17, December 11,
1931, in Rayford W. Logan Papers, Manuscript Division, Library of Congress; Woodson
to Edwin Embree, August 12, 1931, in Julius Rosenwald Papers, University of Chicago
Library. Also see Hubert E. Potter, "A Review of the Life and Work of Carter G. Woodson" (MS in Moorland-Spingarn Research Center, Howard University), Appendix A,
"Interview with Captain Louis R. Mehlinger," 56–57.
5. Charles H. Thompson, Editorial Comment on the Association for the Study of
Negro Life and History, *Journal of Negro Education*, IV (1935), 467; Rayford W. Logan,
"*Phylon* Profile VI: Carter G. Woodson," *Phylon*, VI (1945), 321.

own generation and stature that Woodson viewed himself to be in an adversarial relationship. Although often in a position to assist and advance other scholars with projects that promoted black history, Woodson frequently declined to participate. Beginning in 1933 he would not endorse or participate in any projects financed by whites that he could not control, because he considered them detrimental to his cause and unlikely to advance black history or the professional stature of black scholars. Yet Woodson's presence in the field was so commanding that many scholars overlooked his personality quirks and continued to assist him and to seek his endorsement of projects promoting black history.

Woodson's greatest challenge throughout the 1930s and early 1940s was to keep the association financially stable, and he continued to solicit funds from white foundations. Numerous requests—in 1934, 1936, 1940, and 1941—to the Rockefeller institutions were denied, although each time Woodson demonstrated the educational merits and worthiness of his proposals and often obtained the endorsements of leading white historians. In 1934, for example, Woodson requested funds from the General Education Board to establish an Institute of Negro Culture. He proposed the creation of a center for black music, drama, and art, which would be located in Washington, D.C., to draw upon existing cultural resources and serve the greatest number of people. It would include departments of instruction in each discipline, an auditorium for cultural programs, an area for art exhibits, and a library for rare books and manuscripts. In addition to the capital outlay of about two million dollars for the building, Woodson estimated that sixty-seven thousand dollars would be required annually to maintain and operate the institute. A Board of Trustees drawn from Howard, Atlanta, Dillard, and Fisk universities would be established, and faculty from these institutions would provide instruction at the institute. The General Education Board did not even consider the proposal. Perhaps Woodson believed that he was suggesting the kind of project the board would be interested in funding, but at the same time it is inconceivable that he really believed he could obtain such a large amount of money. At any rate, he was not greatly upset when the proposal was rejected. On several different occasions during the 1930s and 1940s Woodson requested twelve hundred dollars per year from the General Education Board to hire a field worker who would sell books and subscriptions to the *Negro History Bulletin* to black schoolchildren and their parents and teachers. In 1941 Jackson Davis indicated that the project would be funded only if

the individual Woodson had in mind functioned as a curriculum spe-
cialist. While curriculum development would be among the responsibilities of a field worker, it was not the primary responsibility, and
Woodson never received funding.[6]

Woodson also requested financial assistance from the Rockefeller
institutions to continue to collect source materials in African-American
history. Even though he had tangible evidence of success—in the large
collection donated to the Library of Congress and in the letters of recommendation from Manuscript Division chief Jameson—Woodson
was not awarded any funds. At Woodson's suggestion, Jameson tried to
bypass the foundation and wrote to John D. Rockefeller, Jr., hoping
that he might make a personal contribution to continue the collecting
project. Rockefeller, however, merely referred the request to one of the
family foundations.[7]

The inability to raise even a few thousand dollars from white philanthropists caused Woodson to become bitter. "The foundations and
agencies which give so freely to Negro institutions and thereby control
their downsitting and uprising," he asserted, "refuse to aid the Association . . . because it is independent." Woodson lashed out not only
against white philanthropists but also against those blacks who benefitted from their philanthropy, noting that "so-called philanthropy in
the United States . . . has retarded rather than aided the progress of the
race in America." While his statements often sounded bombastic, they
also rang true. After regularly being turned down by white foundations,
Woodson often appealed to individual whites for financial assistance.
In 1935 he wrote to Jameson: "We are living on the nickels and dimes
of Negroes who are not yet on the bread line." Despite these appeals,
Woodson received few contributions from whites during the thirties
and forties. "The whites of considerable means have shown less and

6. Woodson to John Marshall, January 30, 1934, David H. Stevens to Woodson,
February 1, 1934, Woodson to Jackson Davis, December 16, 1940; Davis to Woodson,
December 19, 1940, January 31, 1941, Woodson to Davis, April 12, 1941, Davis, Memo-
randum of Interview with Carter G. Woodson, May 16, 1941, in General Education
Board Records, Rockefeller Archive Center, Tarrytown, N.Y.; Woodson to Sydnor Wal-
ker, April 8, 1936, enclosure in Woodson to Arthur M. Schlesinger, April 8, 1936, Schles-
inger to Walker, April 14, 1936, all in Arthur M. Schlesinger Papers, Pusey Library,
Harvard University; Walker to Schlesinger, April 15, 1936, in Rockefeller Foundation
Archives, Rockefeller Archive Center.

7. Woodson to Jameson, March 20, 24, 1930, Jameson to John D. Rockefeller,
April 1, 1930, all in J. Franklin Jameson Papers, MS Div., LC; Jameson to Woodson,
April 17, 1930, Woodson to Jameson, April 19, 1930, Jameson to Woodson, April 22,
1930, all in Library of Congress Archives, MS Div., LC.

less interest in the work of the Association as the years have passed," he noted in 1938. "They have tended to look unfavorably upon the revelation of truth as shown by scientific investigation."[8]

At the height of the depression and throughout World War II, blacks provided most of the financial support for the association. "It is not an insignificant achievement that during these lean years," Woodson reported in 1934, "the income derived from the poor whom this cause is intended to serve has not diminished." Similarly, in 1935 Woodson asserted that because the majority of his funds "come chiefly from the impoverished Negro element of the United States it must strike the observer as a fine demonstration of self-help." To Woodson this indicated that blacks were "deeply interested in their past [and] have redoubled their efforts to support the work . . . giving now more than ever before in the history of the undertaking."[9]

Beginning in 1935, on the twentieth anniversary of the association's founding, to more aggressively "sell the Association to the people," Woodson inaugurated a $30,000 fund-raising drive, and received $5,500 after writing hundreds of letters to blacks urging them to begin campaigns in their communities. A network of black college professors, students, educational administrators, elementary and secondary schoolteachers, professional groups, women's clubs, fraternities, sororities, and church groups was coordinated through local branches of the association. In the early 1920s, association branches were organized in cooperation with existing clubs, religious groups, and literary societies in large East Coast cities like New York and Philadelphia. By the 1930s the number of branches had increased and extended to smaller cities in the Midwest, South, and Southwest, including Cleveland, Columbus, Cincinnati, Pittsburgh, Hampton, Nashville, Petersburg, Terre Haute, St. Louis, New Orleans, and Houston. The black bourgeoisie in these communities worked through schools and other educational institutions, like the YMCA, to reach working-class blacks, presenting local and family histories to promote Woodson's black history program among a mass audience and to raise funds for it.[10]

8. Woodson, "Annual Report for 1941–1942," *Journal of Negro History*, XXVII (1942), 373–74; Woodson to Jameson, April 29, 1935, in Jameson Papers; Woodson, "Annual Report for 1937–1938," *Journal of Negro History*, XXIII (1938), 409–19.

9. Woodson, "Annual Report for 1933–1934," *Journal of Negro History*, XIX (1934), 343–54; Woodson, "Annual Report for 1934–1935," *Journal of Negro History*, XX (1935), 363–72.

10. Woodson to Schlesinger, September 26, 1935, in Schlesinger Papers; Vincent P. Franklin, "In Pursuit of Freedom: The Educational Activities of Black Social Organiza-

Although many of the association's outreach and fund-raising activities were conducted by its branches, Woodson continued his own efforts to expand interest in Negro history and generate revenue among a variety of audiences through lectures, publications of the Associated Publishers, and articles in the black press. In the mid-1930s, for example, he lectured on Negro history at Civilian Conservation Corps camps. And during World War II, he convinced U.S.O. clubs to subscribe to the *Negro History Bulletin*, making it available to black soldiers.[11]

Since the appeal of the *Journal* was limited to a scholarly audience, Woodson began publishing the *Negro History Bulletin* in 1937 to supplement the other printed materials that the association produced for schoolchildren and the general public. The *Bulletin* was full of photographs of and biographical information on current and past black achievers, and Woodson hoped that its attractiveness and appeal would stimulate the sale of books published by the Associated Publishers. Nine issues were published per volume, to coincide with the school year. Woodson often organized issues around a central theme: abolition and antislavery; blacks in art, literature, science, education, religion, or business; blacks in Africa, Asia, Europe, or Latin America; blacks in regional areas of the United States; and blacks in the military.[12]

Woodson also published regular columns in the *Bulletin* each month. "Persons and Achievements to be Remembered" was a calendar of birthdays of important blacks and significant dates in black history. The "Children's Page" consisted of "School News," which chronicled the activities of teachers and children studying Negro history and celebrating Negro History Week, "Books," which offered suggestions and reviews, and "Questions for Study," which were exercises to be done after reading *Bulletin* articles. And often Woodson published

---

tions in Philadelphia, 1900–1930," in *New Perspectives on Black Educational History*, ed. Vincent P. Franklin and James Anderson (Boston, 1978), 90–95. Also see Woodson's Annual Reports for 1933–1934, 1934–1935, and 1937–1938 in the *Journal of Negro History*. Among the few contributions by whites after 1933 was a $750 matching grant given by the Rosenwald Family Association in support of the 20th anniversary fund, but Woodson had to come up with $750 first. See N. W. Levin to Woodson, July 18, September 11, 1935, in Rosenwald Papers.

11. See Woodson's Annual Reports for the 1930s and 1940s, in the *Journal of Negro History*.

12. Woodson, "Annual Report for 1937–1938," 413–14; *Negro History Bulletin*, I-XI, (1938–39 to 1949–50).

plays, stories, and essays on Negro history written by schoolchildren. Other regular features included "News of Branches" and "Questions Answered," in which Woodson responded to queries on topics in Negro history. He published the names and addresses of information seekers and enlisted the assistance of readers to offer additional information.[13]

Woodson utilized the *Bulletin* as a forum not only to educate and inform but also to offer advice on self-improvement. He lashed out against white racism, oppression, and injustice directed toward blacks. In numerous polemical articles Woodson advocated thrift, avoidance of debt and extravagance, and patronage of businesses owned by blacks, and he described the ways in which black businessmen could improve their services. He cautioned readers against following black politicians blindly, lest they be exploited. Woodson criticized European imperialism in Africa during World War II, and the United States government's treatment of black soldiers. After the war he continued to criticize the government's treatment of black veterans and argued that the United Nations should not allow the United States to join unless it corrected domestic racial problems first.[14]

Because the *Bulletin* had wide appeal, it sold well. Woodson believed it to be of such importance that he sold it below cost at a loss, for he was determined to make it available to a mass audience. As interest in Negro history expanded, schoolteachers and the general public increasingly turned to the association for information. Woodson had only a skeletal staff to respond to these inquiries, and frequently it was necessary that they conduct extensive research to answer the many queries received. Yet he reported that his "staff has cheerfully given assistance without price, despite the fact that many of these inquirers are not members of the Association and do not materially support the work."[15]

13. See, for example, "Calls for Help," *Negro History Bulletin*, XII (April, 1949), 159–61.

14. See, for example, Woodson, "How the Foreign Merchants Exploit the Negro," *Negro History Bulletin*, III (January, 1940), 55–56, "Some Suggestions with Respect to Business and the Depression," *Negro History Bulletin*, III (January, 1940), 57–58, "Development of the Negro Community," *Negro History Bulletin*, VIII (November, 1944), 47–48, "The Deplorable State of the Nation," *Negro History Bulletin*, IX (February, 1946), 119–20, "Dangers of Political Leadership," *Negro History Bulletin*, X (November, 1946), 47–48, "The Unfinished Task," *Negro History Bulletin*, X (February, 1947), 98, and "Keep Our Money at Home," *Negro History Bulletin*, XI (April, 1948), 146.

15. Woodson, "Annual Report for 1940–1941," *Journal of Negro History*, XXVI (1941), 413–20; S. B. Stratton, "Three Years of the Negro History Bulletin," *Negro History Bulletin*, IV (November, 1940), 44. Also see Woodson to Schlesinger, January 18,

From 1936 to 1938 Charles Wesley and Susie Quander, a Washington, D.C., schoolteacher, spearheaded a "Nationwide One-Dollar Sustaining Membership Drive" and were assisted by twenty-seven state chairmen. Echoing Woodson's views about white foundations, Wesley noted that, "A thousand Negroes who will give one dollar to the cause are in the long run of more real value to the Association than many times a thousand dollars from a foundation which desires to direct its publication[s] and influence its thinking." In 1940 Woodson asked those blacks who were able to do so to contribute $25 to a "Silver Anniversary Fund," and raised $7,000.[16]

Luther Porter Jackson, a professor of history at Virginia State College, was instrumental in keeping the association financially solvent. From 1935 until his death in 1950, Jackson worked almost as tirelessly as Woodson to raise money for the association, writing letters, giving lectures, and making personal appeals for funds. Although Virginians took pride in the fact that Woodson was born in their state and were especially receptive to the work of the association, not as much money would have been contributed without Jackson's efforts. Through black organizations, the Jeanes Supervisors, the mail carriers union, and the Virginia Teachers Association, for example, Jackson won financial support for Woodson. Woodson, grateful for Jackson's work, contended that he was "one among ten thousand, for history shows that only this small proportion of the human race is interested in preserving and publishing its record to generations unborn."[17]

1935, April 8, 1936, Schlesinger to Woodson, April 14, 1936, all in Schlesinger Papers; Luther P. Jackson to Woodson, February 20, 1935, in Luther P. Jackson Papers, Johnston Memorial Library, Virginia State University; Woodson to Schomburg, April 8, 1935, in Schomburg Papers; Jameson to Woodson, April 30, 1935, in Jameson papers; Arthur B. Spingarn to Woodson, May 2, 1935, in Arthur B. Spingarn Papers, MS Div., LC; Woodson to Emmett J. Scott, May 2, 1935, in Emmett J. Scott Papers, Soper Library, Morgan State University, Baltimore; and Jameson to Woodson, May 7, 1935, in Library of Congress Archives.

16. Woodson's Annual Reports for 1936–1938, in the *Journal of Negro History;* Wesley to Luther P. Jackson, January 27, 1937, in Jackson Papers; Woodson to Schlesinger, March 26, 1940, in Schlesinger Papers; Woodson to Frank Graham, April 18, 1940, in Frank Graham Papers, Southern Historical Collection, University of North Carolina, Chapel Hill; Woodson to W. P. Few, April 19, 1940, in W. P. Few Papers, University Archives, Perkins Library, Duke University; Woodson to Jackson Davis, June 15, 1940, in Jackson Davis Papers, Alderman Library, University of Virginia; Woodson, "Annual Report for 1940–1941," pp. 413–20.

17. See Jackson to Woodson, January 6, February 4, 20, April 4, 21, 1935, Woodson

Income remained stable during the 1930s, but by the 1940s, Woodson began to have deficits almost every other year and was unable to begin new projects. In seven of the eleven years from 1938 to 1949, Woodson's debts were larger than his income. The most serious crisis came in 1942, when he was $4,000 in debt. However, by 1943, he had managed to pay off most of this amount "through the sacrifices of a faithful staff and of the Director who turns his salary back to the Association as he has done for many years."[18] The following year Woodson appealed to readers of the *Journal* for contributions, noting that he needed $30,000 annually to operate effectively. He requested that four individuals contribute $1,000, eight contribute $500, sixteen contribute $250, and so forth. Woodson's best year during the forties was 1945, when he cleared $3,000 over his expenses. This was an unusual year however, for two wealthy benefactors, Frederic Bancroft and Francis Boyce, had died and bequeathed money to the association. Woodson also received over $300 from Phi Delta Kappa sorority.[19]

Blacks from all classes and occupations appreciated the value of Woodson's work, and the growing popularity of and interest in black history increased black support of association programs. By the 1940s, contributions had come from twenty-eight states and the District of Columbia; and although most blacks who gave contributed less than one dollar, and the majority were unable to give anything, the number of contributions, rather than the amount of each, had substantially increased. "While not a warmly supported undertaking," Woodson noted, "the Association is in no sense an institution dependent upon a dole from without the race." He added that enough blacks "have shown sufficient vision to appreciate the enduring value of this work, and to figure out what it will mean in the remote future to have in print the

---

to Jackson, November 26, 1935, February 7, 1936, Jackson to Woodson, November 18, 1936, Woodson to Jackson, February 18, 1937, Jackson to Woodson, May 15, 1937, Jackson to Mary Smith, May 20, 1937, Jackson, form letter to mail carriers of Petersburg, June 4, 1938, Woodson to Jackson, April 21, 1939, Jackson to Woodson, August 5, 1939, Woodson to Jackson, July 15, 1940, June 12, 1941, January 7, August 26, 1942, April 6, 1943, Jackson to Woodson, November 4, 1945, February 19, October 19, 1948, Woodson to Jackson, August 22, 1947, all in Jackson Papers.

   18. Woodson, "Annual Report for 1942–1943," *Journal of Negro History*, XXVIII (1943), 373–80.

   19. Advertisement at beginning of each issue, *Journal of Negro History*, 1944–1945; Woodson, "Annual Report for 1944–1945," *Journal of Negro History*, XXX (1945), 251–59.

record of the Negro which is now so generally ignored by the chroni-
clers of this generation." And Woodson was not discouraged that "a
larger number do not realize the importance of this movement." This
"should not be attributed to any racial trait," he maintained, "but to an
unfortunate background and to the general inclination of people of all
races to neglect their past."[20]

Despite limited funds in the thirties and forties, Woodson increased his
outreach activities, sponsoring lectures, teacher-training institutes, and
workshops. He also devoted attention to local and family history, and
engaged a mass audience in the collection and dissemination of source
materials for the study of black history. Although Woodson's movement succeeded best in areas with large centers of black population, by
the late 1920s, boards of education in both black and white communities had begun to integrate black history into the curriculum, white
teachers and educational administrators to write to him for advice, and
public libraries to purchase more books on black history.[21]

Woodson provided a forum for participation by blacks of all socio-
economic and educational levels through annual meetings sponsored
by the association. Unlike the annual meetings of the white-dominated
professional historical associations, Woodson's association planned and
developed programs that appealed to both general and scholarly audiences. Program committee members included schoolteachers, club
women, businessmen, and ministers, as well as scholars, to ensure an
assembly that would be entertaining as well as educational. Usually
meetings were held at black institutions, especially churches and
schools. Admission was usually free, and both academic and amateur
historians presented papers. Other regular activities included a "Get
Acquainted Dinner," art exhibits, visits to museums and other cultural
and educational institutions, poetry readings, plays, and musical programs. Woodson appealed to broad popular interests and stimulated
large attendance by inviting black professionals to discuss both the historical background of black participation in the professions as well as
contemporary problems black professionals faced.[22]

20. See Woodson, "Annual Report for 1946–1947," *Journal of Negro History*, XXXII
(1947), 407–16, and his other Annual Reports for the 1940s, in the *Journal of Negro
History*.
21. Woodson, "Woodson Speaks," Washington *Tribune*, December 17, 1935, p. 4,
and Annual Reports during the 1930s, in the *Journal of Negro History*.
22. See Annual Meeting Proceedings for the 1930s, in the *Journal of Negro History*.

Because Woodson was greatly concerned about education, he made the teaching of Negro history—strategies, methods, interpretations, and source materials—a theme for many annual meetings. Club women, ministers, parents, and teachers addressed this topic and received feedback from black children, who were invited to attend Saturday sessions of the meetings. At the gathering in 1933, for example, schoolteachers Arthur D. Wright and Herman Dreer spoke on teaching methods. Impressed with their papers, Woodson published them in the *Journal* to give them exposure to a larger audience. And at the 1936 meeting, attention was given to methods of teaching about black contributions in literature and art.[23]

Cultural and social activities at annual meetings also served an educational purpose. Dinners and receptions enabled conferees from all levels of the black community to become better acquainted with one another, discuss ideas, and share information and resources. Woodson invited black poets, musicians, and artists to make presentations and display their work so as to convey a sense of the richness and pride in black cultural heritage. Participants at the 1931 meeting in New York City attended a dinner sponsored by the white liberal minister Harry Emerson Fosdick at his Riverside Church; a musical program and an interpretive lecture on black music followed. In conjunction with the meeting, the New York Public Library's Harlem branch held an exhibit on Negro literature and art. The 1933 program in Washington, D.C., included musical programs, art exhibits, and poetry readings by Sterling Brown, Countee Cullen, Langston Hughes, and Georgia Douglas Johnson. The Harlem Artists Guild sponsored an art exhibit for the 1938 meeting in New York City, and musical programs were held to commemorate the deaths of Arthur Schomburg and James Weldon Johnson. Writers whose books were published by the Associated Publishers were honored at an authors' breakfast at the 1942 meeting in Washington, D.C. And during the 1945 meeting in Columbus, Ohio, participants visited several libraries and museums to view exhibits on black contributions to Ohio history.[24]

During the 1940s, Negro History Week celebrations became increasingly sophisticated and well attended. Woodson compiled and sold Negro History Week kits, posters, and large photographs depicting various eras in Negro history. Black women's organizations and social

23. See *ibid.*
24. See *ibid.* and for the 1940s.

service groups sponsored lectures and rallies for their members. Libraries, museums, and educational institutions held special exhibits. School systems throughout the country sponsored institutes to help teachers observe the occasion. Teachers assigned students essays on topics in Negro history, helped them write and produce plays, and sponsored oratorical and essay contests.[25]

Woodson credited schoolteachers with ensuring the success of Negro History Week celebrations. He regularly reported on their efforts in the *Journal* and in the black press, highlighting the most creative and innovative activities. In some school systems the immense popularity of the celebration led teachers to establish Negro history study clubs that gave attention to the subject throughout the school year. In 1935 Woodson reported that Delaware, Georgia, and Texas had incorporated Negro history courses into their junior and senior high school curricula, and that boards of education in Columbia, South Carolina, and Birmingham, Alabama, were planning to do so.[26]

By the 1940s white politicians made annual proclamations in honor of Negro History Week and whites began to participate in special events. During Woodson's lifetime the popularity of the celebration was far-reaching to the extent that whites and blacks in Latin America, the West Indies, Africa, the Philippines, and the Virgin Islands also participated in Negro History Week activities.[27]

Meager funds and the drive to bring outreach activities to the masses of black Americans limited Woodson, in his research initiatives, to collecting and disseminating information on primary source materials, assisting other organizations and scholars with their research, and investigating African history and culture and its impact on blacks in the

25. Woodson to Luther P. Jackson, January 8, 1948, in Jackson Papers; Emma K. Cardwell to Nannie H. Burroughs, October 12, 1943, and Burroughs to Paralee Clark, November 22, 1949, in Nannie H. Burroughs Papers, MS Div., LC; Lavonia H. Brown to Mary McLeod Bethune, January 16, 1945, and A. F. Dixon to Bethune, November 3, 1945, in National Council of Negro Women Records, National Archives for Black Women's History, Washington, D.C.; Woodson's Annual Reports for the 1940s, in the *Journal of Negro History.*

26. Woodson, "Woodson Speaks," December 17, 1935, p. 4, and Annual Reports for the 1930s and 1940s, in the *Journal of Negro History;* Roy Wilkins to Arthur B. Spingarn, July 25, 1938, Wilkins to David O. Selznick, July 25, 1938, Wilkins to Charles H. Wesley, July 25, 1938, all in Arthur Spingarn Papers, LC; Wesley to Wilkins, July 30, 1938, NAACP Records, Group II, Series L, Box 13, MS Div., LC.

27. See Woodson's Annual Reports for the 1930s and 1940s, in the *Journal of Negro History.*

diaspora. Although Woodson had been engaged in these activities since the 1920s, they became the focus of his resources and energies during the 1930s and 1940s to the exclusion of other research projects. Unfortunately, the postwar period did not bring relief from financial hardship, and Woodson was unable to broaden his research agenda. "With limited income and uncertain future," he reported in 1946, "the Association has been reluctant to enter upon any new project of research."[28]

During the 1930s and early 1940s Woodson continued to collect primary sources that documented the African-American experience, and he was so successful that the federal government engaged him as a consultant. In 1934 the Federal Emergency Relief Administration funded a pilot project at Kentucky State College directed by Lawrence Reddick to collect oral histories of former slaves residing in Kentucky and Indiana. Woodson served on the advisory board and assisted Reddick in promoting the project. At the 1936 meeting of the association, Reddick presented a paper on the use of slave testimony. More than 250 interviews were collected in the pilot project, and in 1937 it was expanded to other states through the Works Progress Administration's Federal Writers Project. The WPA also sponsored a nationwide survey of nongovernmental historical records, directed by Luther Evans. In 1936 Evans asked Woodson to head an effort to identify and catalog manuscripts of blacks who lived in the District of Columbia. Relying on the technical expertise of his former student Arnett Lindsay, Woodson supervised the cataloging of Frederick Douglass' manuscripts, which were at Cedar Hill, his Anacostia home. In 1938, after the project in the District of Columbia was under way, Evans expanded the survey to include privately owned manuscripts throughout the United States. State chairmen were appointed, and Woodson coordinated and supervised their work. When the nationwide survey was completed in 1941, Woodson tried unsuccessfully to raise funds to publish a guide to black manuscript sources.[29] Almost thirty years would pass before a similar guide was finally published by Walter Schatz.

28. Woodson, "Annual Report for 1945–1946," *Journal of Negro History*, XXXI (1946), 386.

29. "Scholars to Study Ex-Slaves through F.E.R.A." (Press Release), October 17, 1934, in Claude H. Barnett Papers, Chicago Historical Society; Luther Evans to Woodson, March 6, 1936, in Record Group 69, Records of the Work Projects Administration, File 67, National Archives and Records Administration; Luther Evans to Ellen Woodward, December 9, 1938, and Woodward to Evans, December 30, 1938, in the Records

Woodson traveled to Europe during the summers of 1932, 1933, 1935, and 1937, vacationing and collecting research materials on Africa and blacks in the diaspora of the colonial period. He visited rare-book shops, libraries, archives, and museums, searching for documentation of the slave trade and slavery in colonial America, Haiti, and the British West Indies. In 1933 Woodson noted that he had purchased more than three hundred out-of-print books from European dealers and hoped to reissue some of them through the Associated Publishers if he could find the necessary funds. He made arrangements for Abel Doysie, a French scholar-researcher who was hired by the Library of Congress to copy materials from French repositories for its Foreign Copying Program, to undertake similar work for the association. During these trips Woodson also met many European scholars with similar research interests and encouraged them to make their work available to an American audience. He was greatly impressed by the work of several French scholars, and after returning to Washington in the fall of 1933, he enlisted Boas in bringing two of them to the United States for a speaking tour. Woodson's European travels came to a halt when World War II erupted in the late 1930s, but he continued to correspond with those European scholars interested in Negro history, keeping them apprised of his research activities.[30]

Perhaps Woodson's greatest accomplishment during the thirties and forties was providing assistance and encouragement to scholars researching African-American history. Although he was very selective of those he chose to help, if he believed in the historical value of the project and had faith in the individual researcher, he freely gave his time and resources. Numerous white scholars benefited from his knowledge and editorial judgment, as he published their work in the *Journal* in the late 1930s and the 1940s. Woodson traded research notes on slavery

---

of the Joint Committee on Materials for Research, MS Div., LC; Evans to Mr. Morris, April 27, 1939, and Arnett Lindsay to Chief, Division of Manuscripts, September 5, 1939, in Library of Congress Archives; Calendar of the Writings of Frederick Douglass in the Frederick Douglass Memorial Home, Anacostia, D.C., 1940, (Mimeograph in MS Div., LC); Woodson to Melville J. Herskovits, March 22, 1941, in Melville J. Herskovits Papers, University Archives, Northwestern University. Woodson wrote the introduction to the catalog of Douglass manuscripts that was produced by the WPA project.

30. Woodson's Annual Reports for the 1930s and early 1940s, in the *Journal of Negro History*; Woodson to Abel Doysie, September 23, 1933, in Abel Doysie Papers, MS Div., LC; Woodson to Franz Boas, September 18, 1933, in Franz Boas Papers, American Philosophical Society Library, Philadelphia.

with Frederic Bancroft, helped historian Philip Foner gain access to Douglass' papers, and encouraged Thomas P. Martin, assistant chief of the Manuscript Division at the Library of Congress, to pursue research on the British antislavery movement. Woodson also assisted a Catholic priest with research on missionary work among black West Indians in the nineteenth century. In addition to working closely with young black scholars in the 1920s and 1930s, he assisted Harold T. Pinkett in the 1940s with research for his Columbia University dissertation on the efforts of the United States to annex Santo Domingo in the nineteenth century. And he encouraged John Hope Franklin to prepare a biography of George Washington Williams.[31]

Woodson usually refused to help on a publishing project directed by other black scholars if it was financed by whites or would compete with those of the Associated Publishers. For example, he declined to participate in a project directed by Alain Locke in the mid-1930s. Locke, like Woodson, was interested in promoting black history and culture among the black masses and founded the Associates in Negro Folk Education to produce curriculum materials for adult education classes. Locke decided to publish a series called "Bronze Booklets" to stimulate adult interest in Negro history and culture.[32]

Woodson participated in joint projects if he believed that the Associated Publishers would benefit from the collaboration. This was the case when Benjamin Brawley approached him in 1932 with a proposal to publish a series of biographies of prominent black Americans. Brawley would edit and coordinate the project, and Woodson would act as coeditor and publisher of the series. Brawley, formerly a professor of English at Morehouse College and at Howard, had published *A Short*

31. Jacqueline Goggin, "Countering White Racist Scholarship: Carter G. Woodson and the *Journal of Negro History*," *Journal of Negro History*, LXVIII (1983), 355–75; Woodson to Frederic Bancroft, March 14, 1932, in Frederic Bancroft Papers, Butler Library, Columbia University; Thomas P. Martin to Woodson, January 26, 1938, in Library of Congress Archives; Philip S. Foner to author, May 9, 1988, and Harold T. Pinkett to author, May 2, 1988; John Hope Franklin, *George Washington Williams: A Biography* (Chicago, 1985). After Woodson's suggestion, Franklin doggedly researched the life of Williams for the next forty years, and dedicated the book to Du Bois, Logan, Wesley, and Woodson. Also see Woodson's Annual Reports for 1939 through the 1940s, in the *Journal of Negro History*.

32. Eugene K. Jones to Arthur Schomburg, February 4, 1935, Jones to Schomburg, February 15, 1935, and enclosures "Invited to Become 'Associates in Negro Folk Education'" and "Associates in Negro Folk Education," Jones to Schomburg, October 28, 1936, all in Schomburg Papers.

History of the American Negro in 1913 and *A Social History of the American Negro* in 1921, both of which were popular presentations of Negro history. Neither book conformed to the high scholarly standards that Woodson had set for himself, and he was critical of them in reviews published in the *Journal.* Woodson's decision to cooperate with Brawley was probably based on his belief that the series would be financially successful.[33] After Brawley compiled a list of eleven biographies for the series, Woodson tentatively accepted the proposal in October, 1932, and asked Brawley to commission the authors. One of the conditions of the agreement was that the books would be published simultaneously, since Woodson contended that it would be too expensive for the Associated Publishers to bring them out individually.[34]

In November, 1932, Brawley began soliciting authors for the series, hoping to have in hand final drafts of all the manuscripts within two years. Problems arose early on, however, when Woodson disapproved of one of the authors Brawley had commissioned. Woodson wrote that he did not have "an exalted opinion of the gentleman about whom you have written me. I am thinking too, that it would be a mistake to have any more Howard University professors on this staff. If we add any more we should call it the 'Howard Biography'! Such a title would be very appropriate because we now have five scheduled or practically half the authors from one institution."[35]

Despite this initial difficulty, the project continued without further disruption until late summer, 1933, when Woodson began complaining about the division of responsibility for the project. Several authors sought research and financial assistance from Woodson, and he maintained that if he had to give editorial advice, he wanted to be appointed editor. Woodson also doubted that drafts of all the manuscripts would be completed on schedule.[36]

33. Woodson, Review of Benjamin Brawley's *A Social History of the American Negro,* in *Journal of Negro History,* VII (1922), 114–15. For biographical information on Brawley, see John W. Parker, "Benjamin Brawley, Teacher and Scholar," *Phylon,* X (1949), 15–19.

34. Brawley to Woodson, October 20, 1932, and enclosure "Plan of a Series of Negro Biographies," and Woodson to Brawley, October 25, 1932, in Benjamin G. Brawley Papers, Moorland-Spingarn Research Center.

35. Woodson to Brawley, December 21, 1932, in Brawley Papers. Also see Brawley to James Weldon Johnson, November 5, 1932, in James Weldon Johnson Papers, James Weldon Johnson Collection, Beinecke Library, Yale University; Charles Wesley to Brawley, November 11, 1932, Rayford Logan to Brawley, November 18, 1932, Lorenzo Greene to Brawley, November 19, 1932, Miles Mark Fisher to Brawley, December 20, 1932, Arthur Huff Fauset to Brawley, January 16, 1933, all in Brawley Papers.

36. Woodson to Brawley, August 27, 1933, in Brawley Papers.

Unruffled by Woodson's complaints, Brawley kept in close touch with the authors, who assured him that the biographies would be finished on time. By late 1934, however, only a few authors had delivered their manuscripts and Brawley had not relinquished total editorial control. Woodson withdrew his offer to publish the series. Relations between Woodson and Brawley had been worsening because of Brawley's involvement in a project financed by the Phelps-Stokes Fund to publish an encyclopedia of the Negro, and this also may have led Woodson to renege on his agreement with Brawley.[37]

Although discouraged and angry with Woodson, Brawley hoped to get a contract with another publisher, and several of the commissioned authors—Miles Mark Fisher, Arthur Fauset, James Weldon Johnson, Locke, and Rayford Logan—were still committed to publishing their books in his series. In 1935, Brawley received a contract from the University of North Carolina Press and published his own biography of Dunbar. Woodson approached several authors individually to offer them contracts, and the Associated Publishers eventually published Charles Wesley's biography of Richard Allen in 1936.[38]

From the mid-1930s through the 1940s, the Associated Publishers continued to produce scholarly and popular works despite limited funds. Although published in runs smaller than those of the 1920s and early 1930s, more than a dozen titles appeared. Black scholars often turned to Woodson's Associated Publishers because white publishing firms were reluctant to publish books on black topics. Rufus E. Clement, Mercer Cook, A. H. Gordon, Lorenzo Greene, Luther Jackson, Ira De Augustine Reid, W. Sherman Savage, V. B. Spratlin, A. A. Taylor, and Wesley were among those who published with Woodson. In addition, during the 1940s, Woodson paid for the publication of two pamphlets written by Jackson; one discussed black soldiers in Virginia

37. Brawley, form letter to authors in the series, May 27, 1933, Brawley to Miles Mark Fisher, November 22, 1933, Brawley to Charles S. Johnson, November 22, 1933, Logan to Brawley, November 27, 1933, Greene to Brawley, November 28, December 10, 1933, Wesley to Brawley, December 14, 1933, and Johnson to Brawley, April 12, 1934, all in Brawley Papers. See Arthur Huff Fauset, *Sojourner Truth: God's Faithful Pilgrim* (1938; rpr. New York, 1971).

38. Dodd, Meade, and Company to Brawley, June 6, 1934, W. T. Couch to Brawley, August 28, 1934, Logan to Brawley, September 29, 1934, Miles Mark Fisher to Brawley, December 27, 1934, Fauset to Brawley, March 6, 1935, Locke to Brawley, March 29, 1935, Johnson to Woodson, March 30, 1935, Logan to Brawley, April 18, 1935, Greene to Brawley, April 29, 1935, all in Brawley Papers. Also see Charles H. Wesley, *Richard Allen: Apostle of Freedom* (Washington, D.C., 1936); Benjamin G. Brawley, *Paul Laurence Dunbar* (Chapel Hill, 1935).

during the revolutionary war, and the other, black politicians in Virginia during Reconstruction, and they were distributed free of charge to a mass audience.[39]

By the late 1930s the Associated Publishers was so financially hard pressed that authors were asked to finance the publication of their books. Woodson also asked black organizations to assist with publication costs, and several sororities and fraternities gave $100 per year. Individual black scholars were asked to contribute $25. A committee, composed of Woodson, Brawley, and Lorenzo Dow Turner decided what would be published.[40]

Since Woodson exercised total administrative control over the Associated Publishers, he proved to be a difficult and demanding editor. Young black scholars were forced either to comply with his demands or to face the unlikely prospect of securing another publisher. In 1931, for example, Woodson wrote to James Hugo Johnston, who was writing a dissertation titled "The Relations Between Indians and Negroes in Virginia," and offered to publish a documentary volume of materials on miscegenation that Johnston had culled in the course of his research. Woodson, however, was unable to secure funding to publish the volume, and Johnston asked him to return his manuscript so that he could send it to another publisher. Woodson then maintained that he had lost the manuscript, and never returned it. Fortunately, Johnston had a copy, and he sent it to Charles Johnson for evaluation and advice. Upon learning that, Woodson wrote to Johnson and accused him of pre-

39. See, for example, Robert T. Kerlin, *Negro Poets and Their Poems* (Washington, D.C., 1935); Maude Cuney Hare, *Negro Musicians and Their Music* (Washington, D.C., 1936); Jane Dabney Shackleford, *The Child's Story of the Negro* (Washington, D.C., 1938); Woodson, *African Heroes and Heroines* (Washington, D.C., 1939); Winifred B. Hambly, *Clever Hands of the African Negro* (Washington, D.C., 1945); Luther Porter Jackson, *Virginia Negro Soldiers and Seamen in the American Revolution* (Norfolk, Va., 1942), and *Negro Office-Holders in Virginia, 1865–1895* (Norfolk, Va., 1945).

40. Woodson's Annual Reports for the 1930s and 1940s, in the *Journal of Negro History*. Also see Charles H. Wesley, *The Collapse of the Confederacy* (Washington, D.C., 1937); Savage, *The Controversy over the Distribution of Abolition Literature* (Washington, D.C., 1938); Arthur Ramos, *The Negro in Brazil*, trans. Richard Pattee (Washington, D.C., 1939). In addition, other books directed to a scholarly audience were published by the Associated Publishers. These included Woodson, *The Negro Professional Man and the Community* (Washington, D.C., 1934), and *The African Background Outlined* (Washington, D.C., 1936); Wesley, *Richard Allen;* John G. Van Deusen, *The Black Man in White America* (Washington, D.C., 1938); Frank Klingberg, *An Appraisal of the Negro in South Carolina* (Washington, D.C., 1941), Eva B. Dykes, *The Negro in English Romantic Thought* (Washington, D.C., 1942); Mercer Cook, *Five French Negro Authors* (Washington, D.C., 1943).

empting his offer to publish Johnston's work. Johnson, unruffled by Woodson's accusatory letter, urged Johnston to continue to seek a publisher for the book, remarking that he had seen Woodson's "explosions" and was "not unduly excited by them." Woodson also accused Du Bois of interference, even though Johnston had never sent him his manuscript.[41]

Johnston was unable to find another publisher and once again offered the manuscript to the Associated Publishers. He felt some obligation to Woodson, for Woodson not only had paid for all the photostatic copies of the documents that Johnston had collected but also had paid him a salary to conduct the research, even when Johnston was ill for several weeks. Woodson, however, only was interested in publishing a documentary source book on miscegenation, and he instructed Johnston to prepare such a volume and to rewrite the rest of his manuscript as articles suitable for the *Journal*. Johnston did publish two articles, "The Participation of White Men in Virginia Negro Insurrections" and "A New Interpretation of the Domestic Slave System," in the *Journal* in 1931 and 1933, but he would not make miscegenation the focus of a documentary volume, believing that the historical profession would object to such a volume and that he would have difficulty obtaining employment if he complied with Woodson's request. Woodson asserted that Johnston was a coward, and told Johnston that if he were unable to obtain a job, he himself would find employment for Johnston. After this exchange, Woodson apparently thought that Johnston would comply with his request and announced the book as forthcoming. Johnston, however, would not focus exclusively on miscegenation, and Woodson would not compromise, contending that a book with a different focus would not sell as well. Johnston continued to look for another publisher but was unsuccessful. By 1938, Woodson had enough funds to publish Johnston's collection of documents, but Johnston was no longer interested and there were no further negotiations. Johnston's monograph remained unpublished until 1970.[42]

*   *   *

41. Charles S. Johnson to James Hugo Johnston, March 12, 1931, Johnston to Woodson, March 5, 1931, Woodson to Johnston, March 5, 1931, Johnston to Woodson, March 7, 1931, all in James Hugo Johnston Papers, Johnston Memorial Library; Woodson to Du Bois, March 9, 1931, in W. E. B. Du Bois Papers, University of Massachusetts.

42. Johnston to Woodson, May 10, 1932, Woodson to Johnston, May 21, 1932, Johnston to Woodson, February 7, 1933, Woodson to Johnston, February 8, 1933, June 14, 1938, Johnston to Woodson, June 15, 1938, Woodson to Johnston, June 16, 1938, Johnston to Woodson, June 21, 1938, Woodson to Johnston, July 5, 1938, all in Johnston

Despite his frequent clashes with colleagues, Woodson's own scholarly productivity remained high. During the 1930s his interest in Africa peaked, and he undertook several new research projects. Since school-teachers and the general public were most in need of information on Africa, Woodson published *The African Background Outlined* (1936), and *African Heroes and Heroines* (1939) to aid them. In 1936, with the assistance of E. D. Preston, Woodson studied diplomatic relations between the United States and Liberia since the nineteenth century, primarily through the use of State Department records. Woodson failed to obtain grant funds to complete the project, and it remained unpublished. While in Europe, Woodson collected sources on African history and the role of Europe in the slave trade. Although his research trips were interrupted by World War II, his interest in African history continued. In 1946 he reported that he was "still working on men and measures in Africa which have had to do with the opening up of the continent and its development along modern lines." He hoped that his work would "invite attention to the vastness of Africa and the complex problems of conflicting cultures." He was "concerned not only with the natives of the continent but with all Europeans of consequence who have vitally affected their lives and shaped the destiny of Africa." [43] Woodson integrated this material into his *Encyclopedia Africana*, which unfortunately was never published. [44]

Woodson's proposed *Encyclopedia Africana* generated considerable controversy within black scholarly circles because it competed with a similar project initiated by the Phelps-Stokes Fund. Woodson had refused to work on the Phelps-Stokes Fund's project because he had serious misgivings about participating in any activity that he could not direct or control and that brought white funds and black scholars to-

Papers; James Hugo Johnston, "The Participation of White Men in Virginia Negro Insurrections," *Journal of Negro History*, XVI (1931), 158–67, "A New Interpretation of the Domestic Slave System," *Journal of Negro History*, XVIII (1933), 39–45, and *Race Relations in Virginia and Miscegenation in the South* (Amherst, 1970).

43. Woodson, "Annual Report for 1935–1936," *Journal of Negro History*, XXI (1936), 245–55, and "Annual Report for 1936–1937," *Journal of Negro History*, XXII (1937), 405–16; Woodson to Department of State, December 23, 1935, Woodson to Franklin D. Roosevelt, December 23, 1935, Arthur W. Mitchell to Wilbur J. Carr, January 4, 1936, Carr to Mitchell, January 6, 1936; Woodson to Carr, January 6, 1936, all in Record Group 59, General Records of the State Department, File 116.2, NA; Woodson, "Annual Report for 1946–1947," pp. 407–16.

44. See Woodson's Annual Reports for the 1930s and 1940s, in the *Journal of Negro History*.

gether. More than twenty years earlier, Du Bois had planned a similar publication—the "Encyclopedia Africana"—to commemorate the fiftieth anniversary of black emancipation in 1915. In 1909 he formed a committee of black and white scholars in the United States and abroad, and had stationery printed. The lack of funds probably prevented the project from materializing, for there was no further discussion of an encyclopedia until April, 1931, when officials of the Phelps-Stokes Fund decided to hold a meeting to discuss plans for an encyclopedia of the Negro.[45]

The controversy surrounding the encyclopedia of the Negro began at the first meeting, which was held at Howard University in November, 1931. Among the twenty black and white scholars, philanthropists, and educational administrators in attendance were Brawley, James Dillard, John Hope, Charles Johnson, James Weldon Johnson, Mordecai Johnson, Thomas Jesse Jones, Frederick Keppel, Robert Moton, Anson Phelps Stokes, Thomas Woofter, and Monroe Work. Du Bois and Woodson were not invited to this first meeting, and the blacks in attendance protested that fact. Brawley, who was elected secretary of the group, was instructed to invite them, along with Locke, to the next meeting, scheduled for January 9, 1932.[46]

Greatly insulted by his exclusion from the first meeting, Du Bois outlined his reservations about participating in the project in letters to Dillard and Edwin Embree. He would not "sit in on a proposition of this sort as a figurehead," and "could not for a moment contemplate a Negro encyclopedia dominated by Thomas Jesse Jones and Mr. Woofter." He also objected to white domination of the editorial board, asserting that "a Negro encyclopedia that was not in the main edited and written by Negroes would be as inconceivable as a Catholic encyclopedia projected by Protestants." Du Bois would participate only if blacks were given total editorial control, but was willing to accept a racially mixed editorial board. Both Dillard and Embree urged him to participate, and Embree noted that "an omission from the first group more serious than yours was that of Carter G. Woodson."[47]

45. W. E. B. Du Bois to W. B. T. Williams, May 20, 1909, in Archibald Grimké Papers, Moorland-Spingarn Research Center; Du Bois to Schomburg, August 4, 1910, in Schomburg Papers.

46. Robert M. Lester, Memorandum on Conference on the Advisability of Publishing an Encyclopedia of the Negro, November 7, 1931, in Carnegie Foundation Archives, Butler Library; Anson Phelps Stokes to Du Bois, November 9, 1931, in Du Bois Papers.

47. Du Bois to Dillard, November 30, 1931, Du Bois to Embree, December 2, 1931, Embree to Du Bois, December 4, 1931, all in Du Bois Papers.

Woodson also was angry at his exclusion from the meeting. Like Du Bois, he had been omitted because of his outspoken criticism of Thomas Jesse Jones. But even if Woodson had been invited, he would not have attended. When Brawley asked Woodson to join the project, Woodson declined, claiming that since 1922, he had planned "to publish a work of ten volumes, the title of which [would] be the *Encyclopedia Africana.*" Woodson advised Brawley, "Spend your time and energy . . . doing some of the other long neglected tasks which the present undesirable condition of the race requires. There is so much to be done for the Negro that it seems to me unwise for one agency to duplicate the efforts of the other." While no evidence exists to document Woodson's contention that the association had planned to publish an encyclopedia, Rayford Logan maintained that Woodson had been compiling data for such a volume before the Phelps-Stokes project was announced. In addition to his specific objections to the involvement of Jones and the Phelps-Stokes Fund, Woodson believed that whites should not be involved in a project to publish an encyclopedia of the Negro, and that it should be written and edited entirely by blacks. His aversion to the project also stemmed from the racism he had experienced earlier in the 1920s when he wrote entries for the *Dictionary of American Biography.* [48]

Even though he understood Woodson's position, Du Bois believed that whites would control the project unless he became involved. Convinced that his participation would ensure the publication of a better encyclopedia, Du Bois swallowed his pride and accepted the invitation, and the concessions he requested were granted. Although blacks did not have total editorial control over the encyclopedia, Du Bois was appointed editor, Robert Park, who also was not invited to the first meeting, served as assistant editor, and the editorial board was comprised of an equal number of blacks and whites. [49]

Many of the black participants tried to persuade Woodson to join them, and Woodson, in turn, attempted to persuade them to withdraw their support from the project. Writing to Hope, then president of the

48. Woodson to Brawley, November 23, 1931, in Johnson Collection; Logan, interview with author, July 6, 1981, Washington, D.C. On the controversy over the *Dictionary of American Biography,* see Woodson to John Hope, December 24, 1931, in Johnson Collection.

49. See Anson Phelps Stokes, form letter, October 19, 1931, in Johnson Collection; Du Bois to Stokes, December 9, 1931, Brawley to Du Bois, December 15, 1931, Du Bois to Brawley, December 17, 1931, Brawley to Du Bois, December 18, 1931, all in Du Bois Papers; Stokes, form letter, December 31, 1931, in Johnson Collection.

association, Woodson cautioned that "a blunder in this matter may mean that the Negro race may be further afflicted with misrepresentation." The production of an encyclopedia of the Negro by the Phelps-Stokes Fund, Woodson argued, would further pervert writings "on Negro life and history" and would "increase the burdens of agencies like the Association for the Study of Negro Life and History." Hoping that Woodson would reconsider his position, Brawley wrote to him again. Woodson, however, maintained that it was time for "the Negro . . . to construct his own program and carry it out as he sees and understands it." In his view, the Phelps-Stokes Fund was trying to undermine the work of the association, and he tried to dissuade Brawley from participating in the project, arguing that blacks "would be glad to have any person sufficiently interested in our people to provide funds for a scientific appraisal of its achievements." He asserted further that whites did "not appreciate the feeling, thought, and aspirations of the Negro and therefore cannot think black."[50]

Underestimating the animus that Woodson felt toward Jones and the Phelps-Stokes Fund, Du Bois and Anson Phelps Stokes continued to try to compromise with him. Woodson told Du Bois that Stokes tried to bribe him to silence his criticism of Jones. Stokes denied the allegation, and asserted that as a board member, he had been instrumental in getting the Rockefeller Foundation to fund Woodson's association. Maintaining that Woodson's refusal to participate would not cause any hardship for white members on the project, but would hurt blacks, Du Bois naïvely believed that if Woodson had already started a similar project, he should be even more willing to share his resources and cooperate.[51]

The controversy continued throughout the spring of 1932 as Woodson published articles in the black press and the *Journal* criticizing Du Bois, Stokes, and the Phelps-Stokes Fund. In an article in the New York *Age* in June, for example, Woodson asserted, "It is unfortunate that so many of us are hungry." Arguing that he could complete the encyclopedia project in less time with fewer resources, Woodson proposed that the Phelps-Stokes Fund provide him with the money to finish his *Encyclopedia Africana* and invited officials to examine the data he had al-

50. Woodson to John Hope, December 24, 1931, in Johnson Collection; Woodson to Brawley, January 7, 1932, in NAACP Records, Group I, Series C, Box 80.
51. Woodson to Du Bois, January 7, 1932, Du Bois to Woodson, January 29, 1932, Woodson to Du Bois, February 11, 1932, all in Du Bois Papers; Anson Phelps Stokes to Woodson, January 8, 1932, in Phelps-Stokes Fund Records, Schomburg Center.

ready collected. Several months passed before the Phelps-Stokes editorial board decided to accept Woodson's offer and, by then, Woodson had changed his mind and would not produce any documentation on his project. After this incident, no further attempts were made to solicit his cooperation.[52]

Woodson, however, continued his efforts to thwart the Phelps-Stokes project. When he learned that Du Bois and Stokes requested funding from the Rockefeller Foundation, Woodson wrote to Sydnor Walker, of the foundation, arguing that the Phelps-Stokes project would duplicate work that the association had already completed. Woodson then tried to persuade the Rockefeller Foundation to fund his project instead. Neither project received funds.[53]

Woodson was not the only black critic of the Phelps-Stokes project. E. Franklin Frazier also criticized the controversy that erupted over Woodson's exclusion, confiding to Robert Park, who had by then committed himself to the Phelps-Stokes project, that "the group originally called together for the encyclopedia was comprised almost all together of Negro school politicians and people who have the reputation for being 'good-willers' and 'having the right attitude toward the race problem.'" Frazier continued his criticism, asserting in 1936 that the encyclopedia should "be the work of the most competent scholars available for the various topics," and that "the Negro scholars should be invited to contribute articles on the basis of their competency." Like Woodson, Frazier maintained that "the planning and execution of the encyclopedia should devolve upon scholars and not upon interracial 'politicians' or 'statesmen' white or black."[54]

52. Stokes to Brawley, April 19, 1932, and Stokes, form letter to board members, May 20, 1932, in Du Bois Papers; New York *Age*, June 18, 1932, p. 5; Woodson, "And So Miss Bowles Goes the Way of Moorland," New York *Age*, June 4, 1932, p. 4; Dillard to Du Bois, October 23, 1932, Du Bois to Woodson, October 24, 1932, Woodson to Du Bois, October 25, 1932, Du Bois to Dillard, October 26, 1932, Woodson to Du Bois, October 27, 1932, and Stokes to Woodson, January 20, 1933, all in Du Bois Papers.

53. Secretary of E. E. Day to Woodson, October 22, 1932, and Sydnor Walker to Woodson, October 22, 1932, in Rockefeller Foundation Archives; Du Bois to Robert R. Moton, September 26, 1933, and Moton to Du Bois, September 29, 1933, in Du Bois Papers; Anson Phelps Stokes to Frederick Keppel, May 10, 1934, Alvin Johnson to Keppel, April 28, 1934, Leland to Keppel, May 21, 1934, Robert M. Lester to Keppel, Memorandum, n.d., all in Carnegie Foundation Archives; Stokes to Trevor Arnett, April 16, 1934, in General Education Board Records.

54. E. Franklin Frazier to Robert E. Park, August 2, 1932, in E. Franklin Frazier Papers, Moorland-Spingarn Research Center; Frazier to Du Bois, November 7, 1936, Du Bois Papers.

In articles published in the black press and in letters to blacks associated with the project, Woodson continued to criticize the encyclopedia. In June, 1936, he published two articles in the Baltimore *Afro-American*, noting that the encyclopedia was "approved by race leaders financed with the white man's money and written according to his will." Believing that Du Bois had compromised his principles by cooperating with Jones and Stokes "for the hope of a few dollars," and that he "supports their proposition," Woodson asserted that "poverty makes strange bedfellows." Calling other black participants traitors to their race, Woodson asserted that Wesley, Ralph J. Bunche, A. A. Taylor, Logan, and Lorenzo Greene, "men who have distinguished themselves among historical scholars for original treatment and scientific research," also should have been asked to participate. Declaring his independence from white foundations and thus, he believed, his higher morality, Woodson contended that he would publish his encyclopedia "without the aid of the rich foundations," and would "demonstrate that after three centuries of contact with modern culture and seventy-one years of freedom the Negro can do some things for himself without compromising his honor and his manhood." In a response published in the *Afro-American*, Brawley countered Woodson's criticisms and objected to his attacks on Du Bois, Hope, and Stokes. Even Claude Barnett, director of the Associated Negro Press, inadvertently became involved in the fray, as he tried to summarize the positions of both Woodson and the Phelps-Stokes project for his readers.[55]

Readers of the black press and members of the black community were both amused and outraged by the battle between Woodson and the Phelps-Stokes Fund. Believing that Woodson was winning the battle, Schomburg told Locke that "Woodson is supreme on the field of polemics and is wielding his sword challenging anyone who will cross his doorstep and question him about the encyclopedia." Even Schomburg conceded that the battle had gotten out of hand, and suggested

55. Woodson, "An Open Letter to the Afro-American on the Negro Encyclopedia," June 3, 1936, and "Remember 1917" (Press Release), June 17, 1936, in Woodson Collection, Moorland-Spingarn Research Center; [Barnett (?)], "Woodson Cites Brawley's Misrepresentations," (Press Release), June 10, 1936, in Barnett Papers; Brawley, "Statement by Dr. Carter G. Woodson About an Encyclopedia of the Negro in the *Afro-American*, May 30, 1936," (Press Release), May 29, 1936, in Arthur B. Spingarn Papers, Moorland-Spingarn Research Center; Anson Phelps Stokes to Claude Barnett, June 8, 1936, and Barnett, "Woodson and Brawley in Controversy over Negro Encyclopedia" (Press Release), n.d., in Barnett Papers.

that if Locke met Woodson in Paris that summer, he should "see him on the Rue de la Paix and invite him to have some of the refreshing drinks that are served to transients and cool his ardor so that we may all get down to work." Schomburg made several other critical remarks about Woodson's behavior, but in the end, supported Woodson's project, possibly because Woodson invited him to serve on the editorial board of the *Journal* and wanted his assurance of loyalty.[56]

Most blacks, however, sided with the Phelps-Stokes Fund. For example, Francis Grimké, although uninvolved, supported the Phelps-Stokes project, mainly because he felt that Woodson had gone too far in his criticism of black participants.[57] Logan joined the Phelps-Stokes project in December, 1936, because he believed it could obtain funding. Woodson consequently fired him from the association staff. Although Logan tried to go quietly, Woodson publicized what he believed were Logan's transgressions, writing to the executive council members to explain that Logan was fired for working "with those who are trying to cut our throats." Logan, Woodson stated, could not "run with the hare and bark with the hounds." Woodson also took legal action "to enjoin him from making use of the data which the Association paid him $3,000 to compile." Woodson had provided Logan with funds to finish his last year of graduate school at Harvard, and when Logan was unemployed for more than a year, had hired him as a research assistant to prepare articles for the *Encyclopedia Africana*. He maintained that Logan's conduct was "unethical, if not illegal."[58] Compelled to reply to Woodson's charges, Logan wrote the executive council members, urging those members who supported the Phelps-Stokes project to resign from the association. In subsequent years Woodson continued to castigate black participants as dupes "serving the interracial racketeers as hirelings."[59]

Woodson's criticism of the Phelps-Stokes encyclopedia project factored, albeit slightly, into the project's inability to attract funds. Some

56. Schomburg to Locke, July 23, 1936, Schomburg to Georgia Douglas Johnson, June 26, 1936, Woodson to Schomburg, December 18, 1936, April 16, 1937, Schomburg to Richard Pattee, May 5, 1937, all in Schomburg Papers.

57. Francis Grimké to Brawley, June 1, 1936, in Brawley Papers.

58. Woodson to James Dillard, December 23, 1936, in James Dillard Papers, Alderman Library. Also see Rayford W. Logan Diaries, May 6, 1950 (MS in Logan Papers), where he recalled what had happened between the two of them in the mid-1930s.

59. Logan to Dillard, December 14, 1936, in Dillard Papers; Woodson to Schomburg, April 16, 1937, in Schomburg Papers.

white foundation officials believed that funding the Phelps-Stokes project would cause friction among blacks and had to be reassured that Woodson was the only serious black critic.[60] Actually, white philanthropists would not fund the project because they objected to the editorship of Du Bois.

Du Bois should have heeded Woodson's warning, and his own gut feeling about Jones's untrustworthiness, for Jones began criticizing Du Bois early on and in 1933 urged Stokes to withdraw his support from the project. Using a tactic similar to the one used against Woodson more than ten years earlier, Jones argued that Du Bois was too radical, and persuaded grant-funding agencies and white philanthropists to withhold financial support. But Jones did not succeed in having Du Bois removed from the editorship, because Du Bois had many black and white supporters. As long as Du Bois remained the editor, however, foundations would not fund the encyclopedia. For example, Jackson Davis conceded that Du Bois was an able scholar, but admitted he was "identified in the public mind with the propagandist aspect of Negro development." Davis maintained that the General Education Board's executive council would question Du Bois' "ability to resist these influences and devote himself to work of this character with the judicial mind which is expected of an editor of such a work." Logan believed that after Du Bois published *Black Reconstruction* in 1935, white philanthropists became so alarmed that they would never consider funding a project with which Du Bois was involved.[61]

When Guy B. Johnson, of the University of North Carolina, re-

60. Stokes to Thomas Jesse Jones, March 18, 1937, in Anson Phelps Stokes Papers, Sterling Memorial Library, Yale University; Stokes to Jackson Davis, April 9, 1937, Du Bois to Davis, April 16, 1937, Davis, Memorandum on Trip to Atlanta, October 19, 1937, David Stevens, Memorandum on Interview with Anson Phelps Stokes, W. E. B. Du Bois, and Jackson Davis, November 29, 1937, Keppel, Memorandum, on Interview with Jackson Davis, December 13, 1937, all in General Education Board Records; Frederick P. Keppel, Memorandum on Interview with Anson Phelps Stokes and W. E. B. Du Bois, June 10, 1937, Donald B. Young, Memorandum on Encyclopedia, June 10, 1937, Keppel, Memorandum on Interview with Alvin Johnson, June 28, 1937, Keppel to Stokes, June 29, 1937, Keppel, Memorandum, October 27, 1937, Stokes to Keppel, November 17, 1937, Keppel to Stokes, December 20, 1937, Keppel, Memorandum, on Interview with Jackson Davis, January 20, 1938, all in Carnegie Foundation Archives.

61. Jones to Stokes, August 5, 1932, in Stokes Papers; Du Bois to Robert R. Moton, September 26, 1933, and Moton to Du Bois, September 29, 1933, in Du Bois Papers; Jackson Davis to Dumas Malone, February 15, 1938, in General Education Board Records; Logan, interview with author, July 6, 1981; Logan Diaries, July 24, September 9, 1941, January 7, May 26, September 3, November 1, 1942.

placed Robert Park as assistant editor in 1937, whites on the editorial board believed that Johnson would act as a moderating influence over Du Bois, and they hoped that white philanthropists would decide to fund the project. Du Bois, who did not "see how a man who seriously argues that Negro folk songs originated and were developed by white people has exactly the mental balance for this work," was overruled by the board. Stokes and other whites should have heeded Du Bois' objections to Johnson, for Johnson was not committed to the project. He confessed to Charles Dollard of the Carnegie Foundation in May, 1941, that "he had never been the least bit keen about having a hand in an encyclopedia . . . and that . . . he would not have a minute to give to the work during the next three years." [62]

It was also in May, 1941, that Du Bois, discouraged by his inability to secure funding, offered his resignation as editor. But Stokes and others persuaded him to prepare a preliminary volume to offer to grant-funding agencies, in the hope that they would support the final product. Work on the preliminary volume continued during the early 1940s, and it finally appeared in 1945, financed by the Phelps-Stokes Fund. In a long introduction titled "Need of an Encyclopedia of the Negro," Du Bois and Johnson argued that new and changing ideas and information about race and interracial problems had stimulated greater interest in African-American history. They maintained that scholars had begun to tap previously neglected source materials, that there was a need to collect bibliographical and research resources together into a reference manual, and that the preliminary volume could be used to correct the historical record. Despite Du Bois' efforts, publication of the volume did not convince agencies to finance completion of the encyclopedia. [63]

62. Keppel to Stokes, November 9, 1938, David Stevens to Keppel, March 19, 1940, Stokes to Charles Dollard, April 22, 1941, Stokes to Keppel, November 14, 1941, all in Carnegie Foundation Archives; Jackson Davis, Memorandum, on Interview with Charles S. Johnson, March 16, 1938, Charles Loram to Davis, March 16, 1938, Davis, Memorandum on Interview with Robert M. Lester, May 5, 1938, all in General Education Board Records; Du Bois to Logan, January 4, 1939, Logan to Du Bois, January 21, 1939, Stokes to Archibald MacLeish, January 4, 1940, Stokes to Madison Bentley, January 23, 1940, Bentley to Stokes, January 28, June 5, 1940, Du Bois to Stokes, February 20, March 14, 1941, all in Du Bois Papers; Herskovits to Bentley, February 8, 1940, in Herskovits Papers; Du Bois to Stokes, November 1, 1937, in Du Bois Papers; Charles Dollard, Memorandum on Interview with Guy Johnson, May 8, 1941, in Carnegie Foundation Archives.

63. Du Bois, form letter to board of directors of the Negro encyclopedia, May 29, 1941, Stokes to Du Bois, June 6, 1941, Du Bois to Stokes, May 15, 1942, Stokes to Du

Du Bois' radicalism probably did account for the project's not being financed, for other projects in black studies received funds. In 1939 the Carnegie Foundation underwrote the research that resulted in publication of *An American Dilemma* (1944), but was reluctant to fund another project in black studies, satisfied that it had made a substantial financial contribution to the advancement of knowledge and the improvement of race relations. Also in 1939, the American Council of Learned Societies financed the Committee on Negro Studies, which was organized to make recommendations regarding preservation and research projects and was headed by Herskovits.[64]

Although several black scholars served on this committee, Sterling Brown and Lawrence Reddick among them, Herskovits controlled it. Woodson anticipated that situation and declined to participate, contending he was too busy. Herskovits, reluctant to invite Woodson in the first place, probably was pleased.[65]

Herskovits wielded considerable influence among white philanthropists and among white intellectuals such as poet Archibald MacLeish, the Librarian of Congress. He persuaded MacLeish to offer no research support for the Phelps-Stokes project and, similarly, may have caused Arna Bontemps to withdraw the support of the Illinois Work Projects Administration staff. Herskovits also urged grant foundations not to fund the encyclopedia, for he not only objected to Du Bois but also believed it was premature to prepare such an encyclopedia and that Africa was given short shrift. In view of the enormous obstacles Du Bois faced, publication of the preliminary volume was a remarkable accomplishment.[66]

Bois, January 4, 1943, all in Du Bois Papers; Stokes to Dollard, June 19, 1941, in Carnegie Foundation Archives; Guy B. Johnson and W. E. B. Du Bois, eds., *Encyclopedia of the Negro: Preparatory Volume* (New York, 1945), 15–21.

64. John H. Stanfield, *Philanthropy and Jim Crow in American Social Science* (Westport, Conn., 1985), 140–42; Robert L. Harris, Jr., "Segregation and Scholarship," *Journal of Black Studies*, XII (1982), 315–31; Logan Diaries, June 6, September 8, October 18, November 3, 1941, March 7, May 23, 24, 1943.

65. Herskovits to Woodson, February 8, 1940, and Woodson to Herskovits, February 20, 1940, in Herskovits Papers. Also see Herskovits to Mortimer Graves, January 9, 1940, in Herskovits Papers.

66. Herskovits to Madison Bentley, February 8, 1940, in Herskovits Papers; Bentley to Anson Phelps Stokes, June 5, 1940, Du Bois to Stokes, February 20, 1941, Du Bois to Stokes, March 14, 1941, all in Du Bois Papers; Stokes to Arna Bontemps, May 14, 1941, in General Education Board Records.

Woodson, unimpressed with the preliminary volume, was critical of Guy Johnson's participation and maintained that too many race leaders and not enough scholars were involved. He wrote a negative review for the *Journal*, asserting that "the editors have not done themselves much credit." Moreover, he argued that the Phelps-Stokes Fund "should not expect the Negro race to subsidize what has been brought them from so-called friends of the other race." Blacks should compile their own encyclopedia, "rather than await dictation from without and thus keep the race going around in a circle and getting nowhere."[67]

Since Woodson's encyclopedia had not yet been published, his harsh criticism of the Phelps-Stokes Fund's volume was unjustified. In his 1936 annual report, Woodson announced that he had been collecting European source materials during previous summers and had enlisted the aid of European scholars to write articles, but in fact, he wrote all the articles himself. In 1940 he reported that the project to compile a "Dictionary of Negro Biography" had been abandoned and that data collected for the dictionary would be incorporated into the encyclopedia so that he could complete it more quickly. By the mid-1940s Woodson had reduced the number of volumes from the originally proposed ten to six, to be published over the next several years. And it was only in December, 1948, that he appointed an editorial board, which included Mercer Cook, John Hope Franklin, Lorenzo Greene, Dorothy Porter, Benjamin Quarles, Sadie Daniel St. Clair, and Charles Wesley, noting "that mature judgment and special contributions of many scholars" were needed, and that his editorial board had "submitted lists of topics . . . and the names of persons qualified to develop them."[68]

As Woodson grew older his behavior opened him to the charge that he was undermining the very cause he was trying to promote. Difficulties with his executive council and disagreements with white philanthropists over funding for association programs caused Woodson to become bit-

67. Woodson, Review of Johnson and Du Bois' *Encyclopedia of the Negro*, in *Journal of Negro History*, XXX (1945), 340–41.
68. Woodson, "Annual Report for 1936–1937," pp. 405–16, and "Annual Report for 1939–1940," *Journal of Negro History*, XXV (1940), 407–15; Stokes to Du Bois, March 2, 1948, in Du Bois Papers; F. D. Patterson to Jackson Davis, November 20, 1946, in General Education Board Records; Woodson to Luther P. Jackson, December 23, 1948, and Jackson to Greene, April 23, 1949, in Jackson Papers; Rayford W. Logan, "Annual Report for 1949–1950," *Journal of Negro History*, XXXV (1950), 363; Woodson, "Annual Report for 1948–1949," *Journal of Negro History*, XXXIV (1949), 385.

ter and disillusioned with cooperative ventures with whites, and he was increasingly critical and suspicious of blacks who participated in projects that whites funded. His criticism of projects that falsely purported to advance knowledge in black history proved to be accurate. White intellectuals and philanthropists did in fact ascribe an inferior status to black scholars and dominated and controlled nearly all cooperative ventures. Woodson's response to this practice was actually moderate and controlled.

While Woodson's refusal to compromise and his desire always to control any project with which he was associated might be considered weaknesses, they were also his greatest strengths, for he would not allow himself to be drawn into black political power struggles and organizational disputes, nor would he allow his freedom of action to be undermined. The success of his own program was due in large part to his control over all aspects of organizational activity.

Because Woodson's black and white contemporaries viewed him as cantankerous, his accomplishments largely went unrecognized during his lifetime. His intense personal independence, while it frequently generated tensions in his relations with others, did not prevent him from forging the links that made his work enduring. In spite of the enormous obstacles he faced, he made an immeasurable contribution to the advancement of black history. For thirty-five years Woodson successfully and almost single-handedly managed the financial and administrative affairs of the association. In view of the enormous difficulties he faced in maintaining his autonomy and in convincing whites and blacks that his cause was credible and worthy of support, the achievement of so much seminal work in black history seems herculean.

Less well known, but equally important, were his activities in political organizations. Although Woodson considered black history to be his primary preoccupation, he used his scholarship to influence social and cultural change.

SCHOLARSHIP AND POLITICAL ACTIVISM

Woodson's fervent belief that blacks' enlightenment about their history was fundamental to overcoming economic and political powerlessness led him to devote his considerable talents to expanding the base of the Negro history movement. Political activism was secondary among his concerns, because after founding the association in 1915, he was faced with the more pressing need of establishing the scholarly credibility of African-American history. Yet even in the association's formative years, many of its programs were directed to those outside of scholarly circles, to the black bourgeoisie and working-class blacks. Woodson believed that the Negro community needed to be reeducated to appreciate black contributions in America's history.

Woodson ardently believed that education in black history, rather than participation in black protest organizations, was the primary vehicle for the political empowerment of black Americans. At the same time, he believed, albeit somewhat naïvely, that if white Americans were educated about black history, their racism would subside. Like other black scholars—Du Bois, for example—Woodson became more radical as he grew older. After he founded the Association for the Study of Negro Life and History, he increasingly combined scholarly and political activity, viewing his research and writing as a mechanism not only to inform but also to influence the plans proposed by black protest organizations for black social and economic advancement in American society. And, like those of Du Bois, Woodson's ideas for appropriate solutions to the economic and social plight of black Americans in the twentieth century changed several times.

However, Woodson did remain consistent in his distrust of and non-participation in mainstream political activity, and he always refused to declare allegiance to either the Democrats or the Republicans. During

World War I, for example, he argued that blacks "should support representative men of any color or party, if they stand for a square deal and equal rights for all." They should "ally themselves with those men who are fair-minded and considerate of the man far down, and seek to embrace their many opportunities for economic progress, a foundation for political recognition, upon which the race must learn to build."[1]

In Woodson's view, neither party had ever been committed to economic or racial equality for blacks. There is little evidence of his participation in organized political activity during his young adulthood, perhaps because he was occupied with obtaining an education and earning the money to pay for it. Once he had obtained his Ph.D. and secured steady employment, he became active in black social welfare and protest organizations like the National Urban League and the NAACP. Later he became involved in more radical black organizations, joined the Friends of Negro Freedom, and supported Garvey's Universal Negro Improvement Association. Woodson advanced his most radical political views during and after the 1930s, but their social and intellectual origins can be detected at least twenty years earlier.

During the depression, New Deal, and World War II eras, Woodson retained his membership in mainstream black organizations, and at the same time supported more radical groups like the New Negro Alliance with its "Don't Buy Where You Can't Work" campaign, George Schuyler's Young Negro Cooperative League, and the leftist coalition that formed the National Negro Congress in 1935. His experiences in and support of these organizations were pivotal to both the shifts in his economic, political, and cultural posture, and the constancy of his commitment to the popularization of black history.

During the 1930s and 1940s Woodson, disturbed by the low self-esteem of blacks and highly critical of black education and educators, redoubled his efforts to develop an enthusiasm for Negro history among the common black folk as well as the black professional class. In Woodson's view, black educators not only failed to transmit black cultural values through education in black history but also failed to teach blacks to earn a living. Thus, Woodson advocated more than education about the black past; he also exhibited a growing commitment to the principle of using history to effect social change. The miseries caused by the depression and the hopes raised by the New Deal inspired Woodson and other black intellectuals to reassess the relative merits of interracial cooperation and self-help as strategies for black uplift, and

1. Woodson, *A Century of Negro Migration* (Washington, D.C., 1918), 180–81.

to consider the possibility of a complete restructuring of society. Like many others in the mid-1930s, Woodson had become disillusioned with Roosevelt's programs. By the end of the decade he had joined a growing chorus of blacks of all political persuasions in denouncing the New Deal. Although his views on how best to resolve black economic and political problems would shift again, in his advocacy of black political independence, racial solidarity, and above all, the value of black history in promoting these other aims, Woodson remained steadfast.

When Woodson arrived in Washington in the fall of 1909 to teach in its segregated public school system and to work on his dissertation, his primary acquaintances were blacks in his Shaw neighborhood, colleagues in the public school system, and fellow congregants at Shiloh Baptist Church, where he usually worshipped on Sundays. Thus, community, school, and church provided Woodson with contacts among Washington's most politically active black citizens. These people and this environment would influence which political causes engaged his attention.[2]

Woodson's first venture into political activity in Washington may have been his participation in 1911 on the Committee of 200, formed to sponsor a memorial service for the late Justice John Marshall Harlan, the lone dissenter in the *Plessey* v. *Ferguson* case. Local black community activists, predominantly ministers and teachers, comprised the Committee of 200. The memorial service for Harlan was held at Washington's Metropolitan AME Church and consisted of tributes by John Cromwell, Archibald Grimké, Lafayette M. Hershaw, and Robert H. Terrell. Cadets from Armstrong and M Street High Schools served as ushers.[3]

A year following the memorial service for Harlan the same core group of activists founded the Washington branch of the NAACP. Woodson joined the branch and participated in one of its first protests, a letter-writing campaign to obtain equal funding for black schools.[4]

2. Ronald M. Johnson, "From Romantic Suburb to Racial Enclave: LeDroit Park, Washington, D.C., 1880–1920," *Phylon*, XLV (1984), 264–70; Steven Mintz, "A Historical Ethnography of Black Washington, D.C.," in *Records of the Columbia Historical Society of Washington, D.C.*, ed. Kirkpatrick J. Flack (Charlottesville, 1989), 235–53.

3. Program, Memorial Service for John Marshall Harlan, December 11, 1911, in Shelby Davidson Papers, Moorland-Spingarn Research Center, Howard University.

4. See NAACP Membership Brochure, 1912, in Archibald Grimké papers, Moorland-Spingarn Research Center, which indicated that the branch hoped to begin a scientific study of Negro schools.

Although blacks comprised 31 percent of all students in the Washington public school system, black schools received only 23 percent of the funds. The branch also launched a series of protests to obtain funds for the construction of a new academic high school for blacks. There were forty-eight black elementary schools but only three secondary schools: M Street, the academic high school; Armstrong Manual Training High School; and Cardoza, a business preparatory high school.[5]

Although school attendance was not compulsory after age fourteen, 70 percent of black students aged fourteen to eighteen attended school. More probably would have attended had there been room to accommodate them. Several hundred were turned away each year because of the lack of adequate facilities. Believing that every black student who wanted an education should be able to obtain it, Grimké, the NAACP branch president, led the fight to persuade Congress to appropriate funds for the construction of a new black academic high school. Woodson and other branch members wrote letters to congressmen and the Washington Board of Commissioners and finally won their fight when Congress appropriated $610,000 in 1915 for the construction of Paul Laurence Dunbar High School.[6]

When Woodrow Wilson became president and segregated employees in federal government offices, the Washington branch mobilized blacks and sympathetic white Washingtonians in protest. The Committee of Fifty, of which Woodson was a member, was organized to plan and raise funds for public demonstrations. In October, 1913, this group held a rally to protest racial discrimination. Other mass meetings were held over the next few months and a vigorous membership drive was implemented.[7]

5. Archibald H. Grimké to William B. Hartgrove, October 3, 1913, and enclosed Membership List, Grimké to Louis Brownlow, December 26, 1917, and Grimké to the Honorable Champ Clark, December 29, 1917, all in Archibald Grimké Papers. The best account of the activities of the Washington branch of the NAACP is found in Lewis N. Walker, Jr., "The Struggles and Attempts to Establish Branch Autonomy and Hegemony: A History of the District of Columbia Branch of the National Association for the Advancement of Colored People, 1912–1942" (Ph.D. dissertation, University of Delaware, 1979). Also see Brent Henry Thurber, "The Negro at the Nation's Capital, 1913–1921" (Ph.D. dissertation, Yale University, 1973).

6. See J. C. Wright, "History of Dunbar High School," November 23, 1916 (typescript in J. C. Wright Papers, Moorland-Spingarn Research Center); Mary Church Terrell, "A History of the Schools for Negroes in Washington," *Journal of Negro History*, II (1917), 252–66.

7. May Childs Nerney to Grimké, October 8, 1913, and Grimké to Roscoe C. Bruce,

The Committee of Fifty gathered information, conducted surveys, and kept close watch over the Wilson administration to provide the NAACP national office with data on current federal policies on blacks. When Grimké learned that Wilson was planning to impose segregation on Washington's public transportation system, he informed the national office and a letter-writing campaign to Congress was implemented. Because the District of Columbia had no legislative representatives, blacks and whites throughout the country responded, and Congress did not impose Jim Crow streetcars.[8]

Some local branch members, including Woodson, believed that their chapter should be more active. Woodson maintained that their chapter had degenerated into "an organization content with the mere reading of the minutes of the previous meeting and hearing the report of the 'standing' committee." To remedy this situation, in January, 1915, Woodson sent Grimké a long letter that included a detailed proposal for action. Part of the problem, in Woodson's view, was that there was no official headquarters or fixed central gathering place that black citizens could identify as the local branch of the NAACP. Monthly meetings rotated among churches, schools, the YMCA, and the YWCA. Woodson proposed that a permanent headquarters be secured and offered to pay the first month's rent. To recruit new members and solicit subscriptions to the *Crisis*, Woodson suggested that Washington's black neighborhoods be subdivided into twenty-five districts and that Grimké appoint one "deeply interested" branch member to be responsible for each district. "Through these agents," Woodson maintained, "meetings of importance, our urgent needs and the general welfare of the race will be kept before every Negro in the city." Woodson offered to take charge of one district and cautioned Grimké that "this work must not be given to persons seeking employment." If blacks hoped "to win in this life-and-death struggle," they could not "expect an immediate reward for what they do to promote their own cause."[9]

November 2, 1913, in Archibald Grimké Papers. The composition of the Committee of Fifty overlapped with the core group of founders of the NAACP.

8. Nerney to Grimké, December 14, 1914, and Grimké to Nerney, December 18, 1914, in Archibald Grimké Papers; Mignon Miller, "The American Negro Academy: An Intellectual Movement During the Era of Negro Disfranchisement, 1897–1924" (M.A. thesis, Howard University, 1966), 86–91.

9. Woodson to Executive Committee of NAACP Washington Branch, January 28, 1915, in Archibald Grimké Papers. Roscoe C. Bruce also proposed that the branch un-

Woodson had already mastered the sarcastic, biting style that would characterize his commentary on black leadership throughout his career. Not content merely to make a constructive suggestion for change, Woodson believed it was necessary to convince Grimké and the executive committee that they would fail unless they adopted his proposal, and he was forceful and direct in his criticism. The local branch, he argued, would be unable to "hold the attention of our people" if it only continued "bringing them to occasional meetings to hear men harping on our wretched condition while they do nothing adequate to the solution of our problems." It is also likely that Woodson alienated branch leaders and members by his thinly veiled references to their class bias, asserting that "spell-binding orators who have been prodigal [with] their advice should come down from the rostrum and work among the people who have not been reached."[10]

If Woodson had proposed only the acquisition of a permanent headquarters and the means for improved communication among black Washingtonians, it is likely that the branch's executive committee would have accepted his proposal. But he went beyond these suggestions to advocate that agents in the twenty-five districts report on and divert "patronage from business establishments which do not treat both races alike." Although Woodson did not explicitly argue that blacks should boycott white businesses and only patronize black businesses, this is what he envisioned. If the collective economic power of blacks could be harnessed, he believed small black businesses could thrive, and white establishments that continued to do business in the black community would be compelled to treat their black employees and customers with respect.[11]

Woodson's proposal apparently generated a great deal of discussion and controversy. While the branch may have wished to rent a permanent headquarters and certainly desired to increase its membership and bring its concerns to the attention of more blacks in the community, it

---

dertake economic organization similar to that suggested by Woodson. See Thurber, "The Negro at the Nation's Capital," 174. Thurber, however, is incorrect when he says that Woodson withdrew from the NAACP branch after they turned down his proposal; NAACP membership records indicate that Woodson retained his membership through the 1930s.

10. Woodson to Executive Committee of NAACP Washington Branch, January 28, 1915, in Archibald Grimké Papers.

11. Woodson to Executive Committee of NAACP Washington Branch, January 28, 1915, in Archibald Grimké Papers.

feared white retaliation if Woodson's suggestion to boycott white businesses was implemented. Some in the branch suggested that whites might sue. Woodson retorted that he was "not afraid of being sued by white business men" and, in fact, "welcome[d] such a law suit," for it "would do the cause much good." He charged that the branch emasculated his original proposal when it eliminated "the appeal to the colored people on behalf of Negro business." In Woodson's view, it was imperative to "get the support of all the colored business men of the city and use their stores as outposts in touch with a militant center." Woodson insisted that there was "no other way of getting the work of the National Association for the Advancement of Colored People permanently attached to the community." Declaring himself a "radical" ready to act if he could "find brave men" to help him, Woodson asserted that he was unwilling to "direct the work of merely increasing the membership and soliciting subscriptions to the Crisis."[12]

The branch did not take up Woodson's controversial proposal, but he retained his membership and continued to be active. During the 1930s he would renew his call for black economic self-help through the use of boycotts of white businesses. Once again, however, he would be disappointed by the conservatism and lack of unity among black Washingtonians.

Economic and racial tensions remained high during and immediately after World War I. They erupted violently during the "Red Summer" of 1919, when more than twenty-five race riots broke out. In July, Washington, D.C., experienced several consecutive days of rioting. A year earlier, Woodson had warned that violent outbreaks might ensue because of the massive northward migration of southern blacks. In his study of black migration published in 1918, Woodson argued that the black masses must be reckoned with. If sufficient numbers of blacks formed into a "rising laboring class," they could "strike for better wages" and use their "votes to defeat for reelection those officers who wink at mob violence or treat Negroes as persons beyond the pale of the law." Yet, if "this migration falls short of establishing . . . Negro colonies large enough to wield economic and political power," Woodson cautioned, "their state in the end will not be any better than those of the Negroes already there." Just as he had chided Washington's black elite for its failure to bring sufficient numbers of the masses into its

12. Woodson to Grimké, March 18, 1915, in Archibald Grimké Papers.

NAACP program in 1915, he told his black bourgeois readers that "to these large numbers alone . . . we must look for an agent to counteract the development of race feeling into riots."[13]

Although the Wilson administration did not cause the July riot, it bore some measure of responsibility for its outbreak. The city's police force was under the jurisdiction of the commissioners of the District of Columbia, who were appointed by the president. White Washingtonians argued that the police were losing control over what they perceived to be a growing black crime wave. Yet most students of the Washington riot place the blame for its occurrence on the city's white newspapers, particularly the Washington *Post*.[14] Throughout June and early July the white press published numerous articles that exaggerated and sensationalized incidents of blacks' assaults against whites.

Woodson was caught smack in the middle of the riot. He was returning home to his Shaw rooming house late one Sunday night when he "unexpectedly walked into a mob near the corner of Pennsylvania Avenue and Eighth Street." Although Woodson had read about the "race riots in the southwest" in the Washington *Post* that morning and had avoided that area of the city, he "did not think for a moment that a mob had control of the whole section of the city." He observed hundreds of military men running up Pennsylvania Avenue in pursuit of "a Negro yelling for mercy." Fearing for his life, Woodson "took refuge in the deep entrance of a store." After the mob passed him by, Woodson breathed a sigh of relief and started walking towards Eighth Street. But "instead of getting away from mob violence," Woodson soon found himself "facing the most harrowing spectacle" he had ever witnessed. The mob "had caught a Negro and deliberately held him up as one would a beef for slaughter, and when they had conveniently adjusted him for lynching they shot him." Woodson wanted to run hurriedly away, but to avoid attracting attention, he walked quickly to Ninth and M streets, where he "finally boarded a car and came home."[15]

13. Woodson, *A Century of Negro Migration*, 180–81. On the riots, see Arthur I. Waskow, *From Race Riot to Sit-In: 1919 and the 1960s* (Garden City, N.Y., 1966), 21–37, 60–104; Constance McLaughlin Green, *The Secret City: A History of Race Relations in the Nation's Capital* (Princeton, 1967), 190–95; Mary White Ovington, *The Walls Came Tumbling Down* (New York, 1947), 65–66.

14. Waskow, *From Race Riot to Sit-In*, 21–25; Lloyd M. Abernathy, "The Washington Riot of July, 1919," *Maryland Historical Magazine*, LVIII (December, 1963), 309–29; Green, *The Secret City*, 190–95; Roberta Cardwell, "The Washington Riot of 1919" (M.A. thesis, Howard University, 1971). Also see Washington *Post*, July 19, 1919, p. 2.

15. Woodson, Affidavit Concerning Events of July 20, 1919, n.d., in Emmett J. Scott

The riot continued for several more days before it was quelled. The NAACP conducted an investigation and placed major responsibility on the Washington *Post*. Woodson prepared an affidavit recounting his experience in the riot, probably at the direction of the NAACP. He also provided an account to the Baltimore *Afro-American*.[16]

Perhaps because of Woodson's eyewitness account of the Washington riot, as well as his research and writing skills (particularly as exhibited in his work on the history of black migration), he was asked to lend his expertise to the Chicago Commission on Race Relations. The commission was to write a report on the Chicago riot, which was longer and even bloodier than the outbreak in Washington. Headed by Francis W. Shepardson, the state director of registration and education and a professor in the history department at the University of Chicago when Woodson studied there, the commission was to investigate the causes of the riot and propose a plan to improve interracial relations in Chicago and elsewhere. Four months before the riot, Shepardson had corresponded with Woodson seeking information on the *Journal* and assistance in constructing a bibliography of contemporary sociological studies on blacks. It is likely that Woodson was among the scholars hired by Shepardson and University of Chicago professor Robert Park to evaluate the data that was collected by staff researchers in 1920. Park, who was then serving as the president of the association, probably recommended Woodson, and Shepardson concurred.[17]

Park served as a consultant to the commission throughout the inves-

---

Papers, Soper Library, Morgan State University, Baltimore. Although my search of Scott's papers failed to turn up a copy of this affidavit, Professor Maceo C. Dailey, Jr., of Spelman College, who is writing a biography of Scott, kindly provided me with a copy from his own photocopied files of Scott's papers. Also see David L. Lewis, *When Harlem Was in Vogue* (New York, 1981), 19, 23.

16. Woodson, Affidavit Concerning Events of July 20, 1919, in Scott Papers; "Soldiers Try to Terrorize Colored Folk," Baltimore *Afro-American*, July 28, 1919, pp. 1, 4; Waskow, *From Race Riot to Sit-In*, 21–35; James Weldon Johnson, "The Riots: An NAACP Investigation," *Crisis*, XVIII (September, 1919), 243.

17. William M. Tuttle, *Race Riot: Chicago in the Summer of 1919* (New York, 1972), 252–57; Waskow, *From Race Riot to Sit-In*, 60–104; Chicago Commission on Race Relations, *The Negro in Chicago: A Study of Race Relations and a Riot in 1919* (New York, 1968), xv–xxiii; Francis W. Shepardson to Woodson, April 28, 1919, Woodson to Shepardson, May 1, 1919, Shepardson to Woodson, May 5, 1919, all in Archives Miscellaneous, Chicago Commission on Race Relations, 1919–1920, Illinois State Archives, Springfield. Woodson gave the final report of the commission a positive review, although it was unsigned, in *Journal of Negro History*, VIII (1923), 112–14.

tigation, and three of the seven scholars hired to draft sections of the final report were his former students. Like Woodson, Park had predicted that violence would erupt in northern cities after the influx of rural southern black migrants. Unlike Woodson, however, Park did not consider the role of southern white migrants in his estimation of the potential for interracial clashes. Woodson later criticized the commission for its failure to address the impact of southern white migration on the riot.[18]

Woodson canvassed southern whites as well as blacks in January, 1921, in an effort to make "for the Chicago Race Commission a digest of the various plans and suggestions for bringing about amicable relations between the whites and blacks and solving the race problem." The evidence suggests that Woodson sought opinions from "persons who have written or spoken" on race relations and probably confined himself to solicitations from black and white educators, intellectuals, and race leaders.[19]

If the replies of Grimké and Edwin A. Alderman, president of the University of Virginia, were characteristic of others that Woodson received, he may have had a great deal of difficulty reconciling the racial divergence of opinion regarding appropriate solutions to the race problem. Whereas Grimké recommended the abolition of segregation and absolute equality between the races in all areas of public life, Alderman took the opposite view.[20] "The very policy of separateness, to which the South is committed," he argued, "carries with it, or ought to carry with it, a habit of mind towards a backward race . . . causing thinking people to discriminate between the good individual negro and the negro considered as a mere perplexing problem in sociology." With the paternal-

18. Tuttle, *Race Riot*, 252–57; Waskow, *From Race Riot to Sit-In*, 80–81; Chicago Commission, *The Negro in Chicago*, 652–55; Woodson, Review of Chicago Commission's *The Negro in Chicago*, in *Journal of Negro History*, VIII (1923), 112–14, and *A Century of Negro Migration*, 180–81.

19. Woodson to Archibald Grimké, January 19, 1921, in Archibald Grimké Papers; Woodson to James Weldon Johnson, January 19, 1921, and Woodson to William Pickens, January 19, 1921, in NAACP Records, Group I, Series C, Box 80, Manuscript Division, Library of Congress; Woodson to Oswald Garrison Villard, January 19, 1921, in Oswald Garrison Villard Papers, Houghton Library, Harvard University; Woodson to Edwin A. Alderman, January 19, 1921, in President's Office Papers, University Archives, Alderman Library, University of Virginia. Woodson wrote the same letter to everyone; the replies of Villard, Pickens, and Johnson have not been located.

20. Grimké drafted a reply on the back of Woodson's letter, Woodson to Grimké, January 19, 1921, in Archibald Grimké Papers.

ism that was typical of most southern white educators at that time, Alderman asserted that while segregation should remain, whites needed to assume greater responsibility for black education. He acknowledged that "the negro is a mighty industrial asset and must be trained to that end," and added that the Negro was "also a human asset for good or ill, and must receive the training which will equip him for usefulness and loyalty to American ideals."[21]

Alderman's and Grimké's responses to Woodson's letter foreshadowed the coming racial split among the board members of the Chicago Commission over what was acceptable in the final report on the riot. Most contemporary observers asserted that the report had little effect on racial practices in Chicago or on race relations in other parts of the country. Woodson, nevertheless, refused to be discouraged. He remained active and continued his participation in many other enterprises that purported to improve race relations.[22]

To improve race relations by demanding economic and political equality for blacks was the primary reason for the establishment of the Friends of Negro Freedom (FNF) in 1920. Organized by Chandler Owen and A. Philip Randolph, editors of the *Messenger*, the FNF included Woodson among its charter members. Long an admirer of Randolph, Woodson, who had heard Randolph address the December, 1919, meeting of the American Negro Academy on "The New Radicalism and the Negro," termed him a "prophet."[23] Shortly after receiving Owen and Randolph's manifesto, Woodson responded to their call for a new organization, and agreed to attend the convention.

According to Owen and Randolph, the "Negro Problem" was basically one of economics rather than race, and so they devoted most of their attention to economic issues. Four separate committees on labor, tenants' rights, boycotts, and cooperative buying were created. The proposal that Woodson had made to the Washington branch of the

21. Alderman to Woodson, February 3, 1921, in President's Office Papers.
22. Waskow, *From Race Riot to Sit-In*, 84–104; Tuttle, *Race Riot*, 252–57; W. E. B. Du Bois, "Chicago," *Crisis*, XXI (January, 1921), 102; Woodson, Review of Chicago Commission's *The Negro in Chicago*, 112–14.
23. A. Philip Randolph, Chandler Owen, George Frazier Miller, Victor K. Daly, and William N. Colson to Grimké, March 4, 1920, and enclosure "The Call for a New Organization," in Archibald Grimké Papers. In "The Negro and the New Radicalism," Randolph called on blacks to unite and to remain independent of the Democratic and Republican parties. Woodson praised the speech in "A. Philip Randolph, Twentieth Century Prophet," Washington *Bee*, January 10, 1920, p. 6.

NAACP in 1915 was very similar to the economic program espoused by the FNF. Unlike Woodson, however, the FNF did not advocate that white businessmen replace white clerks with black clerks. Nor did the FNF argue that blacks should only patronize black businesses. Rather, Owen and Randolph argued that "the emphasis must be placed on the Negro business man's efficiency, rather than on the prospective Negro patron's race pride." Blacks, they contended, "will buy from a white man who sells cheaply in preference to a Negro dealer who sells similar goods higher, and justly so." As proof of their contention, they cited the failure of Garvey's Harlem-based laundries: appeals to race pride failed to convince blacks to switch their allegiance from white laundries whose prices were lower.[24]

When Owen and Randolph began to focus most of their energies on attacking Garvey rather than on promoting the FNF's economic program, the FNF lost Woodson's support, as well as that of many other black activists. They were unable to contain the tensions between a class-based and a race-based program and were increasingly jealous of Garvey's enormous success in mobilizing grass-roots support in the black community. Owen and Randolph sent out twenty-five letters on September 20 and 21, 1920, soliciting opinions about Garvey's movement. They received fourteen replies and must have been disappointed by Woodson's unwillingness to commit himself to their campaign to oust Garvey and his lack of concern about Garvey's growing influence over the black masses. Although Woodson cautiously replied that he had "given such little attention to the work of Marcus Garvey" that he could not "make an estimate of his career," he actually admired Garvey and supported him, albeit indirectly at first.[25]

Garvey, like Woodson, used history to bolster racial pride among his

24. "Friends of Negro Freedom," *Messenger*, II (April–May, 1920), 5, and IV (August, 1922), 464–66. Also see Theodore Kornweibel, Jr., *No Crystal Stair: Black Life and the Messenger 1917–1928* (Westport, Conn., 1975), 203–61; Judith Stein, *The World of Marcus Garvey: Race and Class in Modern Society* (Baton Rouge, 1986), 43–48, 57–60, 105.

25. Stein, *The World of Marcus Garvey*, 48–50, 161–70, 186–89, 202–206; Tony Martin, *Race First: The Ideological and Organizational Struggles of Marcus Garvey and the Universal Negro Improvement Association* (Westport, Conn., 1976), 319–20, and "Carter Woodson and Marcus Garvey," *Negro History Bulletin*, XL (1977), 774–77; Kornweibel, *No Crystal Stair*, 135–70; "A Symposium on Garvey," *Messenger*, IV (December, 1922), 550–52; W. E. B. Du Bois, "Marcus Garvey," *Crisis*, XXI (December, 1920), 58–60, (January, 1921), 112–15. Also see "Garvey Denounced at Negro Meeting," *New York Times*, August 7, 1922, reprinted in Robert A. Hill, ed., *The Marcus Garvey and Universal Negro Improvement Association Papers* (7 vols.; Berkeley, 1983–1990), IV, 816–17.

followers, and Woodson's writings and the programs of the Association for the Study of Negro Life and History were frequently mentioned in Garvey's newspaper the *Negro World* and in his Harlem-based paper, the *Daily Negro Times*. Woodson also maintained ties with such Garveyites as John Edward Bruce and E. Ethelred Brown (who published an article on Jamaica in the *Journal*). In 1923, hoping to tap into Garvey's enormous popularity with the black masses, Woodson offered to write articles and book reviews for the *Negro World*, which had the largest domestic and international circulation among black newspapers.[26] Later, in 1930, Woodson began writing weekly columns for the *Negro World*. It was also in the 1930s that Woodson was compared with Garvey as he promoted in his book *The Mis-Education of the Negro* what Alain Locke termed "black zionism."[27]

When Garvey died in 1940, Woodson published an obituary in the *Journal* praising him and asserting that he had "attracted a larger following than any Negro who has been developed in modern times." Acknowledging Garvey's tremendous influence over African Americans, Woodson stated that his impact on Africa deserved even greater recognition. He contended that some day Garvey would be credited "as a deliverer of the black people from the 'strangle-hold' of the European imperialists." Woodson also blamed "European imperialists" for Garvey's ouster from the United States, maintaining that "complaints were sent to the United States to the effect that his operations were hostile efforts against the economic imperialists with whom the United States was supposed to be on friendly terms." According to Woodson, local pressure groups like the NAACP and the FNF had little influence on the U.S. government.[28]

When the campaign to deport Garvey was in full swing, the NAACP's popularity waned dramatically among the black masses. Almost half of the new branches established in 1919 and 1920 were inoperative by 1923. And among older established chapters, there was a

26. T. Thomas Fortune to Woodson, December 21, 1923, (in response to Woodson to Garvey, December 15, 1923, which has not been located) in Carter G. Woodson Collection, MS Div., LC. Woodson sent a review of Gertrude Sanborn, *Veiled Aristocrats* (Washington, D.C., 1923), which was published in the *Negro World* on January 5, 1924. A copy of that issue of the *Negro World* is no longer extant.

27. Alain Locke, Review of Woodson's *The Mis-Education of the Negro*, in *Survey*, LXIX (October, 1933), 363–64.

28. Woodson, Obituary of Marcus Garvey, *Journal of Negro History*, XXV (1940), 592.

serious decline in membership. For example, in 1921 the Washington branch was the largest in the country with more than 6,500 members, but by 1924 its membership had dropped below 2,000.[29] Still, that branch remained the most active of all NAACP branches, and its members the most successful fund raisers. In addition to participating in a campaign against lynching, the Washington branch continued its more conservative program of public protests against segregation, a measure endorsed by the national office.[30]

Although Woodson may have been disappointed by the NAACP's inattention to the economic concerns of the masses, he remained active in the Washington branch throughout the 1920s. He took special interest in the NAACP's campaign against lynching and joined in a number of activities designed to lobby state and national legislatures to pass laws against lynching. During the period when he taught at West Virginia Collegiate Institute, Woodson lobbied West Virginia state legislators to pass a state antilynching law. He befriended black legislator Henry S. Capehart and asked James Weldon Johnson and Walter White, NAACP secretary and assistant secretary respectively, to send him the NAACP reports on lynching so that Capehart could make a persuasive case before the West Virginia state legislature. When Woodson returned to Washington in June, 1922, he participated in the Washington branch's silent parade against lynching, which was held on Flag Day. In November, 1922, Woodson patronized and helped raise funds for a testimonial for Robert T. Kerlin at John Wesley AMEZ (African Methodist Episcopal Zion) Church, sponsored by the Washington branch. Kerlin, a white professor of English at Virginia Military Institute, spoke out against lynching and was fired from his position. Woodson's Associated Publishers later published one of Kerlin's books.[31]

29. The *Crisis*, XVII (April, 1919), 284, lists the Washington branch membership as of March 1, 1919, as 6,926. Yet the actual membership records list a different and much lower figure of 1,747 members. For 1920–1927 the Washington, D.C., membership figures were: 1920, 3,368; 1921, 6,621; 1922, 4,921; 1923, 2,313; 1924, 1,791; 1925, 2,402; 1926, 2,378; 1927, 2,480. See "Membership of the Washington Branch of the NAACP" (Report), n.d., in NAACP Records, Group I, Series G, Box 36.

30. On the NAACP's campaign against lynching, see Robert L. Zangrando, *The NAACP Crusade Against Lynching, 1909–1950* (Philadelphia, 1980).

31. Report from Branch Bulletin, March 15, 1921, and Resolution of Protest, May 30, 1922, in NAACP records, Group I, Series G, Box 34; Woodson to James Weldon Johnson, January 25, 1921, Woodson to Walter White, January 25, 1921, White to Woodson, January 27, 1921, all in NAACP Records, Group I, Series C, Box 242; Com-

Woodson also was active in a protest orchestrated by the national office of the NAACP early in 1923 against Harvard University's imposition of segregated dormitory facilities. The Washington branch probably had more black Harvard alumni, including Woodson, among its members than any other NAACP branch, and he eagerly participated in the protest. Harvard president A. Lawrence Lowell implemented segregation in the student dormitories during the fall of 1921 after receiving numerous complaints from southern white students about the black presence in the facilities.[32]

James Weldon Johnson wrote to Lowell in January, 1923, and issued a press release to NAACP members. He called on all Harvard alumni to write letters and send telegrams of protest, which were forwarded to Lowell. In response, Johnson received communications from Raymond Pace Alexander, Du Bois, Grimké, Richard T. Greener, Alexander Jackson, William H. Lewis, Robert Terrell, and Woodson. Alexander also wrote an article for *Opportunity*, and Woodson later wrote a second letter to the Associated Harvard Clubs.[33]

In 1914, Woodson had been invited to join the Harvard Club of Washington. He filled out a membership application, but when the club president visited him and discovered he was black, the invitation was withdrawn. Thus, Woodson was outraged when in the spring of 1923 the Associated Harvard Clubs solicited money from him to endow five professorships at Berea College in memory of Nathaniel S. Shaler, who had held positions at both Berea and Harvard. Especially critical of Harvard, "which under the leadership of its mediaeval reactionary Abbott Lawrence Lowell, has recently shown tendencies to restrict its educational efforts to a particular race," Woodson replied that although he was an alumnus of both Berea College and Harvard University, he

---

mittee of 100, Press Release, June 14, 1922, in NAACP Records, Group I, Series G, Box 34; Program, Testimonial for Robert T. Kerlin, November 20, 1922, in District of Columbia NAACP records, Moorland-Spingarn Research Center.

32. William Pickens, "The Decline of Harvard University," n.d. (Typescript), and James Weldon Johnson, Press Release, January 11, 1923, in NAACP Records, Group I, Series C, Box 270.

33. James Weldon Johnson, Press Release, January 11, 1923, and "Harvard's Most Distinguished Colored Graduates Protest Exclusion of Colored Student from Freshman Dormitory," January 13, 1923 (Typescript), in NAACP Records, Group I, Series C, Box 270; Raymond Pace Alexander, "Voices from Harvard's Own Negroes," *Opportunity*, I (March, 1923), 29–31; Woodson to the Associated Harvard Clubs, April 13, 1923, in College Archives, Berea College, Berea, Ky.

would not support or in any way endorse the segregation practiced by these institutions. Woodson added that "if these institutions . . . are to teach that one race . . . is ordained of God to segregate and exploit the other," both should be closed. "Let them pass into history," Woodson argued, "as a memory of a noble effort which finds no exemplification of the principles of John Harvard and John G. Fee."[34] Yet neither Woodson's protests nor those of other black alumni had any effect on Lowell's policy of segregation.

Later, in the 1930s, Woodson made the same suggestion to black administrators—that their institutions should be closed. He argued that black educational institutions were "mis-educating" black students, failing not only to teach them about their racial and cultural heritage, but also how to make a living. Reiterating the charges he had made since the 1910s, Woodson became increasingly critical of the class bias of the black bourgeoisie during the depression decade of the 1930s. The economic plight of southern blacks, as well as the plight of those who migrated to northern urban ghettos, continued to deteriorate because, he believed, the black bourgeoisie failed to address migrants' concerns. Woodson also remained distrustful of traditional party politics, viewing with dismay the massive shift of blacks from Republican to Democratic affiliation. Once again, he argued that the race should not blindly support any particular political party but should remain independent, voting for the individual candidate who was most committed to racial and economic equality.[35]

During the 1930s, although Woodson remained active in the NAACP and the National Urban League, he was radicalized, supporting the New Negro Alliance and its "Don't Buy Where you Can't Work" campaign and the leftist coalition that founded the National Negro Congress in 1935. He also more vigorously combined scholarly and political activity and brought his views to the masses of black Americans through columns in the black press. In doing so, he continued to espouse ideas he had expressed twenty years earlier.[36]

34. Woodson to the Associated Harvard Clubs, April 13, 1923, in Berea College Archives; W. E. B. Du Bois, "Along the Color Line," *Crisis*, IX (February, 1915), 168; Thurber, "The Negro at the Nation's Capital," 178–79.

35. See, for example, Woodson, "Balance of Power is Sole Political Strength of Group," Baltimore *Afro-American*, September 10, 1932, p. 8.

36. On the organization of the Washington, D.C., chapter of the National Urban League, see Harriet Curtis Hall to Archibald Grimké, April 20, 1925, in Archibald Grimké Papers. A Washington, D.C., branch actually began in the 1940s.

Woodson began publishing weekly columns in the black press, discussing racial problems and offering solutions. In these columns he frequently invoked historical examples to illustrate contemporary themes, bringing to a larger audience the same views he had advanced earlier in books written for a scholarly audience. Although historical themes were mingled with prescriptions to relieve current economic ills, the columns served primarily an educative, not a political, purpose, and Woodson always considered himself an educator rather than a race leader or a politician.

Having taught in black public schools and black colleges from 1909 to 1922, Woodson was convinced that education in black history at all levels of the curriculum was essential to the psychological health of black people. While he recognized that white institutions also denied blacks an education that acknowledged their history and culture, Woodson was especially critical of colleagues trained in black colleges. Although 30 percent of the students in Washington's public schools were black, only a few teachers integrated black history into their American history courses. The situation was similar in educational institutions across the country, and Woodson hoped to provide instruction in black history to a mass audience through the newspaper columns he published in the black press. He believed that history "would dramatize the life of the race and thus inspire it to develop from within a radicalism of its own." "Instead of going to others to find something to admire," he urged, "begin to appreciate yourselves."[37]

Woodson promoted black cultural nationalism in his columns. "The reason we are in the position we are in today," he maintained in one column, "is because we have not studied our race."[38] Characteristically, he linked the political and economic plight of blacks to lack of education in black history. Although many of Woodson's columns contained historical themes, he was concerned with the failure of black education in all of its aspects.

Like many reformers who came of age during the Progressive Era, Woodson contended that improved education was the solution to most problems that plagued contemporary society, including the race problem. He argued that racial prejudice was taught, and that racial attitudes were formed by adolescence and thereafter were difficult to change.

37. Woodson, "What the Negro Has to Dramatize" (Press Release), February 17, 1932, in Claude H. Barnett Papers, Chicago Historical Society.
38. Woodson, "Woodson Talks at Florida A. and M.," Baltimore *Afro-American*, June 11, 1932, p. 10.

Thus, Woodson directed his educational efforts toward whites as well as blacks. He considered improved education for blacks to be even more important than the NAACP's campaign against lynching, and asserted, half seriously, that blacks were lynched because no one respected them. Pamphlets on lynching would not stop the crime, he maintained, and the NAACP was treating only the symptoms of a social disease, not the disease itself. Woodson fervently believed that the program of education that he espoused would improve race relations by teaching blacks to think for themselves. "Real education," he contended, "means to inspire people to live more abundantly, to learn to begin life as they find it and make it better."[39]

Although he had studied the history of black education for more than twenty years, Woodson did not make critical public statements about contemporary black education until 1931. During the spring and summer of that year, he gave a series of speeches on the topic, among them, the commencement speech at Fisk University. He reported in the October issue of the *Journal* that after "looking over the recent college catalogues of the leading Negro colleges," he was convinced that these institutions did not "teach Negroes who they are, what they have done, and what they have to do."[40] Two months earlier he had published an article, "The Mis-Education of the Negro," in the *Crisis'* August issue, which annually was devoted to black education. The thesis of this and subsequent articles in the black press was that black institutions of higher education were educating the black bourgeoisie for roles they would be unable to assume in white society. "The so-called education of Negro college graduates," Woodson said, "leads them to throw away opportunities which they have and go in quest of those which they do not find."[41]

Woodson's article, which appeared at the same time that the Na-

39. Woodson, *The Mis-Education of the Negro* (Washington, D.C., 1933), 29. Also see Woodson, "Woodson Speaks," Washington *Tribune*, December 17, 1935, p. 4; Robert L. Zangrando, *The NAACP Crusade Against Lynching.*

40. Woodson, "The Director Speaks," *Journal of Negro History*, XVI (1931), 344–48. Also see Woodson, "The Negro Graduates" (Press Release), June 24, 1931, in Barnett Papers; Woodson, "Negro Trail Blazers a Necessity," New York *Age*, July 11, 1931, p. 9; Woodson, "Only the Trail Blazer Succeeds in Business," Baltimore *Afro-American*, July 18, 1931, p. 6; Woodson, "Negroes Look in Vain for Help from Without," New York *Age*, July 25, 1931, p. 9.

41. Woodson, "The Mis-Education of the Negro," *Crisis*, XXXVIII (August, 1931), 266–67. Also see Du Bois to Woodson, April 6, 1931, in W. E. B. Du Bois Papers, University of Massachusetts.

tional Association of Teachers in Colored Schools was meeting in Washington, D.C., generated considerable controversy. Howard professor Kelly Miller blasted it, contending that Woodson was too negative in his assessment and failed to give blacks credit for the educational strides they had made since 1865. Morehouse College president John Hope, who at that time was president of the association, also argued that Woodson was too harsh in his characterization of black education. But rather than lightening his negative tone, Woodson became even more critical, saying that he was merely trying "to go to the very seat of the trouble" to demonstrate that blacks "have missed the mark and have strayed away from truth . . . When you give Negroes the facts in their case," he asserted, "they call for flattery and misinformation." [42]

In newspaper articles and the *Mis-Education of the Negro*, published in 1933, Woodson advanced a view of education that was similar to those of both Booker T. Washington and Du Bois. Although he never commented directly on Du Bois' ideas about education, in a speech given at the dedication of Washington's restored birthplace, Woodson described Washington as a brilliant educator who had "revolutionized" black education. [43] While acknowledging the need for a "talented tenth," Woodson argued that members of the black bourgeoisie were unable to provide leadership for the race because they had become estranged from the masses; they had been "emasculated" by their education and were unfit to assume leadership roles. "The majority of this class," he contended, "go through life denouncing white people because they are trying to run away from blacks and decrying the blacks because they are not white." [44]

According to Woodson, three quarters of black colleges should have been closed. Part of the problem was that blacks allowed whites to con-

---

42. Philadelphia *Tribune*, August 8, 1931, Clipping in Kelly Miller Papers, Moorland-Spingarn Research Center; Woodson, "Carter Woodson to Publish Book of Opinion," Chicago *Defender*, January 14, 1933, p. 8; Baltimore *Afro-American*, November 14, 1931, p. 13; Woodson, "Woodson as an Iconoclast," New York *Age*, November 14, 1931, p. 9.

43. New York *Age*, July 2, 1932, p. 1. Most reviews of *The Mis-Education of the Negro* were positive, and Woodson published excerpts of reviews from the white press in the *Journal*. See "Some Notices of *The Mis-Education of the Negro*," *Journal of Negro History*, XVIII (1933), 222–24; "Additional Notices of *The Mis-Education of the Negro*," *Journal of Negro History*, XVIII (1933), 341–50.

44. Woodson, "Woodson Thinks Men of 100 Years Ago Were More Outspoken Against Wrongs," Baltimore *Afro-American*, January 23, 1932, p. 17; Woodson, *The Mis-Education of the Negro*, xxiv. Langston Hughes had a similar impression of Washington's black bourgeoisie. See Hughes, *The Big Sea* (New York, 1940), 206–207.

trol black colleges. Many of the "white presidents of these institutions [were] less scholarly than Negroes who [had] to serve under them." Black students, unfortunately, had more respect for white administrators and teachers, and Woodson cited an informal poll that Langston Hughes had conducted among Lincoln University students to ascertain "whether they desired a Negro to serve as a member of that faculty." Shocked by the students' overwhelming negative response, Woodson contended that if "in seventy-six years Lincoln has not been able to produce a graduate that is qualified to serve as a professor there, the only logical thing to do now is to close its doors."[45]

Woodson went so far as to accuse black administrators of colluding with whites to keep "out of the schools teachers who may be bold enough to teach the truth as it is." The system of education in the United States, he asserted, was "so popular that European nations of foresight [were] sending some of their brightest minds to the United States to observe the Negro in 'inaction' to learn how to deal likewise with Negroes in their colonies." Even after the publication of *The Mis-Education of the Negro*, Woodson continued to rail against the black educational establishment. In 1938, discouraged by the lack of progress, he maintained that "the talented tenth of the race is being used to keep the race in its place."[46]

Graduates of black colleges "mis-educated" black children, lacked a sense of direction and purpose, and had few original ideas. "Men in the professional fields are supposed not merely to use their wits to make money. They should," Woodson maintained, contribute "to the theory and practice of their professions . . . and produce something new to advance the professions in which they serve." Woodson also condemned the black bourgeoisie for their class bias. "With respect to developing the masses . . . the Negro race has lost ground in recent years." Contemporary black professionals were educated merely to "memorize certain facts to pass examinations for jobs. After they obtain these positions," Woodson asserted, "they pay little attention to humanity." Although the "colored man in the North turns up his nose at the crude migrant from the South," Woodson noted, the southern black migrant

45. Woodson, "Woodson Says White College Heads Close Their Homes to Alumni and Students," Baltimore *Afro-American*, March 7, 1931, p. 3; "Thomas Jesse Jones Accused of Writing Underhanded Letters Against Association," Baltimore *Afro-American*, February 7, 1931, p. 3.

46. Woodson, *The Mis-Education of the Negro*, 87, 193, and "The Call for the Negro as a Pioneer," New York *Age*, February 12, 1938, p. 6.

brought to the North "more thrift and actual progress than the Northern colored man ever dreamed of."[47]

Educational curriculum needed to be made relevant to the people being taught. Like Washington, Woodson advocated greater attention to the improvement of basic skills and additional emphasis on vocational education. He further proposed "awakening the masses through adult education." Blacks spent more money on liquor and cigarettes than they did on books, and the situation was worsening rather than improving. Woodson held that African Americans needed to develop a "substantial middle class, a producing class and a type of education that will make a man think and do."[48]

Woodson maintained that the black masses needed to be taught new vocational skills suitable for urban industrial living. "The education of the masses," he concluded, "has not enabled them to advance very far in making a living." Black secondary schools were "teaching Negroes what they can never apply in life or what is no longer profitable because of the revolution in industry."[49] Woodson lambasted the black bourgeoisie, arguing that it had failed to assume responsibility for educating the masses. "Having no thinking class," he asserted, "the Negroes of this country have not mastered the fundamentals of life in producing and providing opportunities for artisans, mechanics, manufactures, and merchants who must lay the foundation for a culture marked by great achievements in politics, history, literature, philosophy, and art."[50]

47. "Woodson as an Iconoclast," 6; Woodson, *The Mis-Education of the Negro*, 55, and "Woodson Thinks Men of 100 Years Ago Were More Outspoken Against Wrongs," 17.

48. Woodson, *The Mis-Education of the Negro*, 97, and "Woodson Talks at Florida A. and M.," 10.

49. Woodson, "Little Use to Learn Tailoring, Shoe-Making in Schools Now," Baltimore *Afro-American*, May 7, 1932, p. 17. Also see Woodson, "Thomas Jesse Jones Accused of Writing Underhanded Letters Against Association," 3, and "Woodson Says White College Heads Close Their Homes," 3; Woodson, "The Mis-Education of the Negro in Economics," New York *Age*, June 6, 1931, p. 4; Woodson, "High School Orators Think That Becoming Great is Easy Task," Baltimore *Afro-American*, July 11, 1931, p. 6; Woodson, "Carter Woodson Sees Youth Breaking Away from Traditions," Baltimore *Afro-American*, March 19, 1932, p. 22; Woodson, "Harvard, Columbia, Princeton Education Has Little Use for Our Students," Baltimore *Afro-American*, April 23, 1932, p. 16; Woodson, "Professor Bone Head Doesn't Teach Negro History in Ham Fat University," Baltimore *Afro-American*, April 30, 1932, p. 16; Woodson, "Nannie Burroughs' School Fills a Real Need," Baltimore *Afro-American*, May 19, 1932, p. 17; Woodson, "Harpers Ferry President Should Be Forced to Leave Storer," Baltimore *Afro-American*, June 11, 1932, p. 9.

50. Woodson, "Carter Woodson Says Close up 75 Per-cent of Negro Colleges,"

Like those members of the black bourgeoisie he criticized, Woodson was ambivalent—if not downright prudish—about some aspects of the culture of the black masses, particularly popular music and ecstatic religion. In a 1931 column he expressed disgust at the masses "howling, crying, singing, dancing, and groveling on the floor in answer to the emotional appeal of an insane or depraved preacher." He also disliked jazz, believing that it had no roots in African music and that it was too erotic; for the sake of "social progress," he hoped that it would be "stamp[ed] . . . out as an evil." [51]

Although he did not relinquish his disdain for jazz, by the late 1930s Woodson had become more tolerant of black working-class culture. To avoid "gruesome misrepresentations of the Negro" while developing art, music, and literature that faithfully captured black life, he said, black artists must steep themselves in the culture of the black masses. "One must be of a people," Woodson exhorted, "before he can become its artist." [52]

Woodson reasoned that because blacks were miseducated, they were particularly victimized by the depression. In 1930 he had helped found

Washington *Tribune*, July 27, 1935, pp. 1, 3. Also see Woodson, "Thomas Jesse Jones Accused of Writing Underhanded Letters Against Association," Woodson, "Selection of Textbooks Which Treat Negro Fairly is Made New Objective," Pittsburgh *Courier*, November 18, 1933, p. 2; Woodson to Arthur A. Schomburg, December 9, 1933, in Arthur Schomburg Papers, Schomburg Center for Research in Black Culture, New York Public Library; Thomas L. Dabney, "The Study of the Negro," *Journal of Negro History*, XIX (1934), 266–307; Woodson, "Woodson Speaks," 4, and "Woodson Raps Move to Force Teachers' Oaths of Loyalty to Government," Norfolk *Journal and Guide*, March 7, 1936, p. 2; Baltimore *Afro-American*, January 8, 1938, p. 2; James D. Anderson, "Secondary School Textbooks and the Treatment of Black History," in *The State of Afro-American History: Past, Present, and Future*, ed. Darlene Clark Hine (Baton Rouge, 1986), 253–74.

51. Woodson, "Scarlett Lady, Bootlegger Live by Dr. Woodson, but Are Not His Neighbors," Baltimore *Afro-American*, November 21, 1931, p. 7, and "Dr. Woodson Tells Why Thoughtless People Laugh at the Wrong Places in Theatres," Baltimore *Afro-American*, February 17, 1932, p. 17, also see Woodson, "Sending the Wrong Negro to Europe," New York *Age*, October 17, 1933, pp. 4–5; Woodson, "Advertizing the Race Abroad," New York *Age*, October 21, 1933, pp. 4–5; Woodson, "The Romance of the Creole," Chicago *Defender*, March 24, 1934, p. 12; Woodson, "The Negro Must Not Despise His Glorious Past," New York *Age*, December 18, 1937, p. 2; Baltimore *Afro-American*, January 8, 1938, p. 2; Woodson, "Monuments of the Race," New York *Age*, March 5, 1938, p. 6; Woodson, "Encouraging the Negro Artist," New York *Age*, March 12, 1938, p. 6.

52. Woodson, "Monuments of the Race," 6.

the Committee for Improving Industrial Conditions Among Negroes in the District of Columbia and directed a survey of black employment in Washington conducted by Lorenzo Greene and Myra Colson Callis. To discern the extent of black unemployment and suggest possible remedies for it, Greene and Callis sent questionnaires to workers and employers and conducted follow-up interviews with respondents. Although Washington's unemployment rate was lower than that in most other urban areas—it was only 3.7 percent in 1930—almost half of those unemployed were black, and blacks formed 27 percent of the population. In their report, which Woodson published in 1931, Greene and Callis also disclosed widespread underemployment; college-educated blacks often worked in menial jobs. Woodson distributed the report to black newspapers, churches, citizens associations, and schools.[53]

Through numerous speeches and columns in the black press, Woodson, serving as the spokesman for the Committee for Improving Industrial Conditions, reminded the black community of the need to increase economic opportunities for blacks. "If we permit foreigners to impoverish us by establishing and controlling businesses which we support," he maintained, then "we ought to starve." Woodson argued that the depression was actually a blessing in disguise for blacks, because it would sharpen their awareness of their oppression and, he hoped, lead to greater racial unity. Deploring divisiveness and lack of solidarity among blacks, Woodson promoted black economic nationalism in his columns. "We here in the District of Columbia," he asserted, "have millions of dollars deposited in banks downtown, where a colored woman is not allowed in the ladies room."[54]

Advancing a view similar to Du Bois' concept of positive segregation, Woodson frequently invoked the phrase "use segregation to kill segregation," and advocated black patronage of black businesses and the organization of neighborhood cooperatives. While isolation and

53. Woodson's Annual Reports for 1930–1931, XVI (1931), 349–58, and 1931–1932, XVII (1932), 391–99, published in the *Journal of Negro History;* Lorenzo J. Greene and Myra Colson Callis, *Employment of Negroes in the District of Columbia* (Washington, D.C., 1931). Also see Samuel W. Rutherford to Nannie Burroughs, October 6, November 22, 24, 1930, January 10, 1931, Rutherford to Robert W. Brooks, February 28, 1931, Rutherford to Burroughs, April 18, 1931, Campbell C. Johnson to Burroughs, January 25, April 11, 1932, all in Nannie H. Burroughs Papers, MS Div., LC.

54. Woodson, "Only the Trail Blazer Succeeds in Business," 6; Woodson, "Scarlett Lady, Bootlegger Live by Dr. Woodson, but Are Not His Neighbors," 7.

segregation were "terrible evils," they offered "an unusual opportunity for the Negroes to organize efficient agencies for their own uplift." Woodson urged blacks to think black and buy black, and to become producers as well as consumers. The black man unfortunately had "learned from the white man how to spend money much more rapidly than he had learned how to earn it." [55]

According to Woodson, black economic advancement could be obtained only through individual black enterprises, and he advocated the creation of small black businesses that would hire only blacks and be patronized by blacks. Blacks should organize neighborhood associations "to develop out of these groups a citywide consumers' league to establish and support enterprises in the area settled by Negroes." [56] Although he had made these same suggestions earlier to the Washington branch of the NAACP, he was hopeful that blacks were finally ready to endorse the program that he proposed. "Sometimes," he asserted, "it is necessary for people to get hungry before they learn to think." [57]

Woodson increased his advocacy of black economic nationalism after he was mugged as he walked up Pennsylvania Avenue on his way home from the Library of Congress. On Friday, the thirteenth of January, 1933, two black thugs put a gun to his head and stole the five dollars he had in his wallet. Shaken by the experience, Woodson was starkly reminded of the difficulties some blacks had in earning a living in legitimate enterprises. Yet he channeled his energies not into castigating the black thugs who had robbed him, but instead into petitioning white employers to hire more black workers. He organized a group of blacks from his Shaw neighborhood and asked them to join him in appealing to whites who owned businesses there. They met first with managers of the A & P and Sanitary grocery stores to persuade them

55. Woodson, "If I Were Living in Atlanta," Pittsburgh *Courier*, December 3, 1932, p. 2; Woodson, "The Difficulty of Learning from the Depression" (Press Release), March 23, 1932, in Barnett Papers. Also see Francille Rusan Wilson, "The Segregated Scholars: Black Labor Historians, 1895–1950" (Ph.D. dissertation, University of Pennsylvania, 1988), 378–87.

56. Woodson, "Males' Lack of Respect for Our Womanhood Is Shameful," Pittsburgh *Courier*, December 17, 1932, p. 2. Although Woodson, in "Why Some Negroes Advocate Segregation," Chicago *Defender*, April 21, 1934, p. 12, denied that the program of economic uplift that he espoused was like that of Du Bois, it was very similar. On Du Bois' view see "Does the Negro Need Separate Schools," *Journal of Negro Education*, IV (1935), 328–35, and *Dusk of Dawn: An Essay Toward an Autobiography of a Race Concept* (1940; rpr. New York, 1971), 173–220.

57. Woodson, "The Mis-Education of the Negro in Economics," 4.

to employ black clerks in branches in their neighborhood. When Woodson failed to convince A & P managers to hire black clerks, he concluded that it was futile to beg whites to employ blacks so that whites could "get richer at their expense."[58]

Woodson then urged blacks to establish their own grocery stores. He invited Albon Holsey, a representative of the National Negro Business League's Colored Merchants Association (CMA), to speak to a group of forty to fifty of his neighbors about setting up a store there. Yet the group was not persuaded that CMA stores would succeed in the Shaw neighborhood. Seven months later John Aubrey Davis, a recent graduate from Williams College, formed the New Negro Alliance with a group of young blacks, who had been disillusioned with the Washington NAACP and its lack of attention to economic problems. In August they picketed Shaw's U Street Grill for firing its only black employee, and the "Don't Buy Where You Can't Work" campaign was launched in Washington. The organization, which survived for almost ten years, was among the most successful and long-lived of such groups throughout the country. Although Woodson did not participate in the picketing of the U Street Grill or of the other establishments that the New Negro Alliance targeted for action, he tried to influence public opinion through his newspaper columns.[59]

Prior to the establishment of Washington's New Negro Alliance, Woodson supported campaigns in other cities, and noted in his col-

58. Woodson, "Dr. Carter Woodson Gets Closeup of Depression and Thereby Is Launched on Another Career as Business Organizer," Chicago *Defender*, January 18, 1933, p. 10. Also see Woodson, "Carter Woodson Sees Youth Breaking Away from Traditions," 22; Baltimore *Afro-American*, May 7, 1932, p. 17.

59. On the "Don't Buy Where You Can't Work" campaigns in Washington and elsewhere, see W. C. Matney, "Exploitation or Cooperation," *Crisis*, XXXVII (January, 1930), 11–12, (February, 1930), 48–49, 67; Albon L. Holsey, "Business Points the Way," *Crisis*, XXXVIII (July, 1931), 225–26; W. E. B. Du Bois, "Buying and Selling," *Crisis*, XXXVIII (November, 1931), 393; George S. Schuyler, "The Young Negro Co-operative League," *Crisis*, XXXIX (January, 1932), 465, 472; Vere E. Johns and George S. Schuyler, "To Boycott or Not to Boycott?" *Crisis*, XLI (September, 1934), 258–60, 274; August Meier and Elliott Rudwick, *Along the Color Line: Explorations of the Black Experience* (Urbana, 1976), 314–32; Michele F. Pacifico, "Don't Buy Where You Can't Work: The New Negro Alliance and Job Campaigns in Washington, D.C., 1933–1941" (Paper presented at Organization of American Historians meeting, Cincinnati, 1983, in Pacifico's possession); Michele F. Pacifico, "A History of the New Negro Alliance of Washington, D.C., 1933–1941" (M.A. thesis, George Washington University, 1983); Eugene Davidson, ed., *The New Negro Alliance Yearbook*, (Washington, D.C., 1939), copy in Moorland-Spingarn Research Center. Davidson lists Woodson among the supporters.

umns that a boycott in New York City was particularly effective. He promoted the efforts of the CMA, as well as those of Schuyler's Young Negro Cooperative League, to form business establishments employing young black college graduates. He purchased shares in CMA stores and regularly bought personal goods from black shop owners. At one speaking engagement he boasted that his "shoes and suit had been made by colored Washington storekeepers" while his necktie "had been made by a colored Baltimore firm."[60]

"What we want to do," Woodson exhorted his readers, "is to learn by co-operation to keep within the race sufficient wealth to lift a larger number above drudgery and provide sufficient leisure to develop the unusual talent of the race." Similarly, in a speech presented at Douglass High School in Baltimore in 1932, Woodson, noting that most of the students' parents were domestics and laborers, urged students "to fit themselves for work as tradesmen, storekeepers and manufacturers," and supply their own needs. As homemakers, black women had a special role to play for the economic uplift of their families, Woodson wrote. He hoped "to arouse the women to the extent of doing their part in making the Negro just as much a producer as a consumer."[61]

In several of his columns, Woodson advocated a return to a simpler time when blacks did not feel the need for luxuries, when they "walked to work in the morning and walked back home . . . had a better appetite . . . enjoyed better health and . . . lived longer." Challenging blacks to change their values, Woodson warned that if blacks were "to escape starvation and rise out of poverty into comfort and ease, they must change their way of thinking and living."[62]

60. Woodson, "Carter Woodson Sees Youth Breaking Away From Traditions," 22; Baltimore *Afro-American*, May 7, 1932, p. 17.

61. Woodson, "Be Radical for Your Own Cause Instead of Foreigners," Baltimore *Afro-American*, August 1, 1931, p. 17; Baltimore *Afro-American*, May 7, 1932, p. 17; Woodson, "Males' Lack of Respect for Our Womanhood is Shameful," 12.

62. Woodson, "The Difficulty of Learning from the Depression" (Press Release), March 23, 1932, in Barnett Papers. Also see Woodson, "The Mis-Education of the Negro in Economics," 4; Woodson, "The Poverty of the Depression Not Alarming" (Press Release), March 30, 1932, in Barnett Papers; Woodson, "Not Hard to Get out of the Bread Line, Says Dr. Woodson," Baltimore *Afro-American*, April 16, 1932, p. 16; Woodson, "Modern Education Fits the Needs of Oppressors of Weaker Peoples," Baltimore *Afro-American*, May 21, 1932, p. 8; Woodson, "We Lose Most by Failure of Other People's Business Concerns," Baltimore *Afro-American*, May 28, 1932, p. 9; Woodson, "Segregation Is Cause of Most of Ills We Suffer in This Country," Baltimore *Afro-American*, July 30, 1932, p. 8; Woodson, "America Under Segregation Policies Sure to Fail," Bal-

At times Woodson damned with faint praise the efforts of other racial and ethnic groups in their quest for economic advancement and upward social mobility, which he believed often was obtained at blacks' expense. Blacks, he argued, lacked the solidarity and thrift that was largely responsible for success in American society. "An Italian comes over here from his country to repair shoes in a community of Negroes, and the Greeks to feed them, the Chinese to wash their clothes, and the Jew to sell their merchandise."[63] Woodson sometimes singled out Jews, whose accomplishments and intense group loyalty he admired. He often exaggerated the economic achievements of other ethnic groups, as well their status vis-à-vis blacks, in the hope that he would goad his readers into action.

Despite the exaggeration and sarcasm in his columns, Woodson's message reached those readers he criticized most—the black bourgeoisie. The shift in Woodson's views on appropriate solutions to blacks' economic and political problems during the depression and New Deal eras in many ways paralleled the larger shift in views within the black bourgeoisie. By the mid-1930s the black middle class in Washington, as elsewhere, was divided over the best means of achieving economic and political equality. Although membership in the local NAACP branch, the New Negro Alliance, and the National Negro Congress overlapped, with the same core group active in each organization, the leaders of these organizations espoused positions that often were at odds with those of rank-and-file members. Contending for preeminence on the agendas for social change in all these groups was the issue of race versus class; some believed that blacks should organize themselves as blacks, regardless of socio-economic status, while others

timore *Afro-American*, August 6, 1932, p. 8; Woodson, "Beware of Leaders, What We Need Now Is Workers," Baltimore *Afro-American*, August 20, 1932, p. 8; Woodson, "White Heads of Colleges Should Be 'Naturalized,'" Baltimore *Afro-American*, August 27, 1932, p. 8; Woodson, "Handkerchief-Headed Political Leaders Got Little for Masses out of Politics," Baltimore *Afro-American*, September 17, 1932, p. 8; Woodson, "We as a Race Agree on Nothing," Chicago *Defender*, December 14, 1935, p. 4.

63. Woodson, "Woodson as an Iconoclast," 6. Also see Woodson, "Accumulating with $100 a month," New York *Age*, January 11, 1936, pp. 6, 12; and for additional comments on Jews in comparison with blacks, Lorenzo J. Greene, *Working with Carter G. Woodson, the Father of Black History: A Diary, 1928–1930*, ed. Arvarh E. Strickland (Baton Rouge, 1989), 383.

believed that black workers should ally themselves with white workers.[64]
The argument of race versus class engulfed and divided the black bourgeoisie across the country. A vivid illustration of the rifts it created can be seen in a bitter power struggle that developed within the Washington branch of the NAACP. It began as a dispute over the election of officers in January, 1937. Cast baldly, the conflict was between the old and new black bourgeoisie, with schoolteachers forming the moderate old guard and young black professionals constituting the group of challengers. Yet the struggle cannot be characterized as merely that of generational conflict, for young and old lined up on both sides. And, as usual, Woodson was involved in the early stages of the struggle.[65]

Nine days before the election of branch officers, William E. Taylor, an attorney and faculty member at Howard University Law School, tried to reserve the branch's regular meeting place at the YWCA but discovered that Delta Sigma Theta sorority had priority in use of the space. He then reserved a room at the YMCA and wrote a letter advising the membership of the change in meeting place. In the same letter, he advocated the reelection of John C. Bruce, a supervisory principal in the public schools, as president and A. S. Pinkett, a realtor and insurance broker, as secretary. Aware that attorney William Hastie had organized a group to defeat Bruce and Pinkett, Taylor apparently did not send a copy of the letter to every branch member, although it is uncertain whether he sent copies only to those members who were likely to vote for Bruce and Pinkett. Hastie then successfully campaigned to have the national office of the NAACP declare the election invalid.[66]

64. On the political divisions within the black bourgeoisie during the 1930s, see Ray Gavins, *The Perils and Prospects of Southern Black Leadership: Gordon Blaine Hancock, 1881–1976* (Durham, 1977), 51–75; John B. Kirby, *Black Americans in the Roosevelt Era* (Knoxville, 1980), 145–70, 211–27; Bart Landry, "A Reinterpretation of the Writings of Frazier on the Black Middle Class," *Social Problems*, XXVI (December, 1978), 211–22; Harvard Sitkoff, *A New Deal for Blacks: The Emergence of Civil Rights as a National Issue* (New York, 1978), 22–37, 139–57, 246–65; Gilbert Ware, *William Hastie: Grace Under Pressure* (New York, 1984), 66–80; Raymond Wolters, *Negroes and the Great Depression* (Westport, Conn., 1970), 183–87, 251–58.

65. For a good summary of the activities of the Washington branch of the NAACP during the 1930s, see Walker, "The Struggles and Attempts to Establish Branch Autonomy and Hegemony." Walker, however, does not deal with Woodson's role in the conflict in the 1930s.

66. William E. Taylor, Form Letter to members of the District branch of the NAACP, January 6, 1937, Harry C. Edwards to Walter White, January 16, 1937, John C. Bruce, Form Letter to members of the District branch of the NAACP, April 28, 1937,

Woodson wrote a letter to the NAACP Board of Directors maintaining that the election was valid. Noting that "there was nothing illegal or irregular about the method of taking the ballot," Woodson
asserted that questioning "the ballot was merely another maneuver in
the fight against the present incumbents, for those of the opposition
were outnumbered by at least four to one." He cautioned the national
office against getting involved in the dispute, for it was perceived that
the "militant minority has the ear of certain National officers in New
York," and he added that at the 1936 election, Hastie's group "ran for
president a man who was not even a member of the organization." [67]

Despite letters from Woodson and other leaders in Washington's
black community, like Nannie Burroughs and YWCA president Julia
West Hamilton, both of whom clearly had no personal stake in the
election, in the end, the national office sided with Hastie. Because Hastie was involved in the legal team that brought the NAACP's segregation cases before the courts, he did have the ear of those in the national
office, and he influenced their decision to declare the election invalid
and to suspend branch operations. Vituperative barbs were exchanged
on both sides as the dispute dragged on for more than two years, and
Bruce and Pinkett continued to act as branch officers, unrecognized by
the national office. When the branch was finally reorganized and operational in 1939, Woodson and other black activists did not rejoin.
Instead they shifted their commitment to other organizations in the
quest for political and economic change. [68]

While the controversy in the Washington branch of the NAACP
brewed, the leadership of the New Negro Alliance likewise debated the
best means to achieve the goal of economic equality for blacks. Once

---

Roy Wilkins, "On the District of Columbia Branch," Memorandum to the Committee
on Administration, April 19, 1937, and "Chronological Statement of Facts Leading to
the Revocation of the Charter of the District of Columbia Branch of the NAACP by the
National Board of Directors," May 10, 1937 (Typescript, author unknown), all in
NAACP Records, Group I, Series G, Box 38; Taylor to Isadore Martin, December 3,
1937, in NAACP Records, Group I, Series G, Box 39; Minutes of the Board of Directors
meeting, April 19, 1937, in NAACP Records, Group I, Series A, Box 22.

67. Woodson to NAACP Board of Directors, February 7, 1937, in Arthur B. Spingarn Papers, MS Div., LC. Spingarn was on the NAACP Board of Directors, and Nannie
Burroughs also provided testimony.

68. After the branch reorganized in the spring of 1939, 64 people joined, but the
membership records indicate that Woodson was not among them. See NAACP Records,
Group I, Series G, Box 38.

again, race versus class emerged as the thorny issue. The realization that creating black-owned businesses would not mean the employment of many people from among the masses caused the group's leaders to modify their earlier stance against cooperation with white working-class groups and labor unions. Similarly, Woodson altered his views and began to take more seriously the ideas espoused by black radicals in the National Negro Congress.[69]

While Woodson had read Marx and was aware of socialist and communist proposals to ease economic problems, he believed in the early 1930s that blacks should organize along racial rather than class lines. He encouraged people not "to sit around waiting for the expected millennium from Communism," but rather, to support local black businesses.[70] Despite his mordant criticism of the black bourgeoisie, he actually was one of their more articulate spokesmen when he railed against black radicals who argued that "these men represent[ed] the capitalistic class which must be overthrown before the ills of society can be cured." It was impossible, Woodson maintained, to "revolutionize the social and economic order so as to place all people alike on the same level and at the same time miraculously retain the initiative and invention which have developed the wealth of the country."[71] Black radicals who had "read and misunderstood Karl Marx and his disciples," were wrong in espousing communism or socialism as the solution to blacks' economic problems, Woodson asserted. "History shows that although large numbers of people have actually tried to realize such pleasant dreams, they have in the final analysis come back to a social program based on competition."[72]

69. On the New Negro Alliance, see Meier and Rudwick, *Along the Color Line*, 314–32; Pacifico, "Don't Buy Where You Can't Work"; Davidson, ed., *The New Negro Alliance Yearbook*. For a good description of the class conflicts in the National Negro Congress, see John B. Kirby, *Black Americans in the Roosevelt Era*, 150–71, 211–21.

70. Woodson, "If I were living in Atlanta," 2. Also see Woodson, "Only the Trail Blazer Succeeds in Business," 6; Woodson, "The Mis-Education of the Negro in Economics," 4; Woodson, "The Inconsistency of Negro Radicals" (Press Release), July 29, 1931, in Barnett Papers; Woodson, "Be Radical for Your Own Cause Instead of Foreigners," 17; Woodson, "Independence in Thinking and Voting Is Needed," Pittsburgh *Courier*, September 3, 1932, p. 2; Woodson, "Shall We Live in the City or Go Back to the Farm," Baltimore *Afro-American*, March 17, 1934, p. 19.

71. Woodson, "Only the Trail Blazer Succeeds in Business," 6. On blacks in the Communist party see Mark Naison, *Communists in Harlem During the Depression* (Urbana, 1983), and Wilson Record, *The Negro and the Communist Party* (Chapel Hill, 1951).

72. Woodson, *The Mis-Education of the Negro*, 186.

But as the Communist party began to tackle such overt manifestations of racism as the Scottsboro case, and intellectuals like Herbert Aptheker made the documentation of black struggles a central part of their appeal to blacks, Woodson's views shifted. In the mid-1930s he began to characterize New Deal programs as "narcotic injections," and argued that they were injurious to the economic health and well-being of black Americans.[73] "Instead of rejoicing over the dole," Woodson wrote in one column, the Negro ought "to clarify his vision in order to take the part of a man in the new order to be built." Referring to the New Deal, he proclaimed, "The best that one can say for the experiment is that it is postponing the inevitable destruction of capitalism."[74]

Woodson had attended the first meeting of the National Negro Congress, held in the Chicago armory in February, 1936, on Frederick Douglass' birthday. Organized by A. Philip Randolph the year before in Washington, D.C., the National Negro Congress was concerned with Italy's aggression against Ethiopia, civil liberties, a hostile white press, the black church, black business, and the plight of both the urban black working class and black sharecroppers. Woodson, along with almost one thousand others, listened for three days to speeches and resolutions offered by Earl Browder, James Ford, and Randolph. Agents from the Military Intelligence Division also attended the meeting and dutifully took note of the proceedings.[75]

73. Woodson to Frederic Bancroft, April 18, 1935, in Frederic Bancroft Papers, Butler Library, Columbia University; Robert Weaver to Woodson, October 24, 1933, and Woodson to Weaver, October 25, 1933, in Robert Weaver Papers, Schomburg Center; Woodson, "That Mischievous Advisor on Negro Affairs," Chicago Defender, April 28, 1934, p. 12; Woodson, "Remember 1917" (Press Release), June 17, 1936, in Carter G. Woodson Collection, Moorland-Spingarn Research Center; Woodson, "No Participation in the Reelection of Roosevelt" (Press Release), September 16, 1936, in Woodson Collection, Moorland-Spingarn Research Center; Woodson, "Accumulating with $100 a Month," 6, 12; Woodson, "The Higher Standard of Living," New York Age, January 25, 1936, p. 6; Woodson, "Woodson Holds Negro Voters Have Not Yet Reached Political Freedom," New York Age, March 21, 1936, p. 19; Woodson, "What Negro Do You Hate," New York Age, March 28, 1936, p. 6; Wilson, "The Segregated Scholars," 432.

74. Woodson, "Negro Content to Go Progressively Down," New York Age, March 19, 1938, p. 6.

75. Resolutions of the National Negro Congress Held in Chicago, Ill., February 14–16, 1936 (Pamphlet), copy in Moorland-Spingarn Research Center; Woodson, "Thousands Throng History-Making Conference in Chicago," New York Age, February 22, 1936, pp. 1–2; J. S. Winslow, Memorandum to the Assistant Chief of Staff of the War Department, February 21, 1936, in Record Group 165, Records of the War Department, General and Special Staffs, File 10110-2666-113, Military Intelligence Division Records, National Archives and Records Administration.

In a column written after returning from this meeting, Woodson lambasted whites who charged that the group was Communist. He asserted further that he agreed with the views espoused by the organizers of the National Negro Congress: "Negroes who are charged with being Communists advocate the stoppage of lynching, the abrogation of the laws of disfranchisement, the abolition of peonage, equality in the employment of labor, the removal of trade restrictions of proletarian oligarchy, the impartial extension of credit by financial institutions, the end of monopoly—in short the chance to earn a living and to be free to enjoy life without the terrors of hunger and mob violence."[76]

Woodson also penned a column in 1936 blasting the New York City school system for forcing its teachers to take an oath declaring their opposition to the Communist party and affirming their loyalty to the U.S. government. Criticizing not only the school system but also white unions for their exclusion of black teachers, Woodson charged that the school system had "become the means for preventing enlightenment rather than for promoting it." The administration was "used to keep the people in such ignorance that they will never interfere with this proletarian oligarchy by socializing skilled labor and professional service."[77]

The racism found among white workers and within their unions kept Woodson from embracing wholeheartedly the working-class coalition espoused by the National Negro Congress. He did not attend the second meeting, in 1937, several sessions of which were held at Philadelphia's Independence Hall to commemorate the sesquicentennial of the Constitution. He did, however, appreciate the group's use of history in appealing to the black and white masses. In his speech titled "The Crisis of the Negro and the Constitution," Randolph paid homage to black revolutionaries Gabriel Prosser, Denmark Vesey, Nat Turner, Harriet Tubman, Sojourner Truth, and Frederick Douglass. Other speakers ad-

76. Woodson, "Why Call the Negro Red," New York *Age*, March 14, 1936, p. 6. Also see Woodson, "Thousands Throng History-Making Conference in Chicago," pp. 1–2; Naison, *Communists in Harlem During the Depression*, 184; Lawrence S. Wittner, "The National Negro Congress: A Reassessment," *American Quarterly*, XXII (1970), 883–901.

77. Woodson, "The Next Oath," New York *Age*, March 7, 1936, p. 6. Woodson later would work with the New York City School Board, its teachers' union, and the NAACP on a project for the school system to secure textbooks that adequately covered black history. Walter White noted that there were in 1941 "current attempts to pin the 'Red Label' on the Teachers Union as a whole." See White to William Lloyd Imes, March 14, 1941, in NAACP Records, Group II, Series A, Box 65.

dressed historical themes, linking past struggles to the existing plight of African Americans. Resolutions were passed praising the Congress of Industrial Organizations for admitting black workers to its unions, and organizers called on black and white workers to unify in the quest for social justice.[78]

When the Popular Front collapsed in 1939, so did Woodson's faith in socialism as an appropriate solution for blacks. While he conceded that blacks had been unable to become self-sufficient despite "all the talk . . . about socializing the professions, community buying and selling, consumers' leagues and joint stock corporations of the people," he was still wary of advocating a coalition with white workers. Noting in 1938 that the "hope long since held out in the program of Communism has been blasted by the dictatorial turn things have recently taken in countries where despotism rather than liberty has become the rule," he was "compelled to inquire what it would mean to the Negro to destroy Capitalism when he has not shown sufficient efficiency to compete with others."[79]

By the late 1930s Woodson had shifted his position again, returning to the view that blacks of all classes needed to unify and remain independent of all political coalitions with whites. Yet he remained friendly with leading black and white radicals, often engaging them in debates about the best course for blacks in their quest for equality. As a result, the Federal Bureau of Investigation surveyed his activities, reporting regularly when he spoke to groups that were considered subversive.[80]

As early as 1917 the Military Intelligence Division and the Bureau of Investigation, as it was called then, compiled files on members of the

78. *Official Proceedings of the Second Meeting of the National Negro Congress, October 15, 16, 17, 1937, Metropolitan Opera House, Philadelphia, PA* (Pamphlet), copy in Moorland-Spingarn Research Center.

79. Woodson, "The Negro at the Cross Road," New York *Age*, March 26, 1938, pp. 6, 11.

80. On Woodson's changing political views, see Woodson, "The Negro Must Appeal to His Own," New York *Age*, August 8, 1931, p. 9; Woodson, "Lack of Church Union Accounts for the Negro in Politics," Baltimore *Afro-American*, September 19, 1931, p. 17; Woodson, "Beware of Leaders, What We Need Now Is Workers, Says Dr. Woodson," 8; Woodson, "Independence in Thinking and Voting Is Needed," 2; Woodson, "Balance of Power Is Sole Political Strength of Group," 8; Woodson, "Plain Speaking," Chicago *Defender*, March 10, 1934, p. 11; Woodson, "Why Call the Negro Red," 6; Woodson, "Woodson Holds Negro Voters Have Not Yet Reached Political Freedom," 19; Woodson, "No Participation in the Reelection of Roosevelt" (Press Release), September 16, 1936, in Woodson Collection, Moorland-Spingarn Research Center; Woodson, "Negro Content to Go Progressively Down," 6.

association's executive council and monitored the *Journal*.[81] Although intelligence agents were much more interested in the ideas of people like Du Bois, Garvey, and Randolph, they also took note of Woodson's outspoken advocacy of black racial pride. Woodson believed that he had been investigated since 1919. It was during that year, Woodson maintained in a newspaper column published in April, 1931, that J. Stanley Durkee attempted to silence his criticism of Durkee's administration of Howard by showing him a letter from the Justice Department that purported him to be of a communist bent.[82] However, records obtained through a Freedom of Information Act request reveal no systematic surveillance of Woodson until 1938, when his books were evaluated by the Dies Committee's investigation of un-American activities.[83]

During the 1940s, Woodson attracted the interest of intelligence agents because of his interactions with historians and writers like Herbert Aptheker and James Ford (both of whom wrote books, pamphlets, and newspaper articles for the Communist party) and because of the attention that his scholarship received in the *Daily Worker*. When Woodson spoke at institutions that were rumored to have ties to the Communist party, such as the Samuel Adams School for Social Studies in Boston, the Jefferson School for Social Studies in New York City, and the Rackham Educational Memorial School in Detroit, agents attended his speeches. Woodson's message, however, hardly could be considered radical, for he merely espoused black equality. In a 1943 speech presented at the Rackham School, agents quoted him as saying,

81. The following associates of Woodson were subjects of Bureau of Investigation reports, all in Record Group 165, NA: William R. Jernegan, a Washington, D.C. minister, and John R. Hawkins, in File 3057, Reel 304; Victor Daly, in File 258421, Reel 672; Charles Roman, in File 267600, Reel 682; Roscoe Bruce, Garnett Wilkinson, George William Cook, who worked with Woodson at Howard, and Archibald H. Grimké, in File BS 202600–48, Reel 925. The Military Intelligence Division also investigated several of Woodson's associates; see the following files in RG 165, NA: Charles Roman, in File 10218–15; Nannie Burroughs, in File 10218–11; Kelly Miller, in File 10218–98, all on Reel 1. On the monitoring of the *Journal*, see Col. John M. Dunn, Acting Director of the Military Intelligence Division, to Anna W. Keichline, February 11, 1919, in RG 165, File 10218–304, Reel 5.

82. Woodson, "The Capstone of Negro Education Becomes the Captsone of Negro Politics" (Press Release), April 29, 1931, in Barnett Papers.

83. On September 9, 1986, I filed a Freedom of Information Act request for FBI files on Woodson and received the files on April 26, 1988, case no. 554f-88, FOIA no. 275,579. The file numbers cited in notes 84 and 85 refer to FOIA/FBI files. Also see *Special Committee on Un-American Activities [Dies Committee]: Public Hearings* (8 vols.; Washington, D.C., 1938–1944), I, 606.

"If the United States [is] to have a real democracy, the unfinished task of the Civil War must be taken up by the reform element of the country and carried out to assure freedom and opportunity for all."[84]

The FBI also monitored Woodson's appearances before groups that were considered subversive, such as the Communist party's fraternal society, the International Workers Order, which contributed funds to the association and supported the observation of Negro History Week. Certain branches of the association were investigated if agents believed that black or white radicals were active members. Even the sales of Woodson's books were monitored; agents staked out supposedly radical bookstores, taking note of books on black history that were best sellers, and Woodson's were among them. Agents continued to monitor the *Journal* in the 1940s and recorded instances in which Woodson favorably reviewed books written by Marxists or those with ties to the Socialist or Communist parties. Yet all the evidence compiled on Woodson pointed not to subversive political activity but to scholarship and advocacy of black equality and racial pride through the study of black history, which agents branded as dangerous.[85]

Throughout the 1930s and 1940s Woodson continued his advocacy of black political independence and retained no ties to any party. Equally critical of both the Democratic and the Republican parties, Woodson asserted that they were "two degenerate parties, being practically alike, merely contend[ing] for the opportunity to do the same thing," which,

84. W. L. Furbershaw, Chicago, Weekly Intelligence Report, November 13, 1943, file number illegible. Also see William J. Bingham, Boston, Weekly Intelligence Report, November 7, 1944, in File 100-766-2511, and agent's name withheld, Boston, Weekly Intelligence Report, November 15, 1944, in File 100-6947 MCG.

85. Agent's name withheld, Pittsburgh, Weekly Intelligence Report, October 19, 1943, in File 100–10516; agent's name withheld, Los Angeles, Weekly Intelligence Report, October 24, 1944, in File 100–14872; James W. Ford, "Detroit Plans Huge Patriotic Celebration to Honor Negro Contribution to America," Clipping from *Daily Worker*, February 13, 1943, and "Wider Goals for Negro History Week," Clipping from *Daily Worker*, February 7, 1945, in File 100-135-5-41; agent's name withheld, New York City, Weekly Intelligence Reports, May 27, June 4, 1946, in File 100-3-47-927; "Noted Negro Historians Laud Haywood's Negro Liberation," Clipping from *Daily Worker*, May 8, 1949, and Guy Hottell, Washington, D.C., Weekly Intelligence Report, March 10, 1950, in File 100-33049-53-32. William A. Nolan, in *Communism Versus the Negro* (Chicago, 1951), 112–15, 236–37, charges that Woodson gave favorable reviews to communist and left-leaning scholars to obtain financial support for the association. While Woodson may have praised the work of such authors, there is no evidence he did so because they made substantial contributions.

in his view, was to keep the black man in his place. Black leaders, Woodson said, "should have had sense to realize that the Republican Party ditched the race in 1876, not in 1932." And if it "[has taken blacks] 56 years to realize that we have been abandoned by those who once professed interest in us," he added, "we thereby demonstrate our ineptitude in politics." [86]

Woodson condemned blacks who were appointed to "'Jim Crow' Federal positions set aside to reward Negro politicians," and maintained that these individuals were paid high salaries not to promote blacks' interests, but to keep the black masses in line for white politicians. He accused black politicians of literally selling out black voters, reporting in 1932 that the Republican machine was trying to rid the party of black politicians because they "were more expensive than the lily-whites." They did not "always stay bought after their initial payment," and needed other "'persuasive gifts.'" [87]

Even Woodson's friends did not escape his attacks. He blasted Emmett J. Scott, head of the National Negro Republican League, charging that he was in collusion with the white Republican machine. John Hawkins, chairman of the Colored Voters Division of the National Republican Committee, had served as president of the Association for the Study of Negro Life and History since 1923 and quit the post because of Woodson's attacks on the Republican party. When G. David Houston, who had written articles for the *Journal*, headed the Negro Inaugural Committee for Franklin D. Roosevelt's installation as president in 1933, he incurred Woodson's wrath. Woodson argued that blacks should boycott the inaugural rather than attend the segregated social activities that Houston was planning. Woodson also condemned the special advisory positions created for blacks in Roosevelt's administration, as well as the "Black Cabinet" headed by Mary McLeod Bethune, who served as president of the association from 1935 to 1950.[88]

86. Woodson, "Lincoln Practical Man, Says Woodson, Who Did Things We Condemn Today," Baltimore *Afro-American*, November 19, 1932, p. 8; Woodson, "Independence in Thinking and Voting Is Needed," 2.

87. Woodson, "The Negro Must Appeal to His Own," 9; Woodson, quoted in Ralph Bunche, "A Brief and Tentative Analysis of Negro Leadership," September, 1940, (Research Notes), in Gunnar Myrdal Project, Reel 2, pp. 117–18, Schomburg Center.

88. Baltimore *Afro-American*, June 20, 1931, p. 1; Woodson, "The Development of Scott's Machine" (Press Release), July 1, 1931, in Du Bois Papers; Woodson, "Dr. Carter G. Woodson Refuses to Serve on the 'Special' Inaugural Committee," Washington *Tribune*, February 3, 1933, p. 4; G. David Houston, Letter to the Editor, Baltimore *Afro-*

While most blacks had jumped on Roosevelt's bandwagon by 1936, Woodson refused to join them, contending that "the Negro should not cast his vote for a party that does not recognize him." When Bishop Richard R. Wright, Jr., a member of the Colored Committee of the National Good Neighbor League, which was organized to promote Roosevelt's reelection among blacks, wanted to use Woodson's name in association with the campaign, Woodson refused. But Wright had already announced that Woodson was a member of the league, so Woodson sent a news release to the black press affirming his independence from any political party and asserting that he would "do nothing to elect or defeat any candidate."[89]

Woodson, however, did not advocate total isolation from national politics or complete black noninvolvement in the New Deal. He supported the election of Oscar DePriest to the House of Representatives in 1929, as well as the election of his successor, Arthur Mitchell, in 1934. Since blacks had not served in Congress since Reconstruction, Woodson conceded that these were important victories and was hopeful that blacks' views finally would be represented. He served as a consultant to the Federal Emergency Relief Administration and to the WPA in collecting slave narratives. Similarly, in 1939 Woodson participated in the meeting on the problems of Negro youth organized by Bethune's Division of Negro Affairs in the National Youth Administration.[90]

Yet during the 1940s Woodson remained unconvinced that Roosevelt's policies were beneficial to blacks. He continued to denounce black leaders who cooperated with white politicians and was particularly critical of southern blacks, whom he viewed as overly eager to align themselves with southern white liberals. In the spring of 1943 a group of more than one hundred white liberals and sixty blacks, includ-

---

American, February 11, 1933, p. 6; Woodson, "That Mischievous Advisor on Negro Affairs," 12.

89. Woodson to Francis J. Grimké, May 22, 1936, in Francis J. Grimké Papers, Moorland-Spingarn Research Center; Woodson, "No Participation in the Reelection of Roosevelt" (Press Release), September 16, 1936, in Woodson Collection, Moorland-Spingarn Research Center.

90. Louis R. Mehlinger to Mary McLeod Bethune, October 24, 1938, Woodson to Bethune, December 10, 1938, Roster of Participants, National Conference on Problems of Negro Youth, January 12–14, 1939, and Aubrey Williams to Woodson, January 19, 1939, all in Record Group 119, Records of the National Youth Administration, Division of Negro Affairs, NA.

ing Gordon Blaine Hancock and Woodson's close collaborator Luther Porter Jackson, met in Durham, North Carolina. Blacks in the group had drafted a manifesto calling for equal opportunity, and whites responded less than enthusiastically, viewing the South's problems as regional and economic in nature rather than racial. While individual whites might have opposed segregation, as a group they would not take a public stand and advocate desegregation of public facilities or institutions. Thus, at the next meeting of the group, whites shifted the focus of the agenda accordingly, creating a Southern Regional Council rather than a Southern Conference of Race Relations, which was what the blacks desired. Essentially the group revived the defunct Commission of Interracial Cooperation but gave emphasis to the special problems faced by southern blacks and whites.[91]

After the group's first meeting in Durham, Woodson penned the article "Negroes Not United for Democracy," published in the *Negro History Bulletin*. He referred to southern black leaders as slaves and lackeys of white racists, saying they had "seceded from the aggressive leadership of the race." Woodson contended that because southern blacks refused to oppose whites, they were defenders of segregation. Although Woodson advocated self-segregation by blacks to promote political and economic advancement, he was an outspoken advocate of desegregation in public facilities. Whenever he was a victim of Jim Crow policies as he traveled on trains, he wrote a letter of protest to the offending railroad company and released a copy to the black press, which published it.[92] Similarly, when one of his staff members was segregated from whites while doing research at the State Department, Woodson wrote to the secretary of state and to Roosevelt to complain of the practice.[93]

Woodson subjected his friend Jackson to the brunt of his criticism regarding what he viewed as blacks' acquiescence to southern whites. Woodson had been chiding Jackson about his political activities since

91. The best discussion of the Durham conference is found in Gavins, *The Perils and Prospects of Southern Black Leadership*, 128–35, 138–60.

92. Woodson, "Negroes Not United for Democracy," *Negro History Bulletin*, VI (May, 1943), 170, 177–78. Also see, for example, Washington *Tribune*, December 2, 1932, p. 1; Woodson to Southern Railway System, April 8, 1941, in Woodson Collection, Moorland-Spingarn Research Center.

93. Woodson to Department of State, December 23, 1935, Woodson to Franklin D. Roosevelt, December 23, 1935, Congressman Arthur W. Mitchell to Wilbur J. Carr, January 4, 1936, Carr to Mitchell, January 6, 1936, Woodson to Carr, January 6, 1936, all in Record Group 59, State Department Records, File 116.2, NA.

his election as president of the Virginia Voters League in 1941, re-
minding him at every opportunity that he was a historian and not a race
leader. Although Jackson used his political activities in Virginia to raise
funds among blacks for Woodson's association, and produced pamphlets in cooperation with the association and the Virginia Voters
League, Woodson would not refrain from his criticism. When Jackson
skipped the annual meeting of the association in the fall of 1943 to
attend the national meeting of the NAACP instead, Woodson asserted
only half jokingly that he had "made a mistake in not going. May God
help you to repent!"[94]

After the Southern Regional Council was incorporated in January,
1944, Woodson again published a derogatory article in the *Negro History Bulletin*, branding as "Uncle Toms" the blacks who agreed to participate in the organization. Greatly offended at this characterization
and the inference that he "was selling out the race," Jackson told
Woodson that he was provoking "an unnecessary unpleasant situation
between us."[95] Woodson, however, did not ease up. When an article
Jackson was writing for the *Journal* became overdue, Woodson quipped
that while he was aware Jackson was "busy solving the race problem in
Virginia" and his "duties as a leader of the race in America" were
"arduous . . . the insignificant efforts like the ASNLH should not be
abandoned altogether."[96]

While Woodson continued his barbs on black leaders during World
War II, he saved his most pointed criticisms for whites. When Roosevelt established the Fair Employment Practices Commission, Woodson
said that blacks "hailed this as a new social charter, a blow to segregation of all sorts and proceeded to make demands under this mandate."
But their hopes were dashed when they realized that Roosevelt's "or-

94. A. A. Taylor to Jackson, July 15, 1941, Charles Thompson to Jackson, April 17,
1944, Woodson to Luther Porter Jackson, November 2, 1943, all in Luther P. Jackson
Papers, Johnston Memorial Library, Virginia State University. Also see Jackson's article
in Norfolk *Journal and Guide*, March 27, 1943, cited in Gavins, *The Perils and Prospects of
Southern Black Leadership*, 131.

95. Woodson, "The Negro in the Present World Conflict," *Negro History Bulletin*,
VII (May, 1944), 171–72; Jackson to Woodson, May 20, 1944 in Jackson Papers. Also
see Woodson to Jackson, May 23, 1944, in Jackson Papers.

96. Woodson to Jackson, July 21, 1945, and Jackson to Woodson, August 8, 1945, in
Jackson Papers. In 1947 Woodson asked Jackson to make a presentation titled "The
Current Voting Status of Negroes in the Southern States," which was based on his po-
litical work, at the fall meeting of the association. See Woodson to Luther H. Foster,
September 3, 1947, in Jackson Papers.

ders can never be faithfully carried out until others who constitute the machinery by which the laws are to be enforced catch up with the procession of the advance guard of freedom." In the aftermath of World War II, Woodson tempered his criticism of white and black leaders and racial advancement organizations, even praising the slow and steady progress made by the NAACP in its legal cases to end segregation. He welcomed the formation of a Washington branch of the National Urban League and its efforts to conduct sociological research on racial problems. He supported the protests waged by the Washington branch of the NAACP against segregation in public facilities and in the city's public schools, and worked with the branch in promoting the celebration of Negro History Week.[97]

In the twilight of his life, Woodson devoted all of his languishing energies to popularizing black history among a mass audience, the cause that always had commanded the lion's share of his attention. Almost twenty years after his death, the Associated Publishers reissued Woodson's *Mis-Education of the Negro* with a new introduction by Charles Wesley. The historian pointed out that black students in the late 1960s found the book still relevant to concerns about the crisis in black education.[98] Indeed, Woodson's ideas remain pertinent even in the 1990s, as does much of the scholarship in African-American history he published.

97. Woodson, "The Negro in the Present World Conflict," 171–72; Gertrude B. Stone to Woodson, August 15, 1941, in District of Columbia NAACP Records; "Summary of Activities of the D.C. Branch of the NAACP for the Month of February, 1946," in NAACP Records, Group II, Series C, Box 26; Two Reports on the organization of a National Urban League branch in Washington, 1945, in National Urban League Records, Series I, Box 133, MS Div., LC. Also see Woodson, Review of Walter White's *A Man Called White*, in *Journal of Negro History*, XXXIV (1949), 225–27; Woodson, "Let Us Have Peace," *Christian Education*, XXIX (December, 1945), 70–71, in which he argued that class and race conflicts would worsen in the aftermath of the war.

98. Charles H. Wesley, Introduction to Woodson, *The Mis-Education of the Negro* (2d ed.; Washington, D.C., 1969), xxii–xxiii.

THE FATHER OF NEGRO HISTORY

Like all scholars, past and present, Woodson was influenced by his life experiences. More than most, however, Woodson, the son of former slaves, was greatly influenced by his early formative years and by the racism and segregation he experienced. In addition, the many roles he assumed—sharecropper, coal miner, high school teacher, Harvard graduate student, college professor, and editor-scholar-administrator—affected his scholarship. The subjects Woodson chose for scholarly examination, as well as the themes and tone of his work, reflect the wide range of these life experiences and roles.

Woodson's personal knowledge of slavery and Reconstruction was anchored in the cultural and political climate of late-nineteenth-century Virginia, where he absorbed in considerable detail the accounts of slavery given by his family and other former slaves. During his youth and early adulthood, Woodson acquired an appreciation for the masses of former slaves and for slave folk culture. The seeds of inquisitiveness were planted then, and he yearned for greater knowledge about the black past. In his scholarship he used his family's history as a window to illuminate the larger black experience.

Despite his Harvard training and his emphasis on careful and extensive documentary research to reveal the variety in blacks' experiences, Woodson's most fundamental perceptions of black history were rooted in the oral traditions of his family. His social origins not only influenced his decision to become a historian, but also were inextricably tied to his identity as a *black* historian. They explain, in part, his devotion to the cause of promoting black history and his struggle against the white historical establishment.

Du Bois maintained that Woodson was a "monographist of the strict

Harvard dryasdust school." Yet it is precisely because Woodson felt so passionate about black history that he tried to be dispassionate in his scholarship, believing that white scholars would then consider it more seriously. Rayford Logan contended that Woodson was a "bundle of contradictions," mean and vindictive, but also kind and generous.[1] Although Logan was describing Woodson's personality, the characterization fit his scholarship as well, for the body of Woodson's work contained multiple themes that could be viewed as contradictory.

Woodson was always unsparing in his criticism of American society and its democratic institutions, but remained ever hopeful that one day blacks would reap the economic, social, and political benefits that white Americans enjoyed. Throughout his scholarly work, Woodson argued that education was the key to racial advancement. In his later writings, however, he attacked black educators and black education. In much of his work Woodson also promoted middle-class values of thrift and industry as the means for black advancement in American society. Yet in his sociological studies of black professionals, he ridiculed the black bourgeoisie for its adoption of these same middle-class values. Woodson himself had absorbed these values and could not have achieved his phenomenal organizational success without the support of the black bourgeoisie.

Simultaneously, it seems, Woodson championed in his writings both black nationalism and integration with white America. At times he argued that race had primacy over class; at other times he argued that black and white workers should organize along class lines to promote social change. He celebrated black American culture in his work, tracing its roots back to Africa, but condemned certain cultural attributes that had African roots, such as ecstatic religion and popular music. Like any other human being, Woodson was a complex person who often changed his mind and held conflicting ideas in tandem. The wide range of his life experiences accounts for the nature of his scholarship.

Both prior to and since Woodson's death, black historians have recognized him as the "Father of Black History" and have drawn upon his work to inform their views of the black experience. Until recently, white historians failed to recognize Woodson's signal contributions to the field. Yet most historians, both black and white, have characterized

1. W. E. B. Du Bois, Review of Woodson's *History of the Negro Church*, in *Freeman*, October 4, 1922, pp. 92–93; Rayford W. Logan to W. E. B. Du Bois, April 29, 1950, in W. E. B. Du Bois Papers, University of Massachusetts.

Woodson as a chronicler and fact-finder whose major achievement was to lay the foundation for future scholars to build on. This profile, while accurate, falls short, for previous scholars have not attempted to analyze Woodson's scholarship as it relates to the range of his life experiences.[2]

Woodson's uncontainable enthusiasm for his subject and his sense of urgency—he saw that there was so much to be done that he allowed imperfectly executed work for the sake of at least tackling a particular subject—account for the unevenness in his work. In fact, he believed that he was laying the scholarly foundation for others to build upon. By covering such a broad range of the black experience, Woodson, and his readers, paid a price, for he often was forced to overgeneralize, blurring distinctions of place, time, character, and class, as he wrote Negro history. Often he failed to introduce or conclude chapters in his books; they merely began at the beginning of his story and ended at the end.

The manner in which Woodson composed his books also explains, in part, both his prodigious output and his more than occasional expository inelegancy. In a 1936 interview with Baltimore *Afro-American* reporter George B. Murphy, Woodson said that he began by poring over files of notes, outlining the material for each book. He then spent each morning dictating chapters to his secretary as he paced back and forth across the room. He had used this same method when he was writing his dissertation; Louis Mehlinger, who was an expert stenographer, took down chapters verbatim as Woodson dictated them. Apparently Woodson found it to be a very efficient method. "I do not have to turn over half a library in order to write a book," he told Murphy, "because I have been writing for 30 years. I could dictate several books merely because I have many of them in mind already."[3] Woodson's secretary then presented him with transcriptions of dictated material, and he rewrote and refined the text, although some of his work appears to have been published as it had been dictated.

Several historians, most recently August Meier and Elliott Rudwick,

---

2. See, for example, Earl Thorpe, *Black Historians: A Critique* (New York, 1971), and *The Central Theme of Black History* (Durham, 1969); Michael Winston, "Carter Godwin Woodson: A Prophet of a Black Tradition," *Journal of Negro History*, LX (1975), 459–63; Benjamin Quarles, "What the Historian Owes the Negro," *Saturday Review*, XLIX (September, 1966), 10–13; Robert L. Harris, Jr., "Coming of Age: The Transformation of Afro-American Historiography," *Journal of Negro History*, LXVII (1982), 107–21; Sterling Stuckey, "Du Bois, Woodson, and the Spell of Africa," *Negro Digest*, XXVI (February, 1967), 20–24, 60–73.

3. Baltimore *Afro-American*, April 25, 1936, pp. 1–2.

have commented on the unpolished quality of Woodson's writings. As early as 1922, Du Bois remarked that "the rapid issuing of books at the rate of one a year during the last four years has not improved their finish and readableness." Ulrich Phillips, who prided himself as a stylist, maintained in a 1929 assessment of Woodson's work that he "did not take pains to save the reader pains." In a review of the seventh edition of *The Negro in Our History*, Paul Lewinson, of the National Archives, complained that the book was "heavily freighted with success stories, empurpled with irrelevant personal descriptions, and marred by outcroppings of feud." Further, he judged that the "balance is bad between the subject 'The Negro,' and the background, 'Our History.'" Earl Thorpe contended that too frequently Woodson interrupted "his historical narrative to moralize or criticize." Perhaps the harshest judgment of all was rendered by Meier and Rudwick, who asserted that "Woodson's books so often today read like archaic pedantry." [4]

For anthropologist Melville Herskovits, however, Woodson's greatest shortcoming was his selective use of sources. In a scathing review of *The African Background Outlined*, Herskovits charged that the "book bristled with undocumented accusations," and that the "bibliographies are incomplete and show a strong anti-white bias." He recommended that Woodson "re-read some of the contemporary sources on Haiti and Brazil." Herskovits was not alone in his charge. Years earlier, in a review of *The Education of the Negro Prior to 1861*, one of the most thoroughly documented of Woodson's books, Marcus W. Jernegan concluded that while the book was "excellent" and a "standard authority in its field," Woodson had failed to use "the most important source for early educational efforts"—missionary reports of the Society for the Propagation of the Gospel. He also failed to make much use of colonial newspapers and plantation records, and "some sweeping generalizations should have been backed up by more evidence." Similarly, Lewinson accused Woodson of not keeping up with contemporary scholarship, and Thorpe criticized him for failing to document the assertions in many of his books, stating that "his first two serious works were his most scholarly from the standpoint of documentation and general ob-

4. Du Bois, Review of Woodson's *History of the Negro Church*, 92; U. B. Phillips to Sydnor Walker, May 9, 1929, in Laura Spelman Rockefeller Memorial Fund Records, Rockefeller Archive Center, Tarrytown, N.Y.; Paul Lewinson, Review of Woodson's *The Negro in Our History*, in *Mississippi Valley Historical Review*, XXIX (1942–43), 130–31; Thorpe, *Black Historians*, 132; August Meier and Elliott Rudwick, *Black History and the Historical Profession, 1915–1980* (Urbana, 1986), 93.

jectivity." Without further substantiation, these charges might stand unchallenged, for Woodson often did not update the bibliographies when he revised successive editions of his books. Yet he was aware of the latest scholarship in southern and black history as demonstrated by the books that he himself reviewed or had reviewed in the *Journal*.[5]

Indeed, by citing secondary sources that often included the same core of about fifty books, Woodson gave the impression that perhaps he did not keep up with the scholarly literature in his field. This core of books, however, encompassed the work of the most respected historians of the time, including nineteenth-century pioneers George Bancroft and Hermann Eduard von Holst. While dissenting from their views, Woodson also included the perspectives of Arthur Calhoun, Frederic L. Hoffman, Thomas Jesse Jones, John McMaster, Phillips, and James Ford Rhodes. He relied heavily on the work on slavery produced in the Johns Hopkins Seminary, and he respectfully noted the work of his mentors Edward Channing, Albert Hart, and Frederick Jackson Turner.[6]

Although he approached them with a very different perspective, Woodson relied on many of the same primary sources his white counterparts did. He used the writings of the founding fathers, travelers' accounts, and edited collections of published source materials. Like any well-trained historian, Woodson read widely in public records—local, state, and federal documents—including wills, tax records, inventories of estates, court records, and military records. He used organizational records, such as those of the American Colonization Society, abolition and antislavery societies, businesses, and churches. Woodson scoured state and local newspapers from the seventeenth through the early twentieth centuries, read local histories of counties and towns, and combed through personal and family papers, letters, diaries, sermons, speeches, tracts, and pamphlets.[7]

5. Melville J. Herskovits, Review of Woodson's *The African Background Outlined*, in *Annals of the American Academy of Political and Social Science*, CXC (March, 1937), 246; Marcus W. Jernegan, Review of Woodson's *The Education of the Negro Prior to 1861*, in *American Historical Review*, XXI (1915–16), 635; Thorpe, *Black Historians*, 118.

6. He cited the scholarship of James Ballagh, John Bassett, Jeffrey Brackett, Eugene McCormack, John H. Russell, Bernard C. Steiner, Edward R. Turner, and J. W. Wright. Frederic Bancroft, Sir Harry Johnston, Frank Klingberg, and George Zook were among the white scholars whose work he admired most. Among black scholars, the works of Du Bois and George Washington Williams were cited often.

7. Especially see the sources cited in Woodson, *The Education of the Negro Prior to 1861* (1915; rpr. New York, 1968), 399–434.

Woodson also differed from his white counterparts in the credulity he gave to black sources, and he was harshly critical of white scholars for ignoring them. He characterized the work of John W. Burgess, William A. Dunning, Walter Fleming, and Rhodes as "biased and inadequate," as they had "rejected the evidence from Negro sources and thus denied the Negro not only the opportunity to testify against the white man but even to testify in favor of himself." Thirteen years before the 1935 publication of *Black Reconstruction*, Du Bois' masterly condemnation of Reconstruction historiography, Woodson had similarly chastised the Dunning school, remarking that there were "no scientific studies of the nation-wide reconstruction in which the Negroes took a part."[8]

Much of Woodson's work was based on previously ignored or unused primary sources—letters, speeches, folklore, and autobiographies—of both free blacks and slaves. In the preface to a group of African stories and myths he published in 1928, Woodson noted that the "folktales of a people are a guide to the understanding of their past." To understand and appreciate Africans, scholars "must hear them speak" for themselves. Unlike his white counterparts, Woodson relied extensively on oral testimony, interviewing free blacks, former slaves, and their former white masters. In his sociological studies, Woodson used sampling techniques and questionnaires, and interviewed hundreds of subjects to gather data. He also used biography to teach about the black experience. Relying on an interdisciplinary method that combined anthropology, archaeology, sociology, and history, Woodson gleaned information from sources that reflected the thoughts, feelings, and experiences of African Americans. Only recently have historians adopted the methods and sources for research first used by Woodson. Indeed, during the last twenty-five years historians have had to rediscover the methods and content of Woodson's pioneering efforts.[9]

An extraordinarily efficient researcher, Woodson collected primary sources to use in his books and then published these sources in edited collections and in the *Journal*. By 1925 the *Journal* devoted at least

8. Woodson, *The Negro in Our History* (9th ed.; Washington, D.C., 1947), 408, 390–91.

9. Woodson, ed., *African Myths Together with Proverbs* (Washington, D.C., 1928), ix. Also see my "Countering White Racist Scholarship: Carter G. Woodson and the *Journal of Negro History*," *Journal of Negro History*, LXVIII (1983), 355–75, and "Carter G. Woodson and the Collection of Source Materials for Afro-American History," *American Archivist*, XLVIII (Summer, 1985), 261–71.

one quarter of its space to first-time publication of primary-source transcripts and documents, thereby encouraging their use by scholars who would otherwise not have known about them. When Woodson reproduced these documents in *The Mind of the Negro Reflected in Letters Written During the Crisis*, he asserted that from "the point of view of psychology of the Negro, which must be taken into consideration as an important factor in the study of history, these letters are of still larger value," for they illuminated the "mind of a people." Although letters of the black elite predominated in this collection, those of ordinary blacks were also published by Woodson. He collected speeches and letters of black women, as well as those of black men. More than two dozen women are represented in *The Mind of the Negro* and *Negro Orators*, ranging from "A Colored Lady," to prominent African-American women like Phillis Wheatley, Ellen Craft, and Sojourner Truth. Truth, he observed, "could move multitudes with untutored language." Although Woodson usually provided more evidence and commentary on African-American men, he did give attention to black women's history, and women figure prominently in his work. Woodson was particularly sensitive to gender roles, recognizing that the experiences of black women as wives, mothers, sisters, and daughters in slavery and in freedom differed from those of their husbands, fathers, brothers, and sons.[10]

Woodson also recognized that socio-economic class differences among black and white Americans partly explained their varying experiences. During the 1920s and 1930s Woodson became increasingly aware of the concept of class and used it more frequently as an analytical tool in his scholarship. Although his use of class analysis was most pronounced in the sociological studies he completed later in his life (when he argued that class differences among blacks served as a barrier to racial unity), he also had acknowledged class differences in his earlier historical analyses of the black experience during slavery and Reconstruction.[11]

*   *   *

10. Goggin, "Countering White Racist Scholarship," 355–75, and "Woodson and the Collection of Source Materials," 261–71; Woodson, ed., *The Mind of the Negro as Reflected in Letters Written During the Crisis* (Washington, D.C., 1926), v–vi; Woodson, *Negro Orators and Their Orations* (Washington, D.C., 1925), 125; Woodson, "The Negro Washerwoman: A Vanishing Figure," *Journal of Negro History*, XV (1930), 249–77.

11. See Woodson, *The Negro Wage Earner* (Washington, D.C., 1930), *The Rural Negro* (Washington, D.C., 1930), *The Negro Professional Man and the Community* (Washington, D.C., 1934), and *The Mis-Education of the Negro* (Washington, D.C., 1933).

With the publication of his first book, *The Education of the Negro Prior to 1861*, Woodson embarked on a scholarly career that, judged by output alone, few of his contemporaries or successors could match. Between 1915 and 1947, when the ninth edition of *The Negro in Our History* appeared, he published four monographs, five textbooks, five edited collections of source materials, and thirteen articles, as well as five sociological studies that were collaborative efforts. Covering a breathtaking array of subjects, Woodson's scholarly productivity and range were incontestably spectacular. Five major themes emerge from an examination of the body of Woodson's work: slavery as a social system, including detailed comparative study of slavery in North and South America; black labor during and after slavery; the importance of the frontier in history, particularly as it affected the black experience; migration as a form of resistance to oppression; and the centrality of religion in African-American culture.

Woodson gave prominence in much of his work to an analysis of slavery as a social system in the Americas. It was inevitable that some form of slave labor would arise in the New World, Woodson asserted, for it resulted from cheap land and a wide-open market for agricultural staples. Concerned less with the community that slaves created for themselves, Woodson made his primary focus the system of relations between white owners and slaves, and the impact of slavery upon the organization of land, labor, agriculture, industry, religion, education, politics, and culture; he covered the period extending from the beginning of the African slave trade through the demise of slavery in the Western hemisphere.[12]

Woodson acknowledged that many African societies practiced slavery, but he insisted that it was mild in comparison with slavery in the Americas. Woodson also noted that certain African societies cooperated with Europeans in promoting the slave trade but that Europeans often stimulated tribal warfare to obtain slaves. He described the horrors of the middle passage, yet contended that slave traders initially cared for their captives' physical needs, for a "loss of too many would have made the voyage unprofitable."[13] When the Atlantic slave trade became illegal in 1808, however, eluding the law became the traders' primary concern and the treatment of slaves was much worse. Wood-

---

12. Woodson, *The African Background Outlined* (Washington, D.C., 1936), 72, and "Negro Slavery," in *European Civilization: Its Origin and Development*, ed. Edward Eyre, (7 vols.; New York, 1939), VII, 561–62.

13. Woodson, "Negro Slavery," in *European Civilization*, ed. Eyre, VII, 561–62.

son was aware that planters in the New World expressed preferences for slaves of certain African ethnic groups, but he asserted that estimates of the number of slaves from each particular stock were often unreliable, because European traders sometimes misrepresented the origins of their cargoes. Woodson noted that authorities differed widely about the total number of slaves exported, with estimates ranging between five million and ten million. However, he concluded that "for every slave imported into America, four or five others had to meet death in numerous wars, in the inhuman drive to the coast, and in the cruel shipment in unsanitary ships hardly sufficient for transporting hogs." [14]

Woodson argued that because of the African presence in Spain and Portugal since the fourteenth century, slave traders from those countries regarded Africans differently than did the British traders. Latin traders believed that slaves were human beings with souls, and whole cargoes of Africans were baptized en masse before the voyage across the Atlantic. British traders, who entered the trade later, did not view Africans as human beings. Woodson did acknowledge, however, that mortality rates among slaves in Latin America were much higher, causing Latin American slaveholders to import more slaves over a longer period of time, and that the sex ratio of those imported was uneven, with a higher proportion of males. In the North American colonies, there was a more balanced ratio between male and female slaves. [15]

Initially, a triangular pattern developed in the trade route of the British, as they brought African captives to the West Indies before transporting them to North America. After this seasoning, some slaves were literate in several languages. When "such mentally developed Negroes proved to be a source of discontent," Woodson wrote, North American colonists "deemed it wiser to import slaves in their crude form directly from Africa." [16]

During the colonial period, slavery in British North America was

14. Woodson, *The Negro in Our History*, 62–68, 71–81, and "Negro Slavery," in *European Civilization*, ed. Eyre, VII, 564–67. Also see Woodson, "The Beginnings of the Miscegenation of the Whites and the Blacks," *Journal of Negro History*, III (1918), 335–53, and "Attitudes of the Iberian Peninsula," *Journal of Negro History*, XX (1935), 190–243.

15. Woodson, *The Negro in Our History*, 68–69, and "Negro Slavery," in *European Civilization*, ed. Eyre, VII, 565.

16. *Woodson, The Negro in Our History*, 110, and "The Beginnings of the Miscegenation of the Whites and the Blacks," 339.

patriarchal, particularly in the northern colonies where there were few slaves. The first Africans brought to the region had a status similar to that of white indentured servants, but by the middle of the seventeenth century, they had become servants for life. Relations between the races during this period were fluid, and class, rather than race, was the primary factor determining status in colonial society. Woodson argued that servants and slaves received equal treatment and that indentured servants were closer in status to black slaves than to white aristocratic landowners. It was inevitable that they would intermarry, and he cited numerous cases, including that of Benjamin Banneker, whose "mother was a white woman who married one of her slaves." [17] Miscegenation among the lower classes was widespread before the white "race as a majority could realize the apparent need for maintaining its integrity" and then pass legislation restricting interracial marriages.[18] Yet the laws were ineffective and served mainly to relegate the offspring of interracial unions to the status of slaves, regardless of the race of the mother.

The nature of slavery in North America changed markedly in the postrevolutionary and early national periods, when slavery became solidified as a social and economic institution in the South. In most northern states slaves were emancipated and slavery was outlawed, while in the South, the number of slaves who were emancipated declined dramatically. The improvement of spinning and weaving techniques during the Industrial Revolution increased the demand for cotton fiber and resulted in the demand for more slaves. Many slaves "endeavored to secure relief by refreshing the tree of liberty with the blood of their oppressors." After 1793, in the aftermath of the French and Haitian revolutions, African-American slaves tried to emulate Toussaint L'Ouverture and were aided and inspired by Haitian slave refugees as well as by free blacks, who were "encouraged to extend a helping hand to their enslaved brethren." [19] In addition to violent and

17. Woodson, "The Beginnings of the Miscegenation of the Whites and the Blacks," 339, and *The Negro in Our History*, 114–16. Although Woodson stated that Banneker's mother was white, it was his maternal grandmother who was white; his mother was a mulatto. See Silvio A. Bedini, "Benjamin Banneker," in *Dictionary of American Negro Biography*, ed. Rayford W. Logan and Michael R. Winston (New York, 1982), 22–25.

18. Woodson, "The Beginnings of the Miscegenation of the Whites and the Blacks," 339.

19. Woodson, *The Education of the Negro Prior to 1861*, pp. 7–8, *The Negro in Our History*, 177, and "Negro Slavery," in *European Civilization*, ed. Eyre, VII, 579. Also see

large-scale insurrections like that of Gabriel Prosser in 1800, there were numerous smaller uprisings and an increase in runaways.

In analyzing slavery, Woodson, like most scholars, concentrated on the antebellum period. Yet in a number of ways his work differed from that of his contemporaries—even that of Du Bois and Frederic Bancroft, whose sympathies also were with the slaves rather than the masters.[20] Unlike other scholars, Woodson devoted considerable attention to slavery in the upper South. He often used Virginia as a case study to illustrate his arguments, not only because he had been studying slavery in Virginia since he had been a graduate student but also because his family had been enslaved there. Given the nature of his familial experiences, it was difficult for him to be objective when writing about slavery, and it was inevitable that he would believe that slavery in the upper South in many ways was worse than in the black belt region.

Aside from Bancroft, Woodson was alone among his contemporaries in arguing that the breakup of slave families was typical in the upper South, that miscegenation between masters and their slaves was common, and that the breeding of slaves for sale had become a big business during the antebellum era. When writing for a scholarly audience, Woodson acknowledged that slavery differed according to region, crop mix, and size of holding. He was less careful, however, in the assessment he provided for high school and college students, as he tended to make sweeping generalizations and was concerned more with describing the evils of the system. In his textbook *The Negro in Our History*, he titled the chapter on slavery during the antebellum period "Slavery at Its Worst." Woodson argued that slavery "reduced the poor whites to poverty, caused a scarcity of money, cheapened land, and confined the South to one-crop farming at the expense of its undeveloped resources." Moreover, he contended, slavery "promoted the formation of wasteful habits . . . prevented the growth of towns and cities . . . shut out industrialism and made the South dependent upon the North or European nations for its manufactures."[21]

For an uninitiated audience, Woodson focused on the physical treat-

Douglas Egerton, "Gabriel's Conspiracy and the Election of 1800," *Journal of Southern History*, LXI (1990), 191–214.

20. See, for example, W. E. B. Du Bois, *The Negro* (New York, 1915); Frederic Bancroft, *Slave-Trading in the Old South* (Baltimore, 1931).

21. Woodson, *The Negro in Our History*, 236–37.

ment of slaves, using the upper South to illustrate the worst aspects of the system. Once the cotton gin came into widespread use in the black belt region, Woodson maintained, not only did slaveholders in the upper South sell their excess slaves but also slaves "were matched by force to produce lusty offspring for field hands." In some parts of the region, enterprising owners "paid special attention to the production of fine-looking mulatto Negro girls," who were in demand in the Southwest.[22]

In Virginia alone, Woodson estimated that 120,000 slaves were sold to the lower South. While awaiting sale by auction houses, slaves were put into pens that "were no more than stables for cattle or horses," and they "were fed upon the coarsest food known to be given to human beings." When they were put upon the auction block, slaves were subjected to "an examination of their teeth and other parts . . . to determine their age and health." Woodson noted, however, that slaves often had some influence "in determining their buyers," when they "aided or impeded the sale by singing their own praises or proclaiming their shortcomings."[23]

Whether they were sold into the black belt or remained in the upper South, Woodson argued that the day-to-day living conditions for blacks were barely tolerable. Slaves were usually sheltered in crude cabins with dirt floors, "so poorly constructed as to furnish little protection from bad weather." They lacked furniture, he maintained, "unless the few stools and beds of straw" that were in slave cabins "be worthy of such designation." Slaves were not only inadequately housed but also poorly clothed and given insufficient food. More benevolent masters permitted their bondmen to grow their own vegetables, and a "few of them were permitted to raise chickens or hogs [but] had to look after these personal affairs at night, on Sundays, or holidays." Slaves also "supplemented their rations by hunting and trapping at night," while others "had to steal to obtain a subsistence, and parsimonious masters encouraged them to do so."[24]

Moreover, Woodson contended, "slaves were generally not cared for when sick," and health care for pregnant women was inadequate; "some worked too hard to bear healthy children." Punishments were "crude and abusive," Woodson maintained, and while slaveholders "no longer

22. Woodson, "Negro Slavery," in *European Civilization*, ed. Eyre, VII, 576, and *The Negro in Our History*, 211.

23. Woodson, *The Negro in Our History*, 216, 221.

24. Woodson, ed., *The Works of Francis J. Grimké* (4 vols; Washington, D.C., 1942), I, vii; Woodson, *The Negro in Our History*, 222, 224.

mutilated Negroes or destroyed them on the wheel as in the eighteenth century, flogging, unmerciful beating and even burning at the stake" were not uncommon. Runaway slaves were "hunted with dogs," and if captured and brought back to their masters, "they were put in heavy iron shackles and collars and sometimes subjected to such tortures as drawing out the toenails." Only a minority of planters, according to Woodson, allowed their slaves to earn their own money by working odd jobs to purchase their freedom.[25]

The greater incidence of manumission in Latin America, as well as a host of other factors, led Woodson to argue that slavery there was less severe. Among the first scholars to examine slavery from a comparative perspective, Woodson arrived at the same conclusions Columbia University historian Frank Tannenbaum would reach almost thirty years later.[26] Woodson examined many of the same sources Tannenbaum would use, and he argued, as Tannenbaum and others would later, that slavery in Latin American societies differed markedly from slavery in the United States. Although in his lifetime Woodson was not given recognition by scholars in the United States for his work on comparative slavery, in the 1930s the British scholar Edward Eyre asked him to prepare an article on slavery for his seven-volume study of European civilization. Only one other scholar from the United States was listed among the fifty-four contributors to *European Civilization: Its Origin and Development.*[27]

In the essay written for Eyre's volume, Woodson provided a systematic comparison of all aspects of slavery in both hemispheres, noting that slaves were "driven as brutes" regardless of where they were enslaved. He identified demographic and settlement patterns, the cultivation of different crops, and the organization of labor as factors that affected the nature of slavery. Woodson noted that "the climate in which [a person] was enslaved might affect his surroundings and . . . determine the attitude of the master towards the slave." When he compared the physical treatment of slaves, Woodson acknowledged that day-to-day living conditions often were worse in Latin America. Yet he cautioned that it was difficult to generalize about physical treatment, maintaining that it varied. For example, he noted that in Brazil, "slaves

25. Woodson, *The Negro in Our History*, 223–24, 225.
26. Frank Tannenbaum, *Slave and Citizen: The Negro in the Americas* (New York, 1946).
27. The other American contributor was Michael J. Gruenthoner, of St. Louis University.

used in the production of coffee did not suffer such hardships as those worked on the sugar plantations or in the mines." He concluded, however, that the "tendency to neglect the slaves and turn out helpless creatures to beg for their living or free them to escape the burden of their maintenance" was less common in Latin America than in the United States.[28]

While the "English never treated their slaves with familiarity, nor smiled upon them, nor spoke to them except when compelled," Latin Americans treated them as members of their family, Woodson maintained.[29] Woodson attributed this benevolent attitude of the Spanish and Portuguese to their encounter with Africans in the fourteenth century, the role of the Catholic church, and the greater incidence and acceptance of miscegenation in Latin America.

The Catholic church played a central role in governing the relations between masters and slaves in Latin America, frequently interceding to protect slaves from excessive cruelty and harsh punishment. Woodson believed that the Church impressed upon slaveholders the view that kind treatment would encourage loyal and diligent workers and prevent rebellion. Further, religious teachings facilitated manumission. Woodson noted that "slave mothers often chose well-to-do god-parents for their infants hoping that some day they would be sufficiently benevolent to provide a way for these children to be emancipated." Besides encouraging religious instruction, the Catholic church also promoted greater access to education. According to Woodson, slaves were allowed to become literate and obtain a vocational education and to use these talents to escape the ordeal of slavery. The greater frequency of and possibility for manumission inspired ambitious undertakings, and Woodson recounted the numerous achievements of Latin American slaves and freedmen.[30]

The liberal attitude of Latin Americans toward miscegenation, Woodson argued, produced "mixed breeds who eventually found their way into the social order." Woodson, in effect, was describing what historian Carl Degler later termed the "mulatto escape hatch." The possibility of rising into this class made the "situation seem more hopeful than it otherwise would have appeared." Whereas the "English ac-

28. Woodson, "Negro Slavery," in *European Civilization*, ed. Eyre, VII, 584–85, 587.
29. Woodson, *The Negro in Our History*, 75.
30. Woodson, "Negro Slavery," in *European Civilization*, ed. Eyre, VII, 586, 590–91, and "Attitudes of the Iberian Peninsula," 190–243.

tually sold their offspring by Negro women," in Latin America they were recognized, elevated, and often manumitted.[31]

The postemancipation period of the two societies also differed owing to the nature of race relations during the slave period. The United States experienced a "devastating war" to abolish slavery, Woodson asserted, while Latin Americans "solved the problem with less disturbance of the peace and without any loss of life." Woodson argued further that contemporary Latin America enjoyed more harmonious race relations than the United States, pointing out that "the Negroes of the United States have encountered every sort of race prejudice and discrimination and have found the doors of opportunity closed in their faces."[32]

Although Woodson gave considerable attention to a discussion of contemporary race relations in the United States and Latin America and traced the differences back to the slave period, he paid less attention to the actual labor that slaves performed in each society. Such was the case in the article he wrote for Eyre's volume, as well as in other pieces on slavery directed at a general audience. Moreover, when discussing black labor in antebellum America, Woodson gave greater consideration to the work of skilled and urban slaves and free blacks than to agricultural labor, in which the majority of slaves were engaged. In *The Negro Wage Earner* and *The Negro Professional Man and the Community*, which are largely devoted to black labor, only two chapters deal with the antebellum period. The detailed analysis of class and occupational stratification, skills required for particular jobs, tasks performed, and the work culture in various occupations that Woodson delivers in discussing black labor in the late nineteenth and early twentieth centuries is notably absent from his discussion of the antebellum period. This imbalance is explained partly by the sources he used. When analyzing slave labor, Woodson perhaps was overly influenced by the experiences of his father and grandfather, who were skilled slaves and hired themselves out. He was more objective when he wrote about the postbellum period, for which he relied on demographic data, surveys, questionnaires, and a wide range of oral interviews.

Whether they worked in urban or rural areas, for one master or for

31. Woodson, "Negro Slavery," in *European Civilization*, ed. Eyre, VII, 567; Carl Degler, *Neither Black nor White: Slavery and Race Relations in Brazil and the United States* (New York, 1971), 226–32; Woodson, *The Negro in Our History*, 75.

32. Woodson, "Negro Slavery," in *European Civilization*, ed. Eyre, VII, 592–93.

different employers as hired help, slaves were driven hard. The treatment of slaves, Woodson noted, "was often determined by what they were required to do." Some planters selected slaves of a particular tribal or ethnic background, believing that physically they were best adapted to performing particular types of agricultural labor. According to Woodson, many slaves were well served by their background; those from African societies in which agricultural labor was collective adjusted more easily to plantation labor requirements. The most physically demanding labor was performed on plantations on which "slaves worked in gangs under masters or their overseers." Laboring on rice plantations was equally rigorous, although more flexible in terms of the time spent in cultivation; "work could be so divided as to assign it as tasks by holding each slave responsible for a definite accomplishment."[33] On smaller farms, slaves were subject to less physically demanding labor, although they performed a greater variety of tasks under closer supervision, as their masters and mistresses worked along side them.[34]

Woodson argued that skilled slaves were usually "better situated than other bondmen." Employed as craftsmen, artisans, and mechanics, on railroads, in textile manufacturing, tobacco factories, and sugar refineries, skilled slaves also were "economically better off than the free Negroes," Woodson contended, "whom they often doomed to poverty by crowding them out of various pursuits of labor."[35] Unlike free blacks, who were barred from certain trades, slaves often served as apprentices under a master craftsman. Upon completing their apprenticeship, they were sold or hired out to practice their trade. Poor whites, Woodson observed, often suffered the same fate as free blacks when they were forced to compete with skilled slaves for jobs. In certain southern cities legislation was passed limiting the number of skilled slaves who could be hired for particular jobs.[36]

Free blacks in both the North and the South were restricted to cer-

33. *Ibid.*, 585; Woodson, *The Negro in Our History*, 223. Also see Woodson, *The African Background Outlined*, 149–55, 168–71.

34. Woodson, "Freedom and Slavery in Appalachian America," *Journal of Negro History*, I (1916), 132–50, and *The Negro in Our History*, 223.

35. Woodson, *The Negro in Our History*, 235. Also see Woodson, *The Negro Wage Earner*, 1–15, and "The Negroes of Cincinnati Prior to the Civil War," *Journal of Negro History*, I (1916), 1–22. Lorenzo J. Greene worked with Woodson on *The Negro Wage Earner*. See Lorenzo J. Greene, *Working with Carter G. Woodson, the Father of Black History: A Diary, 1928–1930*, ed. Arvarh E. Strickland (Baton Rouge, 1989), 177–89.

36. Woodson, *The Negro Wage Earner*, 15, and *The Negro in Our History*, 235.

tain jobs, and most lived in urban areas or towns. Some obtained the education necessary to become doctors, lawyers, druggists, engineers, teachers, and ministers, and they practiced mainly among other blacks. In northern cities, workingmen's associations kept free blacks from working in trades. Those who were skilled usually fared better in southern cities like New Orleans and Charleston, or in cities in border states, like Cincinnati. The majority of free blacks were employed in domestic labor, working as barbers, butchers, coachmen, cooks, day laborers, hairdressers, housekeepers, janitors, laundresses, nursemaids, porters, seamstresses, stablemen, and waiters.[37]

Most blacks remained in the South after the Civil War and were restricted largely to agricultural work. Although "nominal slavery . . . had passed away," many freedmen were dependent upon their former masters who "continue[d] the institution in another form." Woodson provided a detailed analysis of the sharecropping arrangements that blacks negotiated, arguing that neither party benefited since both "tried to give the least and get the most from an impossible situation." Tenants negotiated the best agreements. "The difficulties under which the Negro tenant farmer labored" notwithstanding, Woodson wrote, "tenancy constituted a valuable school of bitter experience through which many Negroes advanced to the status of independent farmer."[38]

After 1890 the majority of blacks remained in the agricultural sector. Those who had acquired skills during slavery had difficulty finding employment because the "rising class consciousness of the whites and the prevailing notion of the unfitness of the Negro" excluded them from factory work.[39] Blacks were restricted to the most physically demanding, lowest paying, semiskilled jobs in railroad construction, mining, lumbering, and brickmaking.

Since black men had difficulties in obtaining work in the postbellum South, the labor of black women often saved their families from starvation. As slaves and freedwomen, their lives were given over to "unrelenting toil" for their families. After emancipation, black women withdrew from agricultural labor, "viewing it as unbecoming in their new status . . . while the Negro men," Woodson maintained, "imitating the whites, tended to limit their wives and daughters to the sphere of

37. Woodson, *The Negro in Our History*, 243–258, "The Negroes of Cincinnati Prior to the Civil War," 1–22, and *The Negro Wage Earner*, 1–15.

38. Woodson, *The Rural Negro*, 45, 51, and *The Negro Wage Earner*, 26–27, 29.

39. Woodson, *The Education of the Negro Prior to 1861*, pp. 97–98, and *The Negro Wage Earner*, 32.

the home." Black women, however, continued to labor outside their homes as domestic workers, cooks, laundresses, day laborers, and nursemaids. "When the husband could not supply or showed indifference to the comforts of home," Woodson observed, the wages black women earned "kept the home as nearly as possible according to the standards of modern times." [40]

Blacks were confined to domestic, manual, and agricultural labor because "only a few of the race had the foresight of the advocates of industrial training." Like Frederick Douglass and Booker T. Washington, Woodson believed that blacks needed practical vocational training rather than classical education, and he praised the establishment of Tuskegee Institute. Similarly, Woodson lauded Douglass for being "wiser in his generation than most of his contemporaries [in advocating] vocational training as the greatest leverage for the elevation of the colored people." [41]

Aside from the lack of vocational skills, illiteracy relegated blacks to the lowest occupations. Woodson estimated that three fifths of black wage earners could neither read nor write in 1890. Among the two fifths who were literate, many were employed as clerical workers in banking and insurance, and although their numbers increased after 1890, most failed to advance beyond the clerical level. The number of blacks in business and the professions was increasing, but it was "insignificant in comparison with the masses of Negro wage earners." [42]

A few ambitious individuals who worked in white businesses and mastered the necessary skills "saved sufficient capital to open similar enterprises of their own on a smaller scale." Many failed, however, because of undercapitalization and a lack of black patronage. The most successful blacks were employed in real estate, banking, and insurance, since whites in these businesses often refused to cater to a black clientele. But even among this group, success came slowly. For example, there were only thirty-two black-owned insurance companies in 1920, and most of these were diversified enterprises. [43]

Black women contributed immeasurably to the development of black

40. Woodson, "The Negro Washerwoman," 270, 273, 276, and Woodson, *The Negro Wage Earner*, 57.

41. Woodson, *The Education of the Negro Prior to 1861*, pp. 298, 301, and *Negro Orators and Their Orations*, 11.

42. Woodson, *The Negro Wage Earner*, 47.

43. *Ibid.*, 120; John H. Harmon, Jr., Arnett G. Lindsay, and Woodson, *The Negro as a Businessman* (Washington, D.C., 1929), 1–40.

businesses, investing the wages they earned as domestic laborers. The "first dimes and nickels with which these enterprises were launched came largely from women of this working class." Firms such as the "St. Lukes Bank in Richmond, the North Carolina Mutual Life Insurance Company of Durham, and the National Benefit Life Insurance Company of Washington," Woodson observed in 1930, "still count among their stock holders women of this noble type."[44]

The economic status of the majority of blacks improved markedly during and after World War I. For the first time the number of blacks employed as domestic and agricultural laborers declined. Jobs in industry and manufacturing that had previously been denied to blacks, as well as jobs in new industries such as food processing, steel mills, and automobile and clothing manufacturing, became available to them.[45]

Although thousands of blacks left agricultural work in the South to take these jobs, many stayed behind. "It requires only a trip of forty-eight hours in the South," Woodson observed, "to prove that the Negroes constitute the working class of that section." The same was true in the North. Northern black workers competed with whites for jobs and were paid lower wages for the same jobs. Yet the "most significant fact in the history of the Negro since the emancipation of the race," Woodson concluded, "has been its success in making a living in spite of terrorism, peonage, and the proscription of trade unions."[46]

While Woodson was hopeful that the black masses would maintain and eventually improve their economic status, he was less optimistic about the black professional class, believing it to be more culturally backward and less race conscious than the masses. In the early 1930s he studied the black professional class, analyzing a sample of twenty-five thousand doctors, dentists, nurses, lawyers, writers, and journalists in the urban South and in the border states, where the majority practiced. Woodson made note of their income, education, family background, marital status, religious affiliation, club and professional memberships, and literary tastes. He concluded that there were too many black professionals and that they were more interested in making money than in contributing to the advancement of their professions or to their race.[47]

Those who attained professional status after emancipation gave little thought to the "functioning of various elements which make possible

44. Woodson, "The Negro Washerwoman," 277.
45. Woodson, *The Negro in Our History*, 507.
46. *Ibid.*, 477–78, 594, 598.
47. Woodson, *The Negro Professional Man and the Community*, xviii.

or impossible the opportunity for work in certain spheres." Black colleges and graduate schools trained an excess of professionals, had lower standards of admission, and often provided a lower quality of education than white institutions. As a result, Woodson argued, black professionals were less likely than their white counterparts to keep up with the professional literature in their fields. Because whites barred them from membership in professional associations, blacks formed their own associations, which tended to emphasize social rather than professional advancement. Moreover, black professionals were dependent upon the black working class to earn a living because educated blacks had "just as much intellectual prejudice against the Negro in the professional sphere as the white man ha[d]."[48]

Only 60 percent of the black population sought the services of black physicians, and in rural areas, blacks were more likely to be treated by white physicians. Woodson viewed black physicians and dentists to be the least socially responsible among all black professionals, noting that the most successful "frittered away much of their energy in quest of material things like fine cars, fine homes, and a fine time." He wrote that black physicians, when attending meetings of the National Medical Association, too often "c[a]me in their fine cars and with their beautifully-gowned wives." Rather than "discussing the proper treatment for tuberculosis or typhoid fever," Woodson observed, "they indulge[d] freely in the merits or demerits of the Pierce Arrow or the Cadillac."[49]

Woodson held nurses, lawyers, and journalists in higher regard. Unlike dentists and doctors, nurses provided unrelenting service to the black community, particularly in the rural South. They were more likely to cooperate among themselves and with other black health care professionals, and they accomplished a great deal with limited resources. Although lawyers usually led the fight for civil rights, Woodson acknowledged that they had a difficult time earning a living. Local bar associations, especially in the South, failed to admit black attorneys, and 20 percent of those who studied law were unable to practice. White judges and juries viewed black lawyers to be less qualified than their white counterparts, and blacks held a similar view, since only 15 percent patronized black lawyers. Woodson gave the highest marks to black journalists and writers, but he admitted that black writers had been unable to create a body of Negro literature or cultivate a black audi-

48. *Ibid.*, 24–25, 319.
49. *Ibid.*, 130, 323.

ence. Black journalists, on the other hand, had a large readership because the black masses purchased black newspapers. By the early 1930s twenty-two papers had "developed into credible weeklies which have become vital forces in the educational, religious, economic, and political life of the Negro." [50]

The majority of black professionals, however, "wasted their savings in quest of the fleeting pleasures of life" and dragged down the entire race. Woodson chided the "so-called" talented tenth for failing to "impress themselves favorably enough upon their own people to secure their whole-hearted support," and for doing "very little to make up for this loss by drawing upon the patronage of the other race." [51] Not only did black professionals fail to measure up to the standards of their white counterparts, Woodson concluded, but also, in terms of their economic progress and race consciousness, they had not advanced as much as the black masses.

Since he had come from a black working-class family, Woodson's greater sympathy for ordinary black folk was not surprising. What was surprising, however, was his sympathy for ordinary white folk, particularly those in the southwestern Piedmont. As Woodson grew up in Piedmont Virginia, lived in West Virginia, and attended Berea College in the Appalachian Mountains, he rubbed shoulders with the sons and daughters of yeoman farmers in the region. Frederick Jackson Turner reinforced this interest in and sympathy for the white yeomanry when he served on Woodson's dissertation committee and influenced his analysis of the effect of the frontier on American character.

In his dissertation, "The Disruption of Virginia," Woodson argued that geographic and economic factors accounted for the secession movement in western Virginia. Covering the early eighteenth century through the antebellum period, Woodson's dissertation fleshed out Turner's contention that sectional conflict was an important historical force, and that understanding western expansion of the frontier was a key to understanding American history. Although blacks were not Woodson's primary focus, the role of blacks was central in his interpretation that slavery retarded Virginia's economic and social progress and caused the secession of the western part of the state. [52]

Woodson's was a social, economic, and geographical interpretation,

50. *Ibid.*, 140, 191, 283.
51. *Ibid.*, 331, 333.
52. Woodson, "The Disruption of Virginia" (Ph.D. dissertation, Harvard University, 1912).

as he argued that class conflict among poor whites, aristocratic planters, and merchant traders was exacerbated by the institution of slavery. Using maps to help illustrate demographic and geographic characteristics—also a Turnerian influence—Woodson asserted that geographic conditions prevented the profitable expansion of slavery to the Western frontier. In his opening chapter, "The Geographic Influence of the Development of an Aristocracy," Woodson revealed that his sympathies were clearly with the poor whites.[53]

Among the first historians to argue that the American Revolution was a social and economic as well as a political upheaval, Woodson traced the causes of secession in 1863 to the economic and religious conflicts in the eighteenth century between the tidewater aristocrats in the east and small yeoman farmers in the west. According to Woodson, German and Scotch-Irish religious dissenters, who settled in the western frontier between the Blue Ridge and Allegheny mountains, were united in their demand for equal rights, and were an important force that brought about the American Revolution. Woodson also described the conflicts between eastern and western Virginia—over internal improvements, expansion of suffrage, and taxation and representation—building toward his thesis that slavery was the ultimate cause of secession. Placing his case study within the context of southern history, Woodson described in one of his final chapters, "Virginia and the South," the development of the proslavery argument, southerners' assertion of the right to hold slaves, and their insistence on the expansion of slavery. In his concluding chapter, Woodson outlined western Virginia's secession from Virginia in relation to the election of 1860, which split the state into political factions that supported Democratic, Republican, southern Democratic, and Constitutional Unionist candidates.[54]

In his later works on the frontier, Woodson refined and amplified the same themes that appeared in his dissertation. Life on the frontier was based on individual equality, and this philosophy carried over into the treatment of slaves, Woodson maintained, for slaves held by yeoman farmers were treated better than those held by large planters. Describing the system of slavery practiced by the yeomanry as "patriarchal," Woodson noted that slaves worked alongside their masters and mistresses and were more likely to have been provided with education and religious instruction.[55]

53. *Ibid.*
54. *Ibid.*
55. Woodson, "Freedom and Slavery in Appalachian America," 132–50.

As the majority of yeomen on the western frontier held no slaves, they "believed that the institution of slavery was an economic evil of which the country should rid itself." They supported antislavery societies, colonization, and gradual emancipation. Woodson acknowledged that coastal planters eventually convinced the frontiersmen to support them in their defense of slavery and that the two united forces during the Civil War, but he believed it was only a temporary alliance. Having grown up and been educated in Appalachia during the post-Reconstruction period, Woodson made the observation that black and white men there "work side by side, visit each other's homes and often attend the same church." Even in the 1910s there was "such a fundamental difference in atmosphere of the two sections, that in passing from the tidewater to the mountains," Woodson noted, "it seems like going from one country to another." [56]

While Woodson most often addressed the influence of the frontier on southern culture, in the mid-1920s he assessed its impact on the larger society. America, he contended, "had developed from aristocracy to frontier democracy . . . to progressivism and . . . almost to socialism." Taking up where Turner had left off, Woodson discerned that since 1890 there had been an "increase of restlessness, pessimism, and revolutionary sentiment," which had been exacerbated by an influx of immigrants who, "no longer able to go west, must remain in our large cities to wage war against the capitalists." Coming just short of calling for an alliance of black and white workers against capital, as he did in the 1930s, Woodson noted that in the nineteenth century, "combination against capital was impossible when land was abundant and individualism was strong." [57]

The availability of free arable land and the freedom to migrate was a theme that Woodson also used to analyze the black experience. Writing in 1918 when black migration was at its peak, Woodson observed that "this new phase of Negro American life . . . will doubtless prove to be the most significant event in our local history since the Civil War." Viewing migration as a form of resistance to racial and class oppression, Woodson not only examined the new life that black migrants built for

56. Woodson, *The Negro in Our History*, 234, and "Freedom and Slavery in Appalachian America," 150.
57. Woodson, *The Negro in Our History*, 530, 533; Frederick Jackson Turner, "The Significance of the Frontier in American History," in *Annual Report of the American Historical Association for the Year 1893* (Washington, D.C., 1894), 197–227, and *The Frontier in American History* (New York, 1920).

themselves on farms and in towns and cities but also assessed the con-sequences of migration for those who were left behind. Woodson chronicled the migrations of blacks during and after the Civil War, as hundreds of refugees fled from their former masters. By the 1870s a massive emigration of blacks from the South had occurred. Woodson estimated that almost one hundred thousand left in search of oppor-tunity in the West. Another group, dissatisfied "with the low remu-neration of farm labor[,] advanced upon [northern] towns in search of industrial employment, where," according to Woodson, "they conse-quently glutted the labor market and reduced the small earnings of those already in such jobs." [58]

The youngest, strongest, and brightest left. Like Frederick Doug-lass, who had warned of the deleterious effects of black migration on those who remained behind, Woodson argued that this massive exodus had been harmful, noting that Douglass had "deplored the fact that education and emigration had gone together." Since the majority of the black population would always remain in the South, Woodson con-tended that they had "been robbed of their due part of the talented tenth." At the same time, he insisted, "educated blacks have had no constituency in the North and . . . have been unable to realize their sweetest dreams." [59]

Woodson acknowledged, however, that there were some gains from migration. Like thousands of other black migrants during this period, Woodson and his family left Virginia for greater opportunity in West Virginia, where they found better jobs, earned higher wages, and even-tually purchased their own home. He noted that as labor became scarce, the "exodus was productive of better treatment for the Negroes" and led to an "increase in their wages in certain parts of the South." [60] Yet race relations did not improve in the South and even worsened by the end of the nineteenth century, as blacks suffered increasing racial op-pression, segregation, and violence at the hands of whites.

Migration intensified during the first decades of the twentieth cen-tury. "Within the last two years," Woodson wrote in 1918, "there has been such a steady stream of Negroes into the North in such large numbers as to overshadow in its results all other movements." As re-

58. Woodson, *A Century of Negro Migration* (Washington, D.C., 1918), v, and *The Negro Wage Earner*, 54.
59. Woodson, *The Education of the Negro Prior to 1861*, p. 304, and *A Century of Negro Migration*, 152.
60. Woodson, *A Century of Negro Migration*, 152.

strictions were placed on white European immigrants, jobs in northern factories and industries opened up for blacks. Because of those job opportunities, Woodson maintained, the "proportion of those returning to the South will be inconsiderable."[61]

Woodson was cautiously optimistic, writing that the entire country would be "benefitted by this upheaval." Even in the South the "decrease in the black population in those communities where the Negroes outnumber the whites will remove the fear of *Negro domination,* one of the causes of backwardness of the South and its peculiar civilization."[62] He was mindful, however, of the great social consequences of migration for racial and class relations, warning that the black masses must be reckoned with lest violence erupt. A little more than a year after his book on migration went to press, dozens of race riots broke out all over the country.

Woodson never underestimated the growing racial and class consciousness of the black masses. In his later writings he discussed Marcus Garvey's attraction among black northern migrants. Unlike other intellectuals, who were chagrined by Garvey's ability to capture the hearts, minds, and paychecks of the black masses, Woodson was not surprised at all, and used similar tactics in appealing to race loyalty to garner financial support for his black history programs in the 1930s.

Woodson was in the vanguard among intellectuals in giving attention to religion early in his scholarly career. Characterizing the black church as the "greatest asset of the race," Woodson demonstrated that religion had been a central element in African cultures and had become even more so in African-American culture. Providing more than hope and inspiration through slavery and freedom, the black church developed as an educational, political, and social institution and served as the foundation for the rise of an independent black culture. Woodson observed that in making the transition to Christianity, African slaves retained many elements of African religious expressions, and that the similarity between African religions and Christianity facilitated religious syncretism.[63]

For the majority of colonial slaveholders, religion served primarily as a method of socialization for slaves. Among Catholic slaveholders in Latin America, Louisiana, and Maryland, however, the Church served

61. *Ibid.,* 167, 174.
62. *Ibid.,* 183.
63. Woodson, *The Negro in Our History,* 591, *The History of the Negro Church* (Washington, D.C., 1921), 1–20, and *The African Background Outlined,* 168–74.

as a moderating force and facilitated better treatment, greater physical freedom, and manumission. After the revolutionary war the status of blacks deteriorated and gave rise to the independent black church movement. Northern black separatists Richard Allen, Absolom Jones, and James Varick broke from white congregations and formed the AME and AMEZ churches. Woodson maintained that initially black church leaders "found it difficult to secure a following," but potential congregants soon "forgot the stigma attached to their radical religious bodies and united freely with their brethren."[64]

After the schism resulting from the establishment of independent black churches, the major denominations in the North continued "to discountenance as far as possible all cruelty of whatever kind in the treatment of slaves," including "that which consisted in selling slaves to those who would . . . deprive these unhappy people of the blessings of the gospel."[65] Later, some northern denominations broke with their southern counterparts over the issue of slavery.

Slaves usually were physically segregated from whites during religious services. Thus, Woodson argued, freedmen in the post–Civil War South left white churches in droves and established independent congregations. Inspired largely by their northern counterparts, southern black churches promoted "education as a means to spread the gospel . . . to enable the laity to appreciate it as the great leverage in the uplift of the man far down."[66] Functioning mainly as educational and social institutions, these churches soon established kindergartens, women's clubs, training schools, and burial and fraternal societies from which independent black businesses developed. As meeting places for kin and neighbors, black churches strengthened the political and economic base of the black community and promoted racial solidarity.

Black conservatives believed that churches should adhere strictly to religious education, while progressives maintained that they should continue their outreach in the economic and political arenas. The progressives won out of necessity. With the spread of racial oppression in the early twentieth century, the role of the black church expanded even more in the political and social arenas, as did the role of the black minister. Frequently he became the moral force leading the movement for civil rights. The "impetus for the uplift of the race," Woodson ar-

---

64. Woodson, *History of the Negro Church*, 6, 71–72, 123.
65. *Ibid.*, 127–28.
66. *Ibid.*, 205.

gued, "must come from its ministry," who could "fearlessly speak for them within the limits of public opinion." [67]

Particularly concerned with the rural black church, Woodson viewed religion in the countryside to be in crisis. Having fewer congregants but three times more churches than their urban counterparts, rural black ministers were less educated and less socially responsible to their parishioners. While these churches had a more important role to play as social welfare agencies, since there were fewer institutional resources in rural communities, Woodson found them sorely lacking. There were "practically no rural churches with a semblance of . . . religious education." Rather, religious education was "of the antiquated order devoted to the dissemination of Biblical Truths and doctrinal matters which have no bearing on the development of the body and character of the individual." Woodson believed that black ministers in the rural South were reactionaries, and argued that they kept "Negroes thinking about the glorious time which they will have beyond this troublesome sphere" and caused "them to forget their oppression here." [68]

Religion in urban black America was not without its problems, however. Church attendance continued to fall off in the 1920s and early 1930s, particularly among the black bourgeoisie. Woodson was dismayed by this pattern, and deplored the growing proliferation of black storefront churches and their attractiveness to the black masses. He was distressed by the "very large following" of Negro ministers "who conduct the storefront churches and work the people up into a frenzy by indulging in religious dances." Displaying his own moral prudishness and class bias, Woodson viewed with disdain black ministers "who have come under the influence of the primitive ideas of sanctification, holiness, and divine healing," and he characterized them as having "more primitiveness than is usually found in the most backward parts of the rural districts." [69]

Among the black masses and the left-leaning black bourgeoisie who had turned away from religion, Woodson worried that radical political organizations would assume the role formerly held by the black church. "The most striking thing in the appeal of the Negro radical element," he noted, writing in the early 1930s, "is that Communism offers every-

---

67. *Ibid.*, 247–49, 281.
68. Woodson, *The Rural Negro*, 168, 149.
69. Woodson, *The Negro Professional Man and the Community*, 317, and *The Negro in Our History*, 591–92.

thing which the church does not offer."[70] Yet Woodson always remained steadfast in his belief that the black church was the only independent power base for blacks, and he argued that the church should be used more effectively to combat political and economic oppression. Only after his death in 1950 did the black church fulfill the role that he had envisioned for it.

Recently scholars have noted that Woodson's work on the black church has remained unsurpassed in many respects.[71] The same can be said for his scholarship in black urban and labor history and especially for his work on slavery in the New World. Despite Woodson's tendency to overgeneralize about the nature of slavery and to be less than rigorous in analyzing the treatment of slaves, his work prefigured scholarly interpretations advanced from the 1940s through the 1970s. Many of his arguments are intact even today, particularly his conclusions drawn about the importance of African culture, the internal slave trade, and the experiences of skilled and hired slaves in the United States. Also relevant today are Woodson's many findings on slavery in Latin America, including the greater frequency of manumission there and the existence of a "mulatto escape hatch," which facilitated better, although more complicated, race relations in contemporary Latin America.

Woodson defiantly challenged white historians' views about the black experience in much of his work. Although in his lifetime he did not win the contested struggle for preeminence—or even acceptance— of a different version of the black past, he constructed a historical framework that is used by contemporary historians of African Americans. In forging a dissenting interpretation of the meaning and relevance of the black experience, Woodson relied on the range of his life experiences. As the son of former slaves, he moved from sharecropper to coal miner to Harvard graduate student to high school teacher to college professor, and, finally, to editor-scholar-administrator, and drew upon the wellsprings of the collective and cultural memories of his family and other African Americans. In doing so, he contributed immeasurably to black historiography and laid the foundation that several generations of scholars have built upon.

70. Woodson, *The African Background Outlined*, 391.
71. See Albert J. Raboteau and David Wills, with Randall K. Burkett, Will B. Gravely, and James Melvin Washington, "Retelling Carter Woodson's Story: Archival Sources for Afro-American Church History," *Journal of American History*, LXXVII (1990), 183–99.

"HIS CAUSE WAS THE PRESENTATION OF THE TRUTH"

Several years before Woodson died, the archivist-historian Harold T. Pinkett had a conversation with him. Woodson jokingly glanced down at his feet and said, "You see these big shoes that I am wearing. It will take some big feet to fill them."[1] Woodson aptly described the problem that confronted his successors as they struggled to ensure that his legacy would endure. Although the legacy that he left to generations of black Americans continues today in the Association for the Study of Afro-American Life and History, Woodson's successors have never accomplished as much as he did with far fewer resources. And while most of the programs he founded still operate, for many years there has been a struggle for control within the association, between professionally trained scholars and interested amateurs—schoolteachers, ministers, lawyers, doctors, and social workers. No one has succeeded as Woodson did in bridging the gap between the history promoted by professionally trained scholars and the needs of the general public, to whom Woodson devoted many of his efforts.

For the most part, contemporary scholars, black and white, have not played as active a role as Woodson did in promoting black history among the masses of black Americans, or in popularizing black history among white Americans.[2] Rather, they have focused their attention on creating a distinguished body of scholarly work in African-American

1. Harold T. Pinkett to author, May 2, 1988.
2. See, for example, Louis R. Harlan, "The Future of the American Historical Association," *American Historical Review*, VC (1990), 1–8, "Social Studies Reform and the Historian," *Journal of American History*, LXXVII (1990), 801–11, and especially "Broadening the Concept of History," *Journal of Southern History*, LVII (1991), 3–14.

history and on achieving recognition in the historical profession. Although Woodson did not achieve recognition from the historical profession during his lifetime, he succeeded in popularizing black history because he trusted and believed in the ability of black people to overcome adversity. Perhaps his success can best be measured by acknowledging that most of the association programs he founded and carried out are still operational, even if they are struggling.

After Woodson died in April, 1950, many of his black contemporaries wrote tributes recognizing his signal contributions to the field of African-American history. In an obituary published in May, 1950, W. E. B. Du Bois acknowledged that "there will be a vast respect and thankfulness for the life of this man," for "under the harshest conditions of environment," Woodson "kept to one great goal, worked at it stubbornly and with unwavering application and died knowing that he accomplished much if not all that he planned." Charles Wesley noted that Woodson "had a spirit of devotion to his cause and his cause was the presentation of the truth." [3]

Heightened black consciousness during the 1960s created controversies between black activists and intellectuals, not only about the role black history and culture would play in fostering social change but also about their content and themes and the appropriate media for their expression. In the midst of the movement to establish black studies programs during the late 1960s, Wesley, then the executive director of the association, praised Woodson's accomplishments and discussed the relevance of his teachings and writings for contemporary African-American educators. The association even reissued a second edition of *The Mis-Education of the Negro* in 1969. [4]

The Mis-Education of the Negro is still in print and is selling more briskly than ever before. In the late 1980s the Washington, D.C., chapter of Marcus Garvey's Universal Negro Improvement Association praised Woodson's insights in *The Mis-Education of the Negro*, urged African Americans to read the 1933 classic, and characterized it as "a key to our freedom as a people." In language that was similar to Woodson's, a UNIA spokesperson argued that the American educational system "was never set up to educate Negroes. It was set up to keep them

3. W. E. B. Du Bois, "A Portrait of Carter G. Woodson," *Masses and Mainstream*, III (May, 1950), 19; Baltimore *Afro-American*, April 15, 1950, p. 7.
4. Charles H. Wesley, Introduction to Woodson, *The Mis-Education of the Negro* (2d ed.; Washington, D.C., 1969), xxii–xxiii.

21st century slaves, who ride around in Cadillacs and who are the most comfortable blacks on earth."[5]

Historians finally have acknowledged Woodson's pioneering contributions to the field of black history. By the 1970s the prevailing interpretations of scholars of southern and Afro-American history in the mainstream of the profession had completely shifted. Many of these scholars relied heavily on Woodson's work and that of other scholars published in the *Journal of Negro History*. Woodson would be pleased to know that black history is now a well-established, legitimate, and respected subject of study, and that its practitioners, many of whom are African American, are recognized as eminent scholars by their peers in the historical profession. And while the black history movement has succeeded in obtaining academic respectability for African-American history and African-American scholars, the psychological and economic benefits to ordinary blacks that Woodson presumed would flow from his efforts are still difficult to discern in the 1990s.

5. Nairo Bota, "An Introduction to the Study of *The Mis-Education of the Negro*," *Garvey Voice*, IX (June, July, August, 1987), 3, 8. On contemporary issues and Afrocentrism see, for example, Jerry Adler *et al.*, "African Dreams," *Newsweek*, September 23, 1991, pp. 42–45.

INDEX